W9-DED-673

THE ETERNAL CHURCH

by

Dr. Bill Hamon

foreworded by

Harald Bredesen
and

Rev. Paul E. Billheimer, Dr. James Lee Beall, Dr. Robert Frost,
Dr. David Kast, Dr. A.W. Rasmussen, Dr. Reg Layzell,
Rev. Ken Sumrall, Rev. Pauline Parham, and Rev. John Gimenez

Christian International Publishers
P.O. Box 27398
Phoenix, Arizona 85061

First Printing 1981   5,000
Second Printing 1982   12,500

The Eternal Church
Copyright © W. S. Bill Hamon, 1981
Printed in the United States of America
All Rights Reserved

International Standard Book Number: 0-939868-00-8 Paper Cover
International Standard Book Number: 0-939868-01-6 Hard Cover

Published by
CHRISTIAN INTERNATIONAL
P.O. Box 27398
Phoenix, Arizona 85061

Typesetting — New Age Type & Graphics, Tempe, Arizona
Printing — Faith Printing Company, Taylors, South Carolina

Dedication

This book is dedicated to Jesus Christ and to all who are members and shall become members of His beloved Eternal Church. More specifically, it is dedicated to my wife, Evelyn, and our three married children and their spouses; Tim and Karen, Tom and Jane, Sherilyn and Glenn, who have faithfully labored with me in the ministry.

In Appreciation

To the faculty and staff of Christian International who have allowed their President to take time to write this book over the last three years. To Rev. Jeff Britt of Texas for his vital help and encouragement. To Rev. Maxwell Morris of Florida and Anne Fadule of California for editorial work. To Ron Lee and Dianne Harder for cover design. To Alice Flemming, Dorothy Rademaker, Carey Lee, Virginia Bedworth for typing and proofreading. To Rev. Tom Morrison and Rev. Gloria Crenshaw for being channels for the voice of the Lord. To all those hundreds of Christian friends who pre-ordered this book making its publication possible. And to all who gave sound counsel and encouragement until the work was completed.

I greatly appreciate my daughter for allowing me to use her wedding picture to portray the Bride of Christ on the cover of this book.

Contents

Capitalization:

Dr. Hamon has taken *Author's Prerogative* in capitalizing certain words which are not usually capitalized according to standard grammatical practice. This is done for the purpose of clarity and emphasis. References to the Church/Bride are capitalized because of Her union with Deity through Jesus Christ.

All Scriptures are taken from King James Version (KJV) except when designated as follows:

NIV	—	New International Version
LB	—	The Living Bible
ASV	—	American Standard Version
RSV	—	Revised Standard Version
AMP	—	The Amplified Bible
Moffatt	—	A New Translation by James Moffatt
Phillips	—	Phillip's Letters to Young Churches

Foreword:

Traveling in Asia Minor today, you might come across a large earthen mound, topped by a cluster of mud huts. "This," you are informed, "is Troy." Actually the foundations of that once great city lie 50 feet down, buried under the debris of succeeding civilizations that have flourished and built one on top of the other.

The medieval church called itself "The One Holy Apostolic Church", but the foundations its apostles had built lay buried under the forms and traditions of successive heirarchies.

Then the great Excavator began His work. His human instrument was Martin Luther. He uncovered "Justification by faith".

"Heresy!" cried his enemies. "Burn him at the stake!"

"Plain Bible truth," retorted his followers, "the corner stone of 1st century Christianity."

When next God used the Anabaptists to bring to light New Testament baptism, Catholics and Protestants alike joined in shouting "Heresy! Don't immerse them, drown them!"

And so it was, and so it is, that the heretics of yesterday are the established churches of today, hounding the heretics that will be the established churches of tomorrow. But God will not stop until He has brought to light every truth, principle, and practice He has from the first intended for His people.

In this book, Dr. Bill Hamon sets out to trace the process, and foresee the ultimate product. In his own words, he "discusses God's plan and purpose for the Church from an overall spiritual perspective, with just enough historical data to portray the origination, deterioration, restoration, and ultimate destination of the Church."

He is writing from a different perspective than mine. He owes no loyalty to any denomination, but only to the truth as he sees it. *The open minded reader may not always agree with his findings, but must agree with his motives, and cannot fail to be enriched, stirred, and edified.*

Harald Bredesen

World-wide Ministry to National Leaders
Author of *Yes, Lord!*

A written history of this kind is an indispensable tool in giving us direction for the future. Dr. Hamon has blessed our generation by adding pieces that it was impossible for us to fill in by ourselves. I admire his thoroughness and research.

Dr. James Beall
Pastor, Bethesda Temple, Detroit, MI
Author of several books such as *The Adventure of Fasting;*
Your Pastor, Your Shepherd; Strong in the Spirit; Let Us
Make Man; School of Holy Spirit; Laying the Foundation;
How to Achieve Security, Confidence and Peace.

The universe was created for one purpose and one alone: to generate, nurture, and educate an Eternal Companion for God's Son, designated in the Word as the Bride, The Lamb's Wife.

The Eternal Church, by Dr. Bill Hamon, recognizes the central importance of the Church, not only in time but, above all, in the age of all ages. According to this monumental work, the Church dominates all history as well as all future events unto the eternities to come. This book breaks virgin soil. So far as I know, it is the first in its field.

Rev. Paul E. Billheimer
Author of *Destined for the Throne;*
Don't Waste Your Sorrows; Love Covers.

Dr. Bill Hamon has skillfully and with sensitivity, traced the life-stream of restoration truth concerning the Church throughout the uneven course of human history. Important prophetic insights help establish our present position in God's unfolding plan, and enable us to practically and personally participate in His glorious end-time purpose.

Jesus prayed that we — as His Body — might be one that the world would have a true witness of God's redeeming love and power. The reader of this book will find himself intrigued, informed, inspired and motivated to be a vital part of that church triumphant in these coming days of challenge and opportunity for us all.

Robert Frost, Ph.D.
Author of *Aglow With The Spirit; Overflowing Life;*
Our Heavenly Father.

I believe Dr. Hamon's book, *The Eternal Church*, expresses the greatest cry of the Holy Spirit in this day and hour. His presentation that God has only one Church and that that Church must come to the unity of faith and spirit before Jesus can return, is of utmost importance. Jesus emphatically stated that the "glory" which the father had given Him was given to the Church that we, the Body of Christ, may be one. Every minister within Christendom is either laboring together with Christ for the unity of the Church or cooperating with the antichrist spirit which is determined to keep the Church fragmented and disunited. All Christians need to be made conscious of Dr. Hamon's emphasis that the next sovereign work of the Holy Spirit is not the Rapture but the maturity of the Saints and unity of the Church — not "going up" but "growing up." **Every Church Minister and Christian needs to Receive the Spirit and Message of this book.**

Pastor John Gimenez
Pastor of Rock Church, Virginia Beach, VA.
Chairman of Washington for Jesus, 1980.
National Chairman, America for Jesus.

Dr. Hamon recognizes that the Body of Christ in our present time did not suddenly come into existence.

He carefully shows that the Church has developed from rich experiences learned in history, and how many denominations have made their contribution to our present Christian society.

I highly recommend this book as a valuable source of study to those interested in the development of the Body of Christ.

David P. Kast, D.Min.
Academic Dean, Christ for the Nations Institute.

I have had the pleasure of reading the manuscript of this work. It gives a tremendous insight into the Church as the many-membered universal Body of Christ. The truths concerning the restoration of the Church are graphically portrayed. The condensed coverage of the Latter Rain Movement is in line with the historical facts. I can verify that Dr. Hamon is personally knowledgeable of the truths of the movement which, on the West Coast, became known as "The Revival Churches" or "Revival Fellowship." This book should be in the homes of all Christian families who are interested in their Christian heritage and future destiny. I especially recommend the book to all Bible students and lovers of the Church of Jesus Christ.

Dr. Reginald Layzell
Founder of two churches.
Author of the book *Unto Perfection*.
He is the "Pastor" spoken of in B.M. Gaglardi's book *Pastor's Pen*.

This book *The Eternal Church* by Dr. Bill Hamon, is written in dignified simplicity and a miraculous clarity concerning the foundation of pentecostalism in experience and message. It will serve well young lives and new believers who seek knowledge which will produce a supernatural ministry that will close the age and bring back King Jesus.

This is an important addition to our pentecostal/charismatic history.

Pauline E. Parham
Daughter-in-law of Charles F. Parham.
Teacher, CFNI, 10 years, worldwide ministry.

This book gives a panoramic view of the Church from its birth to its ministry in the ages to come. It should be a great success for it will be of untold value to the ministry and those who are interested in the present move of God through the Holy Spirit. God continues to move the Church forward unto the day of perfection and full maturity in Christ Jesus. This book should make members of the Body of Christ knowledgeable of God's will and eternal purpose for their lives.

Dr. A. W. Rasmussen
International Secretary of the Independent
Assemblies of God International.
Author, *The Last Chapter.*

At first glance, *The Eternal Church*, may seem like just another book on Church history. However, as the author has unequivocally stated, he has not written from the viewpoint of presenting details of how the Church survived or progressed since its inauguration. Rather, it reveals God's plan and purpose for the Church, emphasizing the slow but deliberate process in which the Church is being brought to maturity.

It is not common in these days to find a book which so thoroughly deals with its subject. Without doubt, this study has demanded the utmost effort in research and selection of truth to be presented.

Dr. Bill Hamon has done his homework well and I highly recommend this book to those who are interested in what Jesus is saying to His Church.

Rev. Ken Sumrall, M.R.S., M.S.
Founder of Liberty Bible College, Globe Missionary Evangelism,
Liberty Fellowship of Churches and Ministers,
and Senior Pastor of Liberty Church, Pensacola, FL.

The
Eternal
Church

Preface

The Spirit and Intention of the Author

This book is presented in the spirit of humility, honesty, and with the sincere prayer that it will be a blessing to each reader. My prayer is that the spirit of wisdom and revelation in the knowledge of the Son of God may rest upon the reader, which will give full knowledge of our inheritance in Christ *(Eph. 1:16-23)*.

There are many spiritual and theological giants who are knowledgeable in the truths of the Church. If they were writing this book, they might have used different terminology and arrangement of material. This does not mean that there are contradictions or confusion concerning the truth presented. Each member of God's family must function and express himself according to the ability given by the Holy Spirit. No two members in the body express themselves the same way. The right hand and the left hand look alike and have the same function, but they fulfill their main ministry of feeding the mouth from opposite directions. If the big toe could see it would have a different perspective of the entire body than, say, the nose would have from its position in the body.

This truth can be further illustrated by the story of the five blind men who were allowed to examine an elephant and then were asked to describe it. The first blind man felt his leg and said, "He is like a round pillar." The second felt his tail and said, "He is like a rope." The third felt his side and said, "He is like a great wall." The fourth felt his tusks and said, "He is like a spear." The fifth felt his ear and said, "He is like a great leaf." They were each right in their description of that which they had experienced, but they were wrong in their overall description because of an inability to see the whole elephant in one panoramic view. They could have argued indefinitely, but their limited view did not change the elephant into something less than it was. It is comforting to know that regardless of how a preacher may describe the Church from his own experience, it cannot change or lessen the totality of the Church. The Word of God says that we see in part and we know in part and we look through a glass darkly. No individual, other than Jesus, has a complete perspective of the overall eternal Church. Hopefully, this book will add another "part" to your understanding of the Church.

Without Bones. Another illustration is that of a good platter of tasty and nutritious fried chicken in which there is a certain amount of bone that cannot be chewed and swallowed. The author has sought to serve this spiritual platter of truth without bone. If you do find a statement or illustration which you feel is bone, do not let it get caught in your throat and hinder you from ingesting the rest of the meat in this book. Lay the bone aside and say, "I don't understand that, I cannot accept that." However, continue to read and receive all the truth that you can find. Perhaps later you will learn that the "bone" was really only a tougher piece of meat than you could chew at the time.

It is not the writer's intention to offend anyone, to speak negatively or derogatorily concerning any religious group, or to propagate any particular doctrine or experience. Rather it is to give a complete and unbiased overview of the Church. What I have written is designed to emphasize the truths concerning the Church.

God has not appointed this author to be a prophet to the nations of the world or to the holy land of Israel but rather, to be a prophet to the *Church*. There are men of God who have prophetic insight concerning the nations of the world. This book is written for members of the great universal Body of Jesus Christ, whose hope is not in their heritage as Americans or Israelis, but in being citizens of the spiritual kingdom of God.

Many books have been written about Jesus and His redemptive work. If all the books in the world were on the subject of Jesus, and if each described His love, grace, and glory from a different aspect, all those billions of volumes would be insufficient to reveal Him fully. Jesus is the greatest love of the author's life, his favorite topic, and the very purpose of his being. Nevertheless, God did not ask the author to write about the dearest thing to his heart but to write about the nearest and dearest thing to the heart of Jesus, which is His Bride, the Church. The writer's purpose is to be instrumental in revealing, to the best of his ability, what Jesus wants to say about His desire, will, and plans for His Bride at this time.

A presentation of church history is not the objective. There are many books which give the history of the Church relating to people, places, dates, and minute details concerning every area of the Church. This writing discusses God's plan and purpose for the

Church from an overall spiritual perspective. Just enough historical data is given to portray the origination, deterioration, restoration, and ultimate destination of the Church. It will seek to reveal God's eternal desire and purpose for His Church.

To gain the full benefit of the truths presented within this book, the reader should have a basic understanding of Church history. To gain a further knowledge of Church history one could enroll in the Christian International College* extension course of Church History or read several good texts on the subject.

*Christian International
Bible College and Graduate School
P. O. Box 27398
Phoenix, AZ 85061
U.S.A.

Introduction

What Jesus Wants

What is the nearest and dearest thing to the heart of God?

What concerns God more than anything else upon Earth?

What does Jesus want from planet Earth?

Jesus came to this Earth for a specific purpose. It was not out of compulsion or constraint, but from compassion. He did not come just to save us from Hell. He came to redeem us unto Himself. What He saved us *for* supersedes anything He saved us *from*. In order to fulfill the eternal purposes, Jesus came to this Earth and took upon Himself a human body. He partook of flesh-and-blood mortality that He might lift humanity to His divine life and immortality. He lived, died, was buried, arose from the grave, and ascended to the Father, sending back the Holy Spirit to perpetuate His purpose and to fulfill His plan concerning man on Earth.

Jesus is Waiting. Jesus is longingly waiting for the day He physically returns to this Earth. Why? What thoughts and desires are taking place within the heart of Jesus at this time? Is our God and Savior, Jesus Christ, a thinking and feeling being? Does He have heart longings, feelings, joy, and excitement similar to what human beings have? Does Jesus still have His human body? Yes! He was born of the virgin Mary, lived as an average human being for 30 years, was manifested as the Son of God for 3½ years, and was crucified upon the cross. That body was then buried in a grave. But the third day the resurrection power of God was activated in that body and it arose an immortal flesh-and-bone body. That body still had every member and organ except blood in its veins. The blood had been poured out for a purpose and was to be presented before the Father as the purchase price for His Bride.

God's Perfect Man. Jesus is still a man. Though eternal and immortalized He continues to have all the positive emotions of man. Our God is alive — body, soul, and spirit. Jesus is, was, and remains God's perfect **man** and man's perfect **God.** His heart did not turn into stone or some substance other than flesh. That heart is full of tender, touchable, compassionate mercy for His own. Every joy, longing, desire, and love we feel for Him and for His return is intensified a million times over in the heart of Jesus in His longing, love, and desire to return to Earth to receive His purchased possession — the greatest treasure of His life.

Prophetic Commission. In 1978, while I was ministering in Atlanta, Georgia, God spoke through prophetic utterance that I was to write a book which was to be the expression of the heart of God and reveal the desires of Christ Jesus. I had been contemplating writing a book on the restoration of the Church. The information given would help Christians understand their Christian heritage, what is taking place in the Church today, and what God has predestined for Christ and His Church. Several years ago I wrote a dissertation entitled *God's Eternal Purpose for Creating the Human Race.* It explained why He placed man on planet Earth, made his body from dust of the earth, and placed him on the planet which was Satan's prison, in a garden containing a tree from which he was forbidden to eat. The dissertation explored eight different reasons why God wanted this new creation living on this particular planet. This book will specialize in the one reason which I believe to be nearest and dearest to the heart of our Lord and Savior, Jesus Christ.

The Greatest Desire of Jesus. The greatest longing and heart desire of Jesus is to receive His Bride, the Church, in her full perfection, beauty, and maturity. He will not and cannot return for His Bride until She is complete with all necessary members, and each member and area of the body is developed to full maturity and womanhood. She will be fully prepared and conformed to Her Bridegroom in thought, attitude, love, power, wisdom, and grace by the time He comes to receive Her. The Book of The Song of Solomon expresses the longing of the Bridegroom for the day when His Bride will be joined with Him. He is ravished with love for Her and desires to be joined with His Bride, but must wait until She is fully developed. He then describes Her with tingling excitement as He beholds Her fully developed in every area of Her being. He is enthralled with Her perfection of beauty and maturity.

The Perfection of the Church-Bride. The Church-Bride will not be an undeveloped little sister, nor a wrinkled, blemished, or worn out old woman. When Jesus returns for His Bride She will be at the peak of Her beauty and performance. She will be performing greater things and be more glorious than She has been in any other generation during Her existence. The perfection of beauty, maturity, ability, and Christ-likeness will be within Her and working through Her. When the King of kings and Lord of lords returns for His Bride it will not be for the purpose of taking Her to some celestial place in the far reaches of the universe to prepare Her for Bridehood. Christ will not return for His Bride until She *is* ready to enter into Her role as Queen of the universe because of Her marriage to the King of the universe. Some speak of a 3½-year or seven-year honeymoon in Heaven before returning to establish Earth as headquarters for a universal reign. Regardless of the honeymoon time, whether it will be five seconds, 3½ years, or seven years, after the honeymoon the Bride will be ushered into the throne room to sit down with Jesus in His Father's throne to begin a co-reign over God's universal domain.

Preparing the Bride. This book reveals that the Church was predestinated and planned from eternity for an eternal purpose. It shows that Jesus purchased His Bride. It portrays His method of preparing the Bride by empowering, purifying, and perfecting Her until She could be presented unto Himself a glorious Church-Bride — without spot, wrinkle, or blemish. His offer to the Church is for Her to preside with Him as co-potentate over His vast universal domain, to perpetuate His presence, purpose, and program throughout the eternal ages to come. I believe Christ has chosen to take approximately 2,000 years to prepare His Bride.

From Birth to Eternal Destiny. The book will show how and when the Church was born, its performance in its early stages of life — its **Origina-**

tion. We will discuss its decline and its time of spiritual Egyptian bondage — its **Deterioration.** It will relate the "time of restitution" or restoration of truth God has used to bring the Church to her present age of maturity — its **Restoration.** It will then venture into some eschatological discussions concerning the truth yet to be restored to the mortal Church. Lastly, it will deal with the restored Church's eternal ministry, or the ultimate **Destination** of the Church.

In summary, the goal of the book is to reveal God's plan for the Church in its **Origination, Deterioration, Restoration,** and **Ultimate Destination.**

A Sequel Planned. This book will have a sequel which will give in-depth scriptural, historical, and factual outlined studies on each of the restorational movements of the Church. Each of the Church types and Doctrines of Christ will be included. There are many books which have been written on the Church from the historical aspect. The student who wants to expand his background knowledge would do well to study them. Christian International University has undergraduate and graduate level extension courses on Church History that cover the history of the Church from the resurrection of Christ to the present time.

An Overview Approach. The book does not give all the details, but will contain a sufficient amount of information to give an overview of the Church from the first coming to the second coming of Christ. It is the jigsaw picture that helps determine where the individual pieces go; the skeleton which provides the overall framework for properly placing the muscles and organs of the body in their correct position. The individual doctrinal pieces in the jigsaw picture of the

Church will be studied in the sequel. This writing will help you grasp the overall picture so that you can rightly divide the Word and properly relate to what God has done, is doing, and will do in the Church.

The Overall Picture. It is much easier to put the jigsaw puzzle together if you have a clear view of the overall picture. You can see that there is blue sky, so you place all the blue pieces in one area, knowing that they have to fit into that section. You place the red barn pieces in another, the green grass pieces in another area, and so on. Once you have the overall skeleton view of the Church in relation to where the Church came from, where it is, and where the Church is headed, you can more easily put Christian doctrine and experience into its proper perspective.

Coming Into Present Truth. Many individuals from various backgrounds are coming into the present truth of what God is doing in this day and hour. They include those with no church background and others with various levels of church backgrounds such as Catholic, Historic, Holiness, Fundamental, Evangelical, Pentecostal, non-denominational, and independent churches. These individuals are coming into a full Christian heritage, rich in "know-so" salvation, with Holy Ghost reality in love, joy, power, liberty in worship, and freedom and faith to possess all the good things of God for spirit, soul, and body. Many do not realize how the wealth of their Christian charismatic heritage was accumulated. The experiential truths which God has taken more than 450 years to restore to the corporate Church, individuals can now receive within a short period of time. For example, a person who thinks he can earn his way to Heaven and who does not know Jesus Christ, may come to the knowledge of present truth. In one or two days he might be born again of the Holy Spirit, be baptized by immersion, sanctified, receive the gift of the Holy Ghost, and be healed of a physical affliction. He may then start worshipping God with uplifted hands, begin expressing praise to God with shouting, clapping, and dancing before the Lord, and receive laying on of hands and prophecy. This would not give him all the biblical knowledge he needs or give him maturity of character, but he would have received most of the experiential truths which God has restored during the last five centuries.

The Trouble With Truth. Every individual down through the years who has been instrumental in restoring certain truths to the Church has had to go outside the camp of status quo Christianity. It is hoped that the reader will gain an appreciation for the Catholic fathers who maintained the truth of the Christian monotheistic faith in one God and in His virgin-born Son, Jesus. Also, respect is warranted for the basics of Christianity as found in the Apostles' Creed and maintained during the Dark Ages, a time of great Church apostasy. During this period there was great persecution and martyrdom from heathen, Moslems, and many other anti-Christian groups. The reader will become knowledgeable concerning the great Protestant movement and the men who sacrificed everything to bring forth the truth of "justification by faith" and establish the doctrine of "Repentance from Dead Works." Likewise, they will become knowledgeable about the men and women used by God to establish the truths that have brought the Church to its present possessions and performance.

Another Restorational Movement Scheduled. Most of the readers of this book will be too young in years, or will not have had the opportunity, to be part of a world-wide sovereign restorational movement. Do not feel left out. The Holy Spirit has not finished His work in the Church. Another restorational movement is scheduled to take place before Revelation 11:15 is literally fulfilled.

Trumpet About to Sound. The trumpet for advancing is about to sound again. Your generation will be challenged to establish the greatest truth and the most revolutionary reality that has ever been revealed to the Church. The truth to be restored to the Church can only be fulfilled by the last generation of the mortal Church. Everywhere I travel throughout the United States and around the world there are those who are catching glimpses of the experiential truth which is to be restored to the Church. The Spirit is preparing and equipping saintly soldiers for the battle of battles and the consummation of the ages. We have a great cloud of witnesses, including the patriarchal forefathers, prophets, early Church Apostles, and Church history leaders, who have paid a price to bring us this far. They have fulfilled the will of God in their generation, but God has left something special for this generation that "they without us should not be made perfect" *(Heb. 11:40)*. They are waiting on us to put the final touches to God's plan so that they, along with us, can enter into our eternal performance with Christ. Therefore let us lay aside every weight that might hinder us in this race while pressing toward the mark for that high calling of God in Christ Jesus *(Phil. 3:14)*. Therefore, ". . . present your bodies as a living sacrifice . . . unto God" *(Rom. 12:1)* that He may use it to fulfill and manifest all truth and prophetic Scripture concerning the Church, and that He may come back for His fulfilled Church and perfected Bride to inaugurate them. The restoration of the Church and the maturing of the Bride will bring Jesus back from Heaven to translate His people into His eternal purpose for them *(Acts 3:20-21)*.

The
Definition
Of The
Church

1

God's
Eternal
Desire

Did God
Want A Church?

The Word of God declares that ". . . Christ also loved the Church," and He "gave himself for it . . . ," that the Church was chosen in Christ before the foundation of the world *(Eph. 5:25, 1:4)*. Jesus paid the ransom price for His Church through the shedding of His life's blood on the cross of Calvary. Jesus desired the Church so strongly that He came to this world and submitted Himself to all the humiliations and limitations of mortal man. He suffered, bled, and died. He endured indescribable agony in body, soul, mind and spirit. Hebrews 12:1,2 reveals that it was ". . . for the **joy** that was set before Him [that Jesus] endured the cross. . ." The Church is the joy that was set before Him. Everything He did while in His mortal body was for His Church. "For God so loved the world that He gave His only begotten Son, that whosoever . . ." *(Jn. 3:16)*. Jesus came to purchase those "whosoevers" and then He sent the Holy Spirit to gather them together into one Body of believers called the Church.

Church Not a Second Choice. The Church is not a second choice of God's. The Church was not planned and instituted after Israel rejected her Messiah. The Church was included in God's eternal plans in the eons of past time, before the foundation of the world. Some say the natural race of Israelites is God's first love . . . that He sent His Son to redeem them, but they rejected Him; therefore God instituted the Church as a secondary business until He could get back to His main business with Israel. In his book, *Destined for the Throne,* foreworded by Billy Graham, Rev. Paul E. Billheimer makes some emphatic statements concerning the role of the Church in God's eternal universal plan.

> The *human race* was created in the image and likeness of God *for one purpose: to provide an eternal companion for the Son.* After the fall and promise of redemption through the coming Messiah, the *Messianic race (Israel)* was born and nurtured in order to bring the *Messiah. And the Messiah came for one intent and only one: to give birth to His Church,* thus to obtain His Bride. *The Church* then — the called-out body of redeemed mankind — turns out to be *the central object, the goal,* not only of mundane history but of all that God has been doing in all realms, *from all eternity.* (Paul E. Billheimer, *Destined for the Throne,* Fort Washington, Pennsylvania, Christian Literature Crusade, 1975. p. 22.)

He presents the cosmology that the creation of the universe and all history related to mankind down through the ages has happened for the sole purpose of producing the Church. He projects the idea that the entire universe in its totality is cooperating with God in His purpose to select and train His Church as His eternal companion. The entire universe is ordered for this purpose, for all things belong to the Church and are for Her benefit *(I Cor. 3:21-23 AMP)*.

The Destiny of the Church. We may conclude that God definitely wanted a Church. His ultimate purpose for the Church is for Her to be an eternal companion of His Son. All power in Heaven and Earth has been given to Jesus. He is King of the universe and head over all things to the Church. When the Church-Bride becomes eternally joined to the Son, then they will sit down together in the Father's throne *(Rev. 3:21)*. When a man and woman are joined together in marriage, God calls them one flesh. The Father will look upon Jesus and His Wife as one. The Bride will equally share Christ's reign, and will perform and relate to God as one with Christ Jesus. It is my belief that the Church, because of Her relationship to Jesus Christ, will become a part of the sovereign eternal headship which perpetuates God's dominion throughout His universal domain. "If we are His children, we share His treasures and all that Christ claims as His will belong to all of us as well! Yes, if we share in His suffering, we shall certainly share in His glory" *(Rom. 8:17 Phillips)*.

Was It Jesus' Will and Desire to Have a Church?

Yes! For He personally declared, "*. . . I will build My Church . . .*" *(Mt. 16:18)*. Notice the implications of each word:

"**I**" Jesus is personally committed to the building of His Church.

"**will**" The Church had not yet been birthed, but was the sovereign will of Jesus Christ. *Will* indicates determination to produce and perfect, regardless of time and effort required.

"build" Suggests a long, slow, drawn-out process *(Eph. 2:20* literal translation, the Church is "being built").

"My" His personal property, pride, and possession *(Eph. 5:25; Acts 20:28).* ". . . Christ . . . gave Himself for it" [the Church],". . . purchased [it] with His own blood" *(Eph. 5:25; Acts 20:28).*

"Church" Establishes at once the distinction between this special, called-out company and every other classification of human being.

Membership a Prerequisite. All the promises of the Bible which refer to the saints ruling and reigning with Christ are qualified by a prerequisite of membership in the Universal Body of Christ. Christ does not work on planet Earth apart from His Church. The Church is His earthly body of expression.

God's Promises Are to the Church. To get in on the promises you must become a living member of the Church, the corporate Body of Christ. The Church is going to fulfill all things, regardless of what the world and certain individual Christians do. The "called out Ecclesia" will perfectly fulfill God's eternal will. This does not mean that every person who starts out in this race is going to win. Everyone who runs this race to the end will win the prize, but those who stop along the way or turn back will not rule and reign with Christ and His Church. The Body can make it without certain members, but a member of the Body cannot make it without staying in the Body. God works with the Church as a whole in dealing with the fulfilling of His overall purpose for the Church. However, the Church consists of particular members which must be dealt with and ministered to on an individual basis. It is the perfecting of each member that makes the whole Body perfect.

One Man — One Church. God never did create a creature called "people." He created a person, one man. The Church is viewed as "one Man," for the Church is destined to be a "perfect Man" *(Eph. 4:13)*. The Church is one Body made up of individual members. The Bible was written to the Church and for the Church, (most books of the Bible begin with "To the Church" or "To the saints"). The Bible is for the enlightenment and for the edification of the Church. It is the power and wisdom of God. It is the power used to bring other members into the Church. The promises of God concerning the present work and future ministry of the Church are not to individuals, but to the Church. For an individual to participate, he must become and remain an active, lively member of the universal Body of Christ, and he must work for its overall fulfillment.

Catching the Heart-Throb of Jesus. If ministers of the Church would catch the heart-throb of Jesus, their efforts would not be in promoting their pet doctrines, denominations, revelations, or experiences, but would be in upbuilding and unifying the Church. Jesus loves every member of His Church whether we do or not. There are truths which cannot be compromised and experiences which cannot be denied for the sake of "getting along," but this does not excuse the hard-headed, narrow-minded, bigoted, self-righteous, unteachable, cold-hearted, and indifferent attitudes held by some ministers of the Church and members of the Body of Christ. Those who have been justified by faith, who have trusted in the blood of Jesus for the cleansing of their sins, and who are filled with and are walking in the Holy Spirit, are members of the one and selfsame Body. If we become exclusive and separate ourselves from the Body in general, we cut ourselves away from God's work, for His greatest love and main work is with the universal corporate Body of Christ, the Church.

2

Why Jesus Established The Church

Why a Church? What we want to discuss here is "Why a Church?" Why was the Church placed here on planet Earth? Why a certain period of time for the mortal Church to function? What purpose could be served by allowing the Church to continue for several hundred and possibly thousands of years? The Church ihas been in existence for almost two millennia (A.D. 30 to A.D. 1980 = 1,950 years).

Why a Mortal Church Age? What is God's purpose in having a dispensation of the Church? Should the Church age last approximately 2,000 years, why is there a need for such a length of time? What is the Holy Spirit commissioned to accomplish during this period of time? Why is it such a long process? What will be the end product? How will the dispensation of the Church age fit into God's eternal plan for man? Will there be another age of God's dealings with man or will the Church bring about the consummation of the ages? Is there a millennial age following the Church age in which there will be a new order established for the functions of man on planet Earth? What will be God's eternal plan and pattern for the function of man and Earth when all human beings have been made immortal? What ministry will the Church fulfill among God's other eternal creatures throughout the endlessness of eternity? Is the Church being called, purchased, and perfected just for this 2,000-year period only, or is the Church being prepared for an eternal position and performance?

The Standard Answers to the question, "Why a Church?" are: God wanted the Church to be a witness, to preach the gospel to the whole world, to "occupy until He comes," to represent Christ to the world, to carry on the work of Christ, to multiply the ministry of Jesus through millions of mortal humans rather than just through the one mortal body that the man, Jesus Christ, inhabited; to demonstrate God's power, to manifest His ministry, to portray His precepts, and to reveal His will for mankind.

All of these questions will be addressed, but at this point we want to show how the Church was prepared, produced, and launched into its mortal ministry on Earth.

The Bible and most theologians agree that the Church is to be an extension of the ministry of Jesus Christ to humanity. Since the Church is to personify Christ as Jesus personified God, then we need to evaluate the life and ministry of Jesus to determine the ministry of the Church.

Jesus' Life and Ministry on Earth

Jesus was supernaturally conceived by the power of the Holy Ghost. God was His Father. He lived a proper life as the oldest child in a human family. He lived a normal (God's norm), mortal, human life for 30 years. He did manual labor, ate, slept, had a social life, and played games as He grew from babyhood, childhood, and adolescence to manhood. At the age of 30 He was launched into His anointed ministry. He was baptized in water, baptized with the Holy Spirit (symbolized by the Dove), then was tempted, tested, and tried by the devil. He submitted His will, His way, and His desires to God. His body was presented to God as a living sacrifice demonstrating the Word, will, and way of God in all of His eternal attributes and glory. Jesus preached, prayed, healed the sick, cast out devils, and raised the dead. He overcame evil with good, blessed those that cursed Him, and did good to those who despitefully used Him. Though Master of all, yet He girded Himself with a towel and served His disciples. He did more than verbally teach — He demonstrated the character of God to mankind.

He then told His followers that He was going away but that He would not be gone for long. He was crucified, buried, resurrected, and He ascended to the Father in Heaven. The early Apostles expected Him to return and establish His kingdom on Earth during their lifetime. However, He has not literally fulfilled that promise in relation to returning in His resurrected, personal, human body. (We are referring to what eschatology calls the "Second Coming.") However, He did keep His promise given in the fourteenth chapter of John. It was fulfilled in a spiritual, rather than in a physical dimension, and was to continue that way for centuries before the literal fulfillment of His promises.

Spiritual Kingdom Before Literal Kingdom. In Acts we have the story of Jesus' final departure. The last thing He told His followers (500 heard His instructions) was ". . . they should not depart from Jerusalem, but wait for the promise of the Father . . ."

(Acts 1:4). He did not want them to be concerned about a natural kingdom with a literal, political fulfillment, but instead wanted them to be concerned about a spiritual kingdom which would come with power after their receiving the gift of the Holy Ghost.

Jesus departed to the Father, and His resurrected human body was seated at the right hand of the Majesty on High. That body will not be seen again by His Church until He returns to transform all of His followers' bodies into the likeness of His glorious body. This will be done by His resurrecting and translating power.

This does not mean that He left His followers as orphans down here on planet Earth. He said in John, "I go to prepare a place for you. . . . that where I am there you may be also," and "I will not leave you comfortless: [as orphans] I will come to you" (Jn. 14:2,3,18). Then He said that the Holy Ghost would come and be to them everything that He had been to them while in His mortal body.

The Church is the Place. Jesus had planned this place for them from eternity. Now all things had been accomplished for this plan to be activated. The spiritual place that Jesus had prepared for them was the **Church,** which is the universal Body of Christ. In that Body there are many "mansions," "dwelling places," "abodes," or "places" for individual members to function.

The Birth of the Church. As they were waiting in the upper room, the climactic time for the fulfillment of the promised Holy Ghost arrived. In the early morning hours of that memorial Jewish feast day called Pentecost it happened. Sweeping in like a mighty wind the uniting, empowering Holy Ghost made them one Body. The **Church** was birthed into reality and life. She entered a new covenant relationship with God. A New Testament had just taken the place of the Old. The 120 saints present were spiritually translated from Mt. Sinai to Mt. Zion. The wind and fire came as the last manifestations of Mt. Sinai, but, as they were transferred to Mt. Zion and entered into the new covenant, a new manifestation was given to them. They began to speak supernaturally in Holy Spirit languages; that is, their born-again human spirits were endowed with Holy Ghost power directing their vocal organs to speak in languages incomprehensible to their natural understanding. The Church had come forth from the womb of Jesus' preparation and had now burst forth upon the world. The second chapter of Acts records the physical signs and manifestations that took place on that day. But many things took place which would not be seen by natural eyes.

From Mt. Sinai to Mt. Zion. The saints were transferred to Mt. Zion which brought them ". . . unto the city of the living God, the heavenly Jerusalem, to an innumerable company of angels, to the general assembly and Church of the firstborn, which are written in Heaven and to God the Judge of all, and to the spirits of just men made perfect, and to Jesus, the mediator of the new convenant . . ." They were ". . . translated out of the kingdom of darkness into the Kingdom of God's dear Son," and were "raised up together and made to sit together in heavenly places in Christ Jesus" *(Heb. 12:22,23; Col. 1:13; Eph. 2:6).*

The Building Begun. The building of the Church had begun. It would be

> ". . . built upon the foundation of the apostles and prophets, Jesus Christ Himself being the chief cornerstone; in whom all the build-

ing fitly framed together groweth unto an holy temple in the Lord: In whom ye also are builded together for an habitation of God through the Spirit" *(Eph. 2:20).*

The personal bodies of the saints had now become the temples of the Holy Ghost. These spirit-filled bodies became the members of the Universal Corporate Body of Christ. Though few in number, this was the beginning of His Church, His Corporate Body on Earth. This Body, consisting of those whom the Holy Spirit baptized into it, had become the dwelling place of God. God had now moved His headquarters from the Tabernacle of Moses to the Church. The Church (true Christianity) is now the dwelling place of God upon Earth.

Christ's New Earth Body. When Jesus was here in mortal flesh, His personal body was the dwelling place of God on Earth. Through that body God revealed and manifested Himself to mankind. Jesus was God manifested in mortal flesh. That dwelling place of God, the personal body of Jesus, was taken to Heaven. But humanity was not left without a physical contact with Christ Jesus, for His **Church** became His Corporate Body on Earth. As God limited Himself to the body of Jesus (the fulness of the Godhead dwelt wholly in the body of Jesus) *(Col. 2:9),* so has Jesus limited His contact with the world to His Corporate Body, the Church. Jesus has invested Himself in the Church. He is able to meet the needs of the world and to fulfill His desire for humanity based on the response and performance of the **Church.** Just as God limited Himself to the body of Jesus for the performance of His will and for the manifestation of His glory, so has Christ Jesus limited Himself to the Church. If the Church believes and responds fully, then Christ is unlimited in His performance. If the Church is lukewarm, indifferent, and insensitive to His desire to manifest mightily His power over all the enemies of the Church and over all binding enemies of the curse, then He is limited in fulfilling what He died to reveal and to fulfill.

An Awesome Responsibility. Fellow members of the great Corporate Body of Christ, what an awesome responsibility and privilege we have as sons of God. Let us analyze our lives and evaluate our faith to see if we are walking worthy of the great vocation wherewith we are called *(Eph. 4:1)*. Are we fulfilling His will and manifesting His glory as He faithfully fulfilled His Father's will and manifested His glory? "[Father,] as thou has sent me into the world, even so have I sent them into the world" *(Jn. 17:18)*.

Fathoming Full Faith. What will happen when we fully fathom and believe that we really are who He says we are; that we can do what His Word declares we can do; that we actually have all that His Word says we have, and that He wants to manifest mightily through us His miraculous *Ministry* to *Mankind?*

3

The
Church
Defined

The term "church" has many meanings among Christendom. It is used to describe a building set aside for religious services. To some it means their local congregation or denomination. To others it means the whole of religious Christian organizations. Some only think of the term in relation to identifying the "Catholic church," "Baptist church," "Pentecostal church," etc. It is essential that we find out how the Bible defines the Church.

Because the **Church** is the main subject of this book and the word **"Church"** is used over and over again, it might be helpful for the author to give his definition.

The Church is the One Universal Many-Membered Corporate Body of Christ

All terms which have the equivalency of this definition will be capitalized. The author feels this emphasis is justifiable based on the calling and joint-heirship of the Church/Bride of Christ. The Bride is destined to be united in marriage with Jesus and co-reign with Him in His eternal God-head function.

What the Church Is and Is Not. The Church is One Universal Body of Believers. It is One Great Corporate Body consisting of multi-millions of members. Jesus said, "I will build My Church," and "He gave Himself for the Church," not churches. The Church is not Judaism improved and continued. It is not a denomination, an organization, or a religious system that propagates certain doctrines and religious rites.

When the word "Church" is spelled with a capital "C," reference is not being made to any specific denomination or any group with particular titles or doctrines, but to the Universal Body of Christ. The one and only true Church is a living organism, a functioning body consisting of many lively members. These members are born-again, Spirit-filled believers who have accepted Christ Jesus as their Savior and Lord.

There will be references to the Church and to the Bride. Most of the time these terms are interchangeable.

It is of urgent importance not to become entangled with definitions and titles. Rather we must discover what it takes to operate according to the highest pleasure and purpose of God and "press toward that mark for the prize of that high calling of God in Christ Jesus" *(Phil. 3:14).*

The Greek word **"ekklesia"** is translated as "assembly" three times and as "church" 112 times. The word **"ekklesia"** is derived from **"ek,"** (out), and

"kaleo," (to call), denoting in historic Greek usage the assembly of citizens called out from their homes to gathering places for special purposes.

Various Theological Definitions of the Church

Bancroft: "The word Church literally means a called-out company and, therefore, it comprises only those who are truly called out from the world by Christ unto Himself, in other words, all true believers wherever found. It is not the aggregate of all churches, composed as they are at present of both true and false professors, nor is it any particular church on earth, although some churches have formed themselves into what they call a church of the whole, or a catholic church.

"The Church is composed of all true Christian believers taken out of all nations, tribes, and tongues, and united with their living head, Jesus Christ during the age from Pentecost to the Rapture. Induction into the Church is the work of Christ through the Holy Spirit." (Emery H. Bancroft, *Christian Theology,* Zondervan Publishing House, Grand Rapids, Michigan, 1955. p. 265.)

Thiessen: "In describing the universal Church of Jesus Christ the Greek word **'ekklesia'** is used. In itself this term means simply a body of called-out people. However, the New Testament has filled it with a spiritual content, so that it means a people called out from the world and from sinful things. It is interesting to note that the English word 'church' comes from the Greek word *'kuriakos,'* which means 'belonging to the Lord.' This adjective occurs only twice in the New Testament as 'Lord's' Supper and 'Lord's'

Day *(Rev. 1:10; I Cor. 11:20).* We might, therefore, give as a secondary definition of the 'church' the following: *A group of people called out from the world and belonging to the Lord.* Yet the former definition recognizes more clearly the fact of the new birth as essential to membership in the true Church." (Henry C. Thiessen, *Lectures in Systematic Theology,* Grand Rapids, Michigan, Wm. B. Eerdmans Publishing Co., 1949. p. 407.)

Robinson: "More fully stated, the one Church of God is not an institutional but a supernatural entity which is in process of growth towards the world to come. It is the sphere of the action of the risen and ascended Lord. All its members are in Christ and are knit together by a supernatural kinship. All their gifts and activities continue the work of Christ by the power of the Holy Spirit, originate from Christ, and are co-ordinated to Him to the final goal. Then the Church will appear in the age to come as the one people of God united in one congregation before the throne, as the one celestial city — the new Jerusalem." (Everett F. Harrison, Gen. Ed., *Baker's Dictionary of Theology,* Grand Rapids, Michigan, Baker's Book House, 1960. p. 123.)

Not a Technical Dissertation

The theological term used for the doctrine of the Church is "ecclesiology." This book is not designed to be a technical dissertation on ecclesiology, but it is designed to be a spiritual overview from God's eternal perspective and purpose. However, a scriptural study of what the Bible has to say about the Church is essential.

4

Scriptural Presentation Of The Church

The Church and the Body of Christ are One and the Same

> *Ephesians 1:22,23* ". . . the **Church,** which is His **Body** . . ."
> *Colossians 1:18* ". . . Christ is the head of the **Body**, the **Church** . . ."
> *Colossians 1:24* ". . . for His **Body's** sake, which is the **Church** . . ."
> *I Corinthians 12:27* ". . . now ye (the church) are the **Body** of Christ . . ."

Paul, the Apostle to the Gentiles and the one who received the greatest revelation of the Church, declares that the Church is the Body of Christ. He states that this truth was not made known unto the sons of men in other ages, but that now it has been revealed to him and other apostles and prophets by the Spirit *(Eph. 3:3-6).*

Only One Church — One Body of Christ

Ephesians 2:16; 3:6; 4:4; Colossians 3:15; Romans 12:4, 5; I Corinthians 12:12-14, 20.

These Scriptures clearly reveal that there is only one Church. Christ has only one Body upon Earth at this time. As God has only one Christ, so Christ has only one Church just as man is to have only one wife. God recognizes only one group of people as His.

Those who have Christ in them and have been baptized into Christ are known as the Body of Christ, the Church. "For by one Spirit are we all baptized into one body, whether we be Jews or Gentiles, whether we be bond or free." God does not have a black church and a white church or a Jewish church and a Gentile church. For as the physical body has variously functioning members performing as one, so it is with the Body of Christ.

Members of the Same Body. Isn't it wonderful to know that we are a part of the whole Body of Christ and that every person who has been born of the Holy Spirit is in the same Body? My sins were washed away by the blood of Jesus on July 31, 1950 at an old-fashioned brush arbor meeting in Oklahoma. Two nights later I was baptized with the Holy Spirit, and the following Sunday the preacher took me to the river and baptized me in water. I have continued to walk in Christ going from glory to glory and faith to faith unto this present moment. Because there is only one Body of Christ, every individual who has received Christ is in the same Body. We are brothers and sisters in the great family of God, whether we appreciate that fact or not, or whether we agree on every doctrine or express our worship to God in the same manner.

Christians Do Not Function Alone. The Body can function without certain members but no member can function without the Body. If a Christian separates himself from the great corporate Body of Christ and seeks to function alone and be a law and entity unto himself, he will begin spiritually to wither and die. This is one reason why the Bible declares for us not to forsake the assembling of ourselves together *(Heb. 10:25).* It has been said that there will be no Christians recognized in Heaven by their tags here on Earth, whether they are called Catholics, Protestants, Fundamentalists, Evangelicals, Pentecostals, Charismatics, or whatever. God pays no attention to the name on the building where the saints gather to worship. Man looks on the outward and is proud of the group into which he has been baptized and has membership. God pays no attention to these things. He looks directly into the heart to see if Christ lives there and to see how much of that life is surrendered to God.

The Body of Christ One As Jesus and the Father Are One

Saints of God, hear what the Holy Spirit has to say to the 20th Century Church. The day has dawned and the timing of the Lord is drawing near for the fulfillment of the prophetic prayer that Jesus prayed in St. John 17. Everywhere I travel throughout the United States, Canada, and around the world I hear ministers saying, "It's time we become one." A desire and willingness for divine unity is arising within the hearts of those who are in tune with what God is doing today.

His Prayer Will Be Fulfilled. Jesus prayed *(Jn. 17)* for all true believers in Him to be one as He and His Father are one. No prayer of Jesus goes unfulfilled. That prayer will be fulfilled before the second coming of Jesus. The prophetic statement in Isaiah 52:8 declares that we shall see eye to eye when the Lord shall bring again Zion. Many react to that statement by saying, "If that is the truth then I'll be glad when everyone sees it like I do." (No doubt **all** of us will have to do some adjusting before it's all over.)

Holy Ghost Pressure. God seemingly has allowed the Church to "get by" with its divisiveness. Presently in the church world there exist jealousy, criticism, condemnation, denominational pride, sectarian spirits, *and* argumentative and divisive spirits over doctrines, revelations, and experiences. These occur among Christian denominations, within non-denominational groups, and among church members in local assemblies. Be assured that these days are over for the Bride. This divisiveness will no longer be tolerated by the Holy Spirit. Time is running out. The day of the Bride being presented to the Bridegroom is near. Judgement is beginning at the house of God, the Church. Holy Ghost pressure is being placed upon and within the Bride to come to perfection.

Spirit of unity. Each one who makes up the Bride of Christ will have nothing in his heart, attitude, or thinking that will hinder him from being one with all other members in the local and Universal Corporate Body of Christ. All members in the Bride of Christ will have a love and unity with each other just as Jesus and His Father have a love and a unity between Themselves. Each member of the Body will know his place and ministry. They will "not thrust one another, they shall not break their ranks but each shall walk in his own path" *(Joel 2:8).* There will be no sense of inferiority or superiority, but, instead, there will be a spirit of unity, love, and oneness just as Jesus and

His Father had when Jesus prayed that prayer. This prophetic prayer of Jesus will be fulfilled.

Are our lives and attitudes helping to fulfill that prayer or are our lives a hindrance to its fulfillment? If there are any of the following carnal attributes in any members of the Church they will have to be purged: spiritual pride, resentment, jealousy, know-it-all/have-it-all attitude, our little group is the elected few in the Bride, an independent/self-righteous spirit of exclusiveness; too historical, evangelical, and conservative to fellowship with the demonstrative and liberated charismatics; or too spiritual and too advanced in revelation and worship to fellowship with those less spiritual in manifestations of the Spirit. For these members to make Bridehood it will be necessary for God to take them through the baptism of fire to burn out all that is wood, hay, and stubble so that nothing may remain but the pure gold of Christ's love, nature, and character *(I Cor. 3:13)*.

> "Holy Father, keep through thine own name those whom thou hast given me, that they may be **one, as we are** . . . Neither pray I for these alone, but for them also which shall believe on me through their word; That they all may be **one;** as thou, Father, art in me, and I in thee, that they also may be **one** in us: that the world may believe that thou hast sent me. And the glory which thou gavest me I have given them; that **they may be one even as we are one:** I in them, and thou in me that **they may be made perfect in one;** and that the world may know that thou hast sent me, and hast loved them, as thou hast loved me *(Jn. 17:11, 20-23)*.

Becoming a Member in the Body of Christ

There is nothing you can do of your natural self to become a member in the Body of Christ. You cannot join it; you must be born, translated, or adopted into the Church. It can only come of, through, and by the Holy Spirit.

John 3:3-7 One must be born of the Spirit.
Romans 8:15 Sons of God by Spirit of adoption.
Romans 8:16 The Spirit itself bears witness with our spirit that we are the Children of God.
I Corinthians 12:13 Baptized into the Body of Christ by the Holy Spirit.
Colossians 1:13 Must be translated into the Kingdom of God's dear Son.
Ephesians 5:30 We are members of His body, of His flesh, and of His bones.

Roll Book in Heaven

There is no possible way that one can become a member of the Church (which is the Body of Christ) by putting his or her name on some independent or denominational church roll book. The **roll book** is in **Heaven.**

Luke 10:20 Names written in Heaven.
Ephesians 2:19, Philipians 3:20 Our citizenship is in Heaven.
Revelations 21:27 Names are written in the Lamb's Book of Life.

How Do We Become Members of His Body, His Flesh and of His Bones?

The only way a lower realm of life can be lifted up to the realm of a higher life is for it to be taken up and transformed into that higher realm of life. The lower realm of life has *to die and forsake its way* of life and take on the nature of the higher way of life. The following analogy will illustrate this truth.

> Minerals can be taken up and transformed into plant life.
>
> Plants can be taken up and transformed into animal life.
>
> Animal flesh can be taken up and transformed into human life.
>
> Human life can be taken up and transformed into Christ's life.

God's ultimate purpose for us is for our self-life to be completely taken up and transformed into Christ's life. When we came to Christ we died with Him. We have died to our old way of life and now "our life is hid with Christ in God." "I live; yet it is not I that liveth but Christ that liveth in me . . ." "that the life also of Jesus might be made manifest in our body . . . in our mortal flesh" *(Gal. 2:20; II Cor. 4:10,11; Col. 3:3)*.

Who Decides the Member's Place of Function?

> *I Corinthians 12:18* God sets the members in the Body as it pleases Him.
>
> *Romans 9:16* Not of him that willeth or runneth but God that sheweth mercy.
>
> *Romans 1:1; Ephesians 1:1* Paul was **called** by the **will of God** to be an Apostle.

I Corinthians 12:11 The Holy Spirit divides out the gifts and ministries to every man severally as He wills.

No Man Can Determine Your Ministry. No mortal man has the power to choose your place of function in the Body of Christ. Likewise, no man can separate you from the Body of Christ. You may volunteer into the armed forces, but the military authorities decide which place of service you will fill, according to where you would best fit and where you are needed most. You may choose to serve, but God makes the decision of how, where, with what, and with whom you serve. A member may increase and expand his gifts and ministries by faithfulness in using what he has received. A prophet of God or the Presbytery may be used to reveal your calling and ministry but only the Holy Spirit can impart and ordain ministry. The Holy Spirit may do this sovereignly, or He may speak and flow through a human channel.

What Part of Man Becomes a Member of the Body of Christ?

Not only man's spirit and soul but his flesh-and-bone body becomes the temple of God and becomes a member of the Corporate Body of Christ.

I Corinthians 6:13 " . . . now the **body** is not for fornication, but for the Lord: and the Lord for the **body."**

I Corinthians 6:15 ". . . know ye not your **bodies** are the members of [Body of] Christ."

I Corinthians 6:19 ". . . know ye not that your **body** is temple of Holy Ghost."

I Corinthians 6:20 ". . . glorify God in your

body which is God's."
I Corinthians 3:16 ". . . ye are the temple of God."
II Corinthians 4:10,11 ". . . life of Jesus should be manifested in our **body,** . . . our **mortal flesh.**"
I Thessalonians 5:23 ". . . I pray God your whole spirit, soul and **body** be preserved blameless unto the coming of our Lord Jesus Christ."

Our Bodies Part of Redemption. The death, burial, and resurrection of Jesus Christ provided redemption not only for man's spirit and soul but for his body also. Every member in the Eternal Body of Christ will be a whole person — body, soul, and spirit. The saints whose bodies have died will receive that part of the redemption of their bodies through resurrection. The last living generation will receive their bodily redemption through translation when their flesh-and-bone bodies are changed from mortality to immortality, from corruptible to incorruptible, from temporal to eternal. The Corporate Body of Christ, though called and equipped during the age of time, is designed and destined to function throughout the ages of eternity. God has already provided for and decreed that His Church will be transformed into an eternal body capable of functioning in the spirit world throughout the universe as well as functioning in the physical world on planet Earth.

Headquarters of the
Church and Membership Roll Book

Ephesians 1:22, 4:15, 5:23; Colossians 1:18, 2:19; I Corinthians 11:3; I Timothy 2:5.

Christ Jesus is the one and only head and headquarters of the Church. The head is neither St. Peter nor any of the early Apostles. No man, religious organization, or city is the head or headquarters of the Church. Jesus alone has been appointed by God to be head over all things to the Church. Christ has anointed the five gifted ministries of Ephesians 4:11 to minister to his Church until it reaches maturity. There are men of God called to be leaders with divine delegated authority, but God never intended for any man or any group of men here on Earth to be the head of the Corporate Body of Christ. No man or system has been ordained of God to control the free will and conscience of another. Each man (member of the Church) shall give an account of **himself** to Christ, the head of the Church. There is one mediator between God and men; that is the **man** Christ Jesus.

Local Church Membership is Good. It is good to be affiliated with a local congregation and to have your name in a local church roll book. However, this does not guarantee a person that his name is in the roll book of the Eternal **Church.** The roll book containing the true members of Christ's Body, the Church, is in Heaven. No mortal man can put another person's name in the book or take it out. No religious leader or Christian organization can pluck a member out of the heavenly Father's hand.

Corporate Body of Christ
vs. the Personal Body of Jesus

The Scriptures emphatically teach that there is only one Body of Christ and the Church is that Body. Therefore, some have erroneously taught that this does away with the personal body of Jesus Christ. The Church is the only physical body that Jesus has, and all that we will ever see literally of Jesus is Him manifested in His many-membered universal Body, the Church. Further, the physical body with which God clothed Himself was just for His time on Earth so that He might die mortally on the cross for man's redemption. Finally, they conclude that the body was discarded when He returned to Heaven.

Jesus Still Has Body. Does Jesus presently have His earth-born, flesh-and-bone body in Heaven? Was the body of Jesus that hung on the cross and then placed in a grave disintegrated into gases and a new body created of spiritual material? If so, then that would have been a re-creation, not a resurrection. Jesus' body was not re-created, it was resurrected. That same human body which was born of the virgin Mary, walked the shores of Galilee, hung on the cross of Calvary with nails piercing through the hands and feet, and then was placed in a grave — is the same flesh-and-bone body that arose from that grave. Now that is a resurrection!

Jesus Rose From Grave. Paul taught that this truth concerning the resurrection of Jesus' body is the foundation of the Christian faith. In fact, he boldly states, "If Christ be not risen from the dead then is our preaching vain [worthless, of no value, void], and your faith is also vain and you are yet in your sins" (I Cor. 15:12-26). If Christ was not bodily raised from the dead then no one will ever be resurrected. If Christ was not raised from the dead then it is ridiculous for me to record the history of the restoration of the Church and to write about the eternal Church.

Thank God we believe and we know that Jesus was born with a human body of the virgin Mary. Jesus was the same as any other human baby, but with one all-important difference — God was His Father. He was begotten of God. Jesus is the only begotten Son of God. God the Father provided the sperm cell that joined with the egg cell in the womb of Mary producing the body of Jesus. The Holy Ghost overshadowed Mary and a supernatural conception took place. Jesus was a generic son with the genes of God for His patterned process of development. It has been stated that the blood for the body of the human baby comes from the father.

> "Conception by the Holy Ghost was the only way the virgin birth could be accomplished. Mary nourished the body of Jesus and He became the *seed of David, according to the flesh.* The Holy Spirit contributed the blood of Jesus. It is sinless blood. It is divine blood. It is precious blood, for there has never been any other like it." (M. R. DeHaan, M.D., *The Chemistry of the Blood,* Grand Rapids, Michigan, Zondervan Publishing House, 1971. p. 35.)

Jesus had God's divine blood flowing through His veins; that is the reason the blood of Jesus can cleanse from every sin. Jesus was man in His physical body, but He was God in His life and blood purity.

True Bible-believing Christians actually believe that their God and Savior took on a human body through the process of conception and birth. He lived for 33½ years in that mortal body and then gave himself bodily for the redemption of the world on the cross. Jesus in His physical body went through all the horrors of the crucifixion until He could cry "It is finished!" Thank God, He did not say, "I am finished," but He said the accomplished work of redemption was completed. Jesus in His spirit body left that physical body hanging on the cross and went and preached to the spirits in prison. His dead body was placed in a grave. At the end of three days and three nights Jesus' spirit returned to that tomb and immediately the resurrection power of Jesus Christ began to saturate every molecule, cell, and atom of that body. The light grew instantly as bright as a thermo-nuclear explosion. His body was glorified, that is, it was made immortal, indestructible, and incorruptible. The atoms in His body were released from the time and space restrictions that mortal bodies have. The angels did not have to come and unwrap the grave cloth covering His body from head to foot. He simply arose by passing through it, just as He later passed through the locked door where the disciples were meeting.

Jesus Took Body to Heaven. Jesus took His human-born, resurrected body to Heaven. He will always have that flesh-and-bone body. One of the reasons God created the human race in His own image and likeness was to have a creation with the power of procreation, providing God with the opportunity to fulfill His eternal desire and plan to father a son in His own image and likeness. Adam was a created son by the hands and breath of God; Jesus was a generated son, a seed from the loins of God. Jesus was the seed of Abraham by Mary, but He was the direct seed of God and the first-born in the lineage of those who are spiritually born of God. God is literally the Father of our Lord Jesus Christ. Jesus is in all reality the only begotten Son of eternal God. Eternal God fathered the physical body of Jesus. That body was crucified, buried, resurrected, and re-inhabited by Jesus. It was immortalized and "eternalized." Jesus' flesh-and-bone body is the only human body in the triune Godhead. ("For in Christ there is all of God in a human body" *Col. 2:9 L.B.)*

Blue Print for Human Race. Christ was before all things and by Him all things exist. According to God's divine foreknowledge the human race was patterned after His blueprint for the body of Jesus. Therefore, God planned from eternity to have a son with a body, soul, and spirit — an earth body as well as a spirit body. The birth, life, death, and resurrection of Jesus was planned before Adam was created and placed on planet Earth. From God's perspective mankind came into existence because of God's eternal plan for His Son and His Bride-To-Be. From man's perspective Jesus came into existence as a mortal being because of mankind's need for redemption. Both perspectives are true, it is just a matter of whether you are viewing it from God's eternal plan or from man's need.

This short discussion reveals three of the things that motivated God to create mankind with the power of procreation and to place him (mankind) on planet Earth.

1. To beget a son in His own image in a human body; to personify Himself to mankind in that body — God manifested in the flesh.

2. To have this Son born with a mortal body in order for Him to live, to suffer, and then to die upon the cross to reveal God's love and provide redemption for humanity.

3. To call out a group of redeemed humanity which would make up a great Body to be purified, perfected, and then presented to the Son as His eternal Bride. The Bride is as precious to God the Father as is Jesus; for She is not an in-law but an in-Christ daughter of God.

Body of Jesus — Body of Christ

May we conclude from our logical scriptural presentation that the Corporate Body of Christ does not do away with the fact that Jesus still lives and reigns in His personal resurrected human body? The fact that Christ is coming to be glorified in His saints and to manifest Himself mightily in His sons does not eliminate the literal return of the Son of God in the clouds to receive unto Himself His bodily resurrected and translated Bride-Body.

Personal Body of Jesus vs. Corporate Body of Christ. The personal body of Jesus is the head of the Church and the saints make up the body of the Church. The Church is not called the body of Jesus but the Body of Christ. The name "Jesus" refers always in Scripture to the personal human body of our Savior. ". . . Thou shalt call His name Jesus" *(Mt. 1:21).* "Jesus — **'Jesous'** — is a transliteration of the Hebrew 'Joshua,' meaning 'Jehovah is salvation,' i.e., 'is the Savior,' 'a common name among the Jews.' It was given to the Son of God in incarnation as His personal name" (W. E. Vine, *An Expository Dictionary of New Testament Words,* Nashville, Tennessee, Thomas Nelson Publishers, 1939, p. 604). The word "Christ" *(Christos* in Greek) means "anointed." It is used in the Old Testament to describe the priests, prophets, and kings who in Greek are called *"hoi christoi Theou."* "the anointed of God." Jesus was the Christ, the only person ever anointed by God to be the promised Messiah. Because Jesus has anointed His Church to be His representative on Earth it can rightly be called the "Body of Christ," but it cannot be called the body of Jesus. The Scriptures never speak of "Jesus in you," or speak of the Church as the body of Jesus, but they do say "Christ in You," and "Ye are the Body of Christ." Jesus was resurrected in His human body, and He still personally dwells in that body which is seated at the right hand of God making intercession for the saints. However, through the Holy Ghost He is now dwelling in His Many-Membered Corporate Body, the Church, the Body of Christ.

The
Origination
Of The
Church

1

The Church Eternal

God Planned the Church With Jesus. The Church was conceived in the mind of God from eternity past. The Church was in the mind of the Eternal from the beginning and was planned and ordained before the foundation of the world *(Eph. 1:4)*. The concept of the Church is as eternal as Christ Jesus Himself. Though the Church was birthed during a particular time on Earth, yet it has always been. For this reason it can rightly be called *The Eternal Church*. It was prefigured throughout the Old Testament biblical record. It was *concealed* in the *womb* of the *Old Testament* and then was *birthed* in the *New Testament*. The *death* of Jesus on the cross *paid* the *redemptive price* for every person who would become a member of the Church. The *resurrection* of Jesus *authorized* the bringing forth of the Church, and the coming of the *Holy Spirit* on the day of Pentecost gave *birth* to the Church.

Jesus Christ purchased the Church through the giving of His life's blood on the cross, and He confirmed it by His resurrection *(Acts 20:28; Eph. 5:25-27; Eph. 2:13-16; Col. 1:18-29; I Pet. 1:18,19)*,

Jesus Provided All things for the birth, growth, and maturity of the Church *(Jn. 17:4; 19:30)*. He planned, purchased, produced, and empowered it. He made provisions for its perfection and presentation to Himself as a glorious Church/Bride without spot, wrinkle, or blemish — perfect in purity and maturity.

Jesus in His human body purchased the Church, but it is through the work of the Holy Spirit that He is building the Church. A correlating analogy: David, king of Israel, received by divine revelation the blueprint for the Temple of God. He then gathered gold, silver, and brass and made provisions for all the other material needed to build the temple. He then gave it to Solomon, who directed the building of the temple until it was finished. Jesus provided all things for the building of the Church. He then commissioned the Holy Spirit to take His provisions, birth the Church, and continue to work with the Church until every part is in place and the whole is perfectly complete.

The ministry of the eternal Godhead became involved in producing the Church. Jehovah God gave His Son Jesus to the world for the redemption of the Church. Jesus Christ gave the Holy Spirit to the Church for its empowerment, preservation, and perfection. The Holy Spirit gives each individual member of the Church the ability to communicate with God in a new prayer and praise language of the Spirit: a dynamo generating inner life and power.

Thus, according to the eternal plan of God, the Church was brought into existence on the day of Pentecost. It originated in the mind of God in eternity past and it was manifested on Earth at that time. The Church was birthed and started on its journey to ultimate fulfillment and maturity.

2
The Church Age

Theologians have divided man's existence on Earth into different periods of time called "Dispensations," "Covenants," and "Ages." A *Dispensation* is a period of time during which God works with man according to a set of divine rules and principles which man must follow in order to have fellowship with God and to fulfill His will. The pattern of God's plan and purpose for that generation is established at the beginning of the Dispensation and continues to be God's will and way for man until He changes the pattern after which another Dispensation is initiated.

Two Theological Concepts. Some prefer to use the word Covenant or Age instead of Dispensation. There are extremists in "Dispensational Theology" and in "Covenant Theology." However, both are principles by which we designate when, where, and how God has worked with mankind since mankind's time on Earth. A beginning and end is shown, but do not conclude that a New Covenant or Dispensation abolishes the Old Covenant or the Old Dispensation. The Old arrangement was not abolished when the New one was ushered in (e.g., Conscience was not abolished when Human Government was brought in; Promise was not abolished when Law was brought in).

The Old Remains.   A New Covenant supersedes the Old Covenant. All of the Old that is in agreement and workable with the New remains. The Old Testament (Covenant) in the Bible was not abolished when Jesus came and ushered in the New Testament (Covenant). The Bible is still one inspired book. It is not an Old Testament that is obsolete and a New Testament that is valid. However, many changes were made. Ceremonial laws and sacrifices were superseded by Christ's one eternal sacrifice. Grace superseded law; Mt. Zion superseded Mt. Sinai; the spiritual temple of God — the Church — superseded the tabernacle of Moses. The law was not abolished but fulfilled.

The Old Testament is the New Testament concealed. The New Testament is the Old Testament revealed. The New Testament makes a statement of truth but one must go to the Old Testament to gain the typological background and details. What is contained in the Old Testament in history, types, and shadows is explained in the New Testament.

The Old, The Pattern of the New

I Corinthians 15:46 reveals the simple order that God has established relative to the progression of truth and to the creation itself. This principle is evident everywhere in the Scriptures: first, the Old Creation, then the New Creation; first darkness, then light; first a Garden of Eden, and then the Tree of Life; the Garden of God and then the real Tree of Life; the First Adam, then the Last Adam; first the Passover, then the Lamb of God which taketh away the sin of the world; first Law, then Grace. The end of the Old is the beginning of the New; out of that which is destined to pass away there comes forth that which is destined to remain.

One of the main purposes for dividing God's dealings with man into Covenants, Dispensations, and Ages is to help rightly divide the Word of truth. You must know to what "Age" the Scripture is speaking for proper interpretation and application. The chronometrical principle in the science of biblical interpretation reveals that one must determine to what age the Scripture relates before correct application can be made. To determine to what period or age of time the verse is referring, evaluate whether it refers to the Eternal Ages Past, the Age of Creation, the Age of Re-creation, the Age of Patriarchs, the Age of Israel as a Nation, the coming of the Messiah and the Church Age, the Age to Come, or to the Eternal Ages.

Each Makes Way For Next. The ages are successive; each age makes way for another. The New Age is greater than the previous because it moves into a higher level in the eternal purposes of God. Each age reveals more of God's will, of His way, and of His desires for humanity. The Age of Law revealed more than the Age of Promise. The Church is greater than both the Age of Promise and the Age of Law; the Age to Come and the Eternal Ages will supersede all previous ages.

Divisions Within Ages. Within each of these ages there are shorter periods of time referred to as times, seasons, days, weeks, months, years, "The Last Days," and "The Latter Days." This book will concentrate on the Church Age. The dispensation of the Church includes the "Early Days" of the Church, the "Years" of the Dark Age, "Times" of Restoration, "Last Days" and "Time of the End."

The following are eight *Dispensations* and *Covenants and the Period of Time* they cover:

Dispensation	Covenant	Period of Time
Innocence	Edenic	From the creation to the fall of man
Conscience	Adamic	From the fall of man to the deluge
Human Government	Noahic	From the deluge to the call of Abraham.
Promise	Abrahamic	Abraham to the law given at Mt. Sinai
Law	Mosaic	Mt. Sinai to the first coming of Christ
Grace	Church	From the crucifixion to the second coming of Christ
Millennial	Kingdom	From Christ's second coming to the end of the millennial reign
Universal	Everlasting	End of millennial into eternity

Covenants Correlated

God, at the beginning of the Dispensation of Promise, established the Covenant of Circumcision. This was the method whereby man could show his desire for fellowship with God and his obedience to God's will. This continued until God ushered in the Dispensation of the Law through Moses at Mt. Sinai. When the Mosaic Covenant went into effect many new rules, precepts, and actions were required in order for man to have fellowship with God and to do His will. These sacrifices, feasts, offerings, and even the Tabernacle ceremonies and worship continued to be God's will for man until Jesus came, ushered in the Dispensation of Grace, and established His Covenant with the Church. Though man drifted away from the Law, misinterpreted and perverted it by mixing in heathen worship and customs so that there was little resemblance to the original pattern and precepts which God gave Moses at Mt. Sinai, God's Word, His will, and His way for man's justification, sanctification, and spiritual manifestations have remained the same. God did not change His mind, His method, or His means of man's fellowship with God during the 1,500 years of the Law.

Same Church Covenant. Jesus' death, His burial, and His resurrection provided the means whereby man could be cleansed from his sins and could be justified by faith through the grace of God. He then established and ushered in the Church Age on the day of Pentecost. We are still serving the same Christ, in the same Dispensation, under the same Covenant, and we are members of the same Church as were the early Christians. We have access by faith into all the things of God as related in the New Testament. Though we are living in the latter part of the Church Age, we still have rights to the same provisions and experiences of the early Christians.

Important Questions. One should ask, "Am I enjoying all the benefits and blessings that God gave me at the beginning of the Church Age? Am I walking in the same principles and precepts that Christ Jesus established? Am I experiencing the same type salvation, sanctification, baptism, love, and spiritual manifestations that Christ gave and that were demonstrated in the early Church? If not, then why not? Has God changed? Has there been any new revelation from God changing God's will for man since the writings of the New Testament? Are there any scriptural or divine reasons why everything that happened in the Book of Acts should not still be happening in the Church today? Is not the whole New Testament still the rule book, the pattern, and the guiding principle for the Church today?"

Jesus Never Changes. Though preachers, teachers, and theologians have changed, Christ Jesus remains the same today as yesterday. Men have drifted away from the New Testament pattern for the Church: They have misinterpreted it, perverted it, and reduced it to religious form and ritual, thus robbing it of its power and purity. Some have even mixed heathen customs, practices, and beliefs with it so that it has little resemblance to the original pattern, precepts, and manifestations which were established when Christ ushered in the Church Age.

A Personal Recommendation to Restudy Book of Acts. The writer strongly urges each person to read this book and restudy the Book of Acts with a completely open mind. Do not read it just to find out what the early Church was like, but read it to find out what God's true Church is supposed to be. Compare your personal experiences to those of the Christians in the Book of Acts. If you are a teacher or preacher, compare your teaching, your preaching, your power, and your spiritual manifestation to that of the ministers of the Book of Acts. Christ has only one Church (Body of believers) on this Earth. The Church started with Christ's first coming and it will continue in force until His second coming.

A Prayer of Blessing Upon the Reader. My prayer for you is the same as that of the Apostle Paul to the Ephesian Christians in Ephesians 1:16-23. I trust that before you have finished this book and your study of the Book of Acts you will have received the same spiritual experiences as the early Christians, that your witnessing, your teaching, and your preaching will be with the same power bringing about the same results. Nowhere in God's revelation (to the Church, to mankind through Jesus' life on Earth, through the demonstration of His will and way for the Church as revealed in the Book of Acts, or in the Epistles) is there any indication that a human being today cannot participate in all of the teaching and experiences of the New Testament Church Age. May you comprehend, believe, and receive all that the Holy Spirit has restored to this present time, thereby becoming "established in the Present Truth" *(II Pet. 1:12).* Be a believer! *(Mk. 9:23; Jn. 14:12-14; Mk. 16:16-20).*

3

The Church
In The
Book Of Acts

Luke the Writer

The Book of Acts records the birth and ministry of the new-born Church. The human author was Luke, the beloved physician. The divine author was the Holy Spirit. Luke declares that he was inspired by the Holy Spirit to write his first letter (St. Luke) to Theophilus to give him an accurate account of the earthly ministry of Jesus Christ, the Messiah. Luke covers the life of Jesus from His birth to His crucifixion and ascension. His second letter (Acts) to Theophilus continues from where the first letter stopped. The Gospel of Luke portrays the Christ that Paul stated they had known "after the flesh" *(II Cor. 5:16)*. The Book of Acts reveals the resurrected Christ whom they now knew "after the Spirit." The first letter reveals the life and supernatural ministry of Christ Jesus through His personal human body. The follow-up letter reveals the life and supernatural ministry of Jesus Christ through His corporate Body, the Church.

Titles Given Acts. The present title of the book is *The Acts of the Apostles,* normally referred to as "the book of Acts," or when a scriptural reference is used, *Acts 1:8,* etc. Throughout history "the book has been called by a variety of names besides the one it currently holds: *The Acts of the Ascended and Glorified Lord, The Book, The Demonstration of the Resurrection, The Gospel of the Resurrection, The Acts of the Holy Spirit, The Gospel of the Holy Spirit,* and sometimes called the *Fifth Gospel.*" (Adam Clarke, *Clarke's Commentary,* Volume 5, New York, New York, Abingdon Press. p. 679.)

The writer believes that either the title *The Acts of the Holy Spirit in the Church* or the *Acts of the Church* would be the most accurate one. Acts records the ministry of the Church, not just the ministry of the Apostles. For instance, Chapter Eight records the results or *Acts* that took place when a deacon was led of the Holy Spirit to preach a revival in Samaria.

Probable Date When Written. Not all Bible historians agree on the exact date of biblical happenings, but most are no more than two or three years apart in their dates concerning the chronology of the Book of Acts. Seemingly, Luke was a constant companion of the Apostle Paul. Undoubtedly he travelled with Paul to Rome and stayed there and ministered to him during his imprisonment. He wrote the Book of Acts while in Rome, in A.D. 63.

Acts Spans First 30 Years of the Church. The Book of Acts starts with the ascension of Jesus and moves to the outpouring of the Holy Spirit in the year A.D. 30; the stoning of Stephen and conversion of Paul approximately three years later; Paul's first visit to Jerusalem after his conversion around A.D. 35; the conversion of Cornelius, the Gentile, about 10 years after the Church was birthed on the Day of Pentecost; Paul's ministry and missionary journeys covering 30 years, A.D. 33 to A.D. 63; Paul's arrest while in the temple trying to please the Christian Jews and elders at Jerusalem concerning his teaching on the Law and Christianity, A.D. 60, 30 years after the origination of the Church.

The "Exodus" of New Testament. The Book of Acts is the *Exodus* of the New Testament, the story of God leading a body of believers out of the bondage of Judaism into the promised land of Kingdom living in the Church. Chapter One is the transition time of the Church from their *physical presence* walk with Jesus to their *spiritual presence* walk. It is the time of labor pangs for the birthing of the Church. The following statement alliterated with the letter "P" gives a description of what was occuring at this time. It was the preliminary pause prior to Pentecost when Christ was persistently preparing His purchased people and appointed Apostles with a proper perspective of His predestinated plan: purifying their purpose from that of parleying for political position with a potentate to that of perservering in praise, patience, and prayer for the promised power which they would perceive and possess at the outpouring of the Holy Spirit.

Progressive Work of Holy Spirit. It took years for the Holy Spirit to fully deliver the Church in precept and practice from the bondage of the Law. It was 10 years after the origination of the Church before the Apostles realized that non-Jews could become Christians without becoming Jews first. Thirty years after the birth of the Church the Jerusalem congregation was still trying to keep the Law and promote Christianity, too. In fact, it was not until the destruction of Jerusalem in A.D. 70 that Judaism and Christianity were forever separated and recognized by the world as two separate entities.

The Book of Acts does not record all of the performances of the Church, any more than the Gospels record all of the teaching and miracles of Christ.

What the Holy Spirit did inspire to be recorded is sufficient to give us the teachings, experiences, and ministry of the New Testament Church. If a person should list every belief and practice of the Church as expressed in the Book of Acts and the other Epistles, he would find quite a contrast between the early Church and many of the modern Christian denominations.

Church Not Man Made. The Church is not a man-made institution. It does not exist nor operate on natural laws or religious forms. The Church operates on spiritual laws and functions in the supernatural. Its power is not in political prestige, secular positions, wealth, or fame, but in the power and demonstration of the supernatural ministry of the Holy Spirit. The blueprint and pattern recorded in the Book of Acts portrays the Church as a supernatural people operating in supernatural principles.

Miracles and the Supernatural in the Book of Acts

"Take the Miracles out of the Book of Acts, and there is little left. However much critics may disparage the Evidential Value of Miracles, the fact remains that God made abundant use of Miracles in giving Christianity a start in the world." (Henry H. Halley, *Halley's Handbook,* Grand Rapids, Michigan, Zondervan Publishing House, 1965. p. 564.)

Dictionary Definitions of Natural, Supernatural, Miracles

(The New Webster Dictionary of English Language.)

Natural: "In conformity with the ordinary course of nature: not unusual or exceptional." (That which can be understood by the natural mind and explained by human reasoning.)

Natural religion: "The doctrine that there is no interference of any supernatural power in the universe." (That God only works through nature and human wisdom and ability.)

Supernatural: "Being above and beyond that which is natural, supernatural phenomena. Abnormal or extraordinary." (That which cannot be understood or explained by natural reasoning and human wisdom.)

Supernaturalism: "The doctrine that religion and the knowledge of God requires a revelation of God." (The natural mind must be illuminated and regenerated into a spiritual mind to understand divine things.)

Miracles and Miraculous: "An effect in the physical world which surpasses all known human or natural powers and is therefore ascribed to supernatural agency." *Miraculous—* "Performed by or involving a supernatural power: a miraculous cure." *(Theologically* — God speeding up the laws of nature or superseding, bypassing, or overriding the natural laws.)

The New Testament Church — The Church of the Supernatural

As Genesis is the book of beginning for the natural human race, so the Book of Acts is the book of beginning for God's supernatural human race. Those in the Church have a supernatural birth. They are born again, born of the Spirit from above. Each is a new creature, a new creation which is created in Christ Jesus unto a new and higher way of life. Those in the Church have a supernatural calling.

They are Sons of God, members of the spiritual Body of Christ, God's new kind, type, and race of human beings.

According to *Webster's Dictionary,* "race" is "a large body of persons who may be thought of as a unit because of common characteristics." The Church is a body (unit) of believers who have been made partakers of Christ's divine nature (characteristics). They are spiritual beings living in an earthly, mortal body. They are born of the Spirit, baptized with the Spirit, and manifest the gifts and fruits of the Spirit. True Christians are different from all the rest of God's created beings in Heaven or Earth. The Church consists of a new race of beings.

Original Race, Then Hebrew Race. At the beginning of man's history in the year one, God created the human race. Approximately 2,000 years later God called Abraham forth to become the head of a new race called Hebrews. They were to be God's special race to possess a particular piece of land and be God's called-out natural race, a chosen natural nation to represent the Eternal to all other nations.

Now New Race. Four thousand years after Adam and 2,000 years after the call of Abraham God established a whole new race. God sent His Son to be the model from which all in this new race would be patterned. The new race were Sons of God, members of the corporate Body of Christ, a supernatural people, a spiritual nation possessing the spiritual kingdom of God. Members of the new race have eternal inner life within mortal bodies. The new race is the present Church.

After approximately 2,000 years have expired God will activate a new race of humanity. The new eternal race will be the resurrected and translated sons of

God who will not only have eternal inner life but will have immortal and indestructible physical bodies. The Church is designed and destined to function eternally as Christ's immortal human race.

Jesus, the First of the Supernatural Race

Jesus had a supernatural conception, a supernatural ministry, a supernatural sacrifice, and a supernatural resurrection. Jesus started the Church with a supernatural experience of supernatural fire and wind, and caused them to speak with supernatural tongues; that is, a language above and beyond their natural understanding and ability. He caused supernatural signs and wonders to be wrought by the hands of the Church. God confirmed His Word spoken by the Church members with Supernatural healings and miracles.

To the spiritual Christian in the Church, the supernatural is to be natural for him. It is to be the expected, not the unexpected; the normal, not the abnormal. *For example:* modern man's miraculous *machinery* (electricity, tape recorders, telephone, radio, cameras, cars, airplanes, rockets, television, explosions from TNT to atom and hydrogen bombs), although not supernatural, might seem so to primitive man.

That which seems to be miraculous, unfathomable, and supernatural to the unspiritual man living in the jungle of sin, materialism, and dead religion, is the every day norm to those living in the Church and seated in heavenly places in Christ Jesus. The uncivilized man would never believe without proof; if it were demonstrated first, then he would believe.

"Jesus began both to **do** and then **teach**" *(Acts*

1:1). The Book of Acts is the **doing** and **demonstrating** of the Church. The Epistles are the teaching and instruction of the Church.

The Miraculous and Supernatural Recorded in the Book of Acts

The following are miraculous supernatural experiences found in the Book of Acts:

Christ's Ascension to Heaven *(1:9)*.

Pentecost, a miraculous visible manifestation of supernatural wind and fire. Supernatural speaking in other tongues *(2:3)*.

Wonders and Signs done by the Apostles *(2:43)*.

Healing of the lame man at the temple gate made a deep impression on the whole city *(3:7-11; 4:16,17)*.

God answered prayer by an earthquake *(4:31)*.

Ananias and Sapphira died by a stroke from the Lord *(5:5-10)*.

Signs and wonders, by the Apostles, continued *(5:12)*.

Multitudes from surrounding cities were healed by Peter's shadow *(5:15,16)*. (It reads like the days of Jesus in Galilee.)

Prison doors were opened by an angel *(5:19)*.

Stephen wrought great wonders and signs *(6:8)*.

In Samaria, Philip did great miracles and signs. *(8:6,7,13)*. Multitudes believed, were saved and healed, and demons were cast out.

Saul was converted by a direct voice from Heaven *(9:3-9)*.

Agabus prophesied about a famine coming to Jerusalem *(11:28)*.

At the word of Ananias, scales fell from Saul's eyes *(9:17,18)*.

In Lydda, Peter healed Aeneas, and the whole region was converted to Christ *(9:32-35)*.

In Joppa, Peter raised Dorcas from the dead, and many believed on the Lord *(9:40-42)*.

Cornelius was directed by an angel who appeared supernaturally to send for Peter. After believing in Christ Jesus Cornelius received the Holy Ghost and supernaturally spoke in other tongues *(10:34-48)*.

A voice from God sent Peter to Cornelius and convinced the Jews later that Peter was right *(10:9-22; 11:15,18)*.

A prison gate opened of its own accord *(12:10)*.

The blinding of a sorcerer led the Proconsul of Cyprus to believe *(13:11,12)*.

Paul did signs and wonders in Iconium, and a multitude believed *(14:3,4)*.

At Lystra, the healing of a cripple made the multitudes think that Paul was a god *(14:8-18)*.

Narration of signs and wonders convinced Jewish Christians that Paul's work among Gentiles was of God *(15:12,19)*.

In Philippi, Paul healed a soothsayer, and an earthquake released Paul and Silas from prison, and the jailor was miraculously converted *(16:16-34)*.

In Ephesus, 12 men spoke in tongues and special miracles done by Paul made the Word of the Lord to prevail mightily *(19:20; 19:6,11,12;)*.

In Troas, Paul raised a young man from the dead *(20:8-12)*.

In Melita, the healing of Paul's hand from the viper's bite made the natives think Paul was a god; and Paul healed all in the island that had diseases *(28:3-6,8,9)*.

Dreams and visions were received by Peter, *(10:3)* Paul *(9:3,4)* and John *(Book of Rev.)*.

Philip was bodily transported by the Holy Spirit from one geographical area to another. *(8:39,40)*.

Supernatural Angelic Visitations

Angels delivered the apostles from prison *(5:19)*.

An angel spoke to Philip — directing him *(8:26)*.

The angel directed Cornelius to find a preacher so that he could be saved *(10:3,7,22; 11:13-18; 15:5-11)*.

The angel awakened Peter, talked to him, directed him, and delivered him out of prison *(12:7-11,15)*.

The angel of the Lord killed Herod *(12:23)*.

An angel stood by Paul, talked to him, encouraged him, and then preserved him and the whole crew *(27:33)*.

4

The
Early
Church

Seventy-Year Period
from A.D. 30 to A.D. 100.

To record the history of a particular subject or period of time becomes a monumental and seemingly insurmountable task. Thousands of pages have been written containing endless amounts of information available in vast volumes of recorded history covering every area of mankind, including his religious history.

Not a Technical Dissertation. The author has personally read and studied numerous volumes covering the history of the Church. Being fully familiar with the history of the Church concerning people, places, dates, councils, doctrines, denominations, etc., it becomes extremely difficult to condense all of it into a short space. This book does not attempt to be a thesis or doctoral dissertation which would require documentation and a long bibliography in order to be accepted by an institution of higher education. However, a sufficient Bibliography of good research sources will be given in order to direct the reader to an endless study in this field if he or she so desires. All statements have been checked to make sure they are historically accurate.

A Volume of Thousands of Pages. There are thousands of interesting stories and historical events concerning people and places, many having a direct influence in either the deterioration, preservation, propagation, or restoration of the Church of our Lord Jesus Christ. To expound briefly on each would produce a volume containing thousands of pages. Though the material is greatly condensed it will be enlightening, educational, and will be significant in laying a foundation for understanding the institution that is the Church.

Nothing More Important. It was stated earlier that the nearest and dearest thing to the heart of Jesus is His Church. Nothing is more important, for it is an integral part of His being and purpose. To understand the Body of Christ is to understand Jesus, for Jesus and His Church are one. He is the head of the Church which is His Body. The Head and Body are one complete embodiment united by one source for its life. If you have a desire to be one with Jesus, then become as involved in the Church as Christ is.

The Spiritual Hidden Church

There are two churches in the world today which evolved from the early Church. Sometimes they are united as one, and at other times they are two separate entities. They are the Structural Church and the Spiritual Church.

The Structural Church

The Structural Church involves the church buildings, organizations, man-made programs, policies, and politics of the Church. It is those things which can be produced by religious Christian leaders without the supernatural works of God. The natural things help to fulfill the spiritual.

The Spiritual Church

The Spiritual Church consists of those things which cannot be produced except by being one with Christ and by moving in the supernatural power of the Holy Spirit. The Spiritual Church is the assembly of saints and true believers who are supernaturally born of the Spirit. The Structural Church is the physical structure where they congregate.

> The spiritual hidden church is not a formal structure or an organization with an administration and other external features. For this reason it is called "hidden" (by some "invisible"). It is the church which is meant in the Ecumenical Creed "I believe in one holy, Apostolic, catholic (Christian) church." Only those in whom Christ is active are members of that church. It is designated also the body of Christ, the pillar of truth, the temple of God, the communion of saints. It has the gift of the Holy Spirit. (Earl S. Meyer, *The Church From Pentecost to the Present,* Chicago, Illinois, Moody Press, 1969. p. 12.)

In relating church history it becomes quite difficult to isolate the members of the Spiritual Church or identify them as such. The Spiritual Church is in and among the churches which teach the gospel. The names and places mentioned will only be the peak of the iceberg of people who were involved in making church history. State schools teach the history of their nation to help develop intelligent patriotism, so also a study of the Spiritual Church from its conception to the present will help Christians develop a greater loyalty to this Eternal Institution of which they are a part.

Minoring in the Structural Church. Only a part of the natural, historical, and structural functions of the Church is presented. Hopefully, just enough to give a clear picture of the Spiritual Church in its history, present ministry, and future work.

Expansion of The Early Church

The Church started on the day of Pentecost. The Church Age began at that time and will continue until the literal Second Coming of Jesus Christ. Everything found in Acts (the truths, principles, gifts and fruits of the Spirit, the miracles and ministries of the apostle, prophet, evangelist, pastor, and teacher) were not intended only for the first generation Church but for the whole Church Age.

The New Testament Canon. All of the books of the New Testament were written before the close of the First Century of the Church. It was many years later before they were all accepted, compiled, and canonized into the 27 books of the New Testament.

Based on research in tradition and history, the writer believes that all (except John) of the 12 Apostles, plus Paul, and most of the original ministers of the Church had been martyred by the end of the 60s. James was beheaded in Jerusalem by Herod; Paul was beheaded in Rome; Peter, Andrew, and Simon were crucified; all the rest were martyred by different means in different parts of the world. It is supposed that only John died a natural death.

The First 40 Years. Before the initial 40 years of the new-born Church had transpired, the first generation believers had spread around the world. Though the Church leaders were still having problems making the transition from the Mosaic covenant to the Church covenant, it did not hinder their propagation of the Good News.

Church Birthed by Supernatural. The Church was not birthed in doctrine or church creed. It was birthed by the supernatural and into the supernatural power of God. The first Christians believed and practiced *(Mk. 16:16-20; Jn. 14:12; Mt. 10:8)*. When they preached the gospel they expected the Word to be confirmed with signs following. They did not preach a dead sermon but proclaimed a living Christ who was able to do through them what He did through His personal body: heal the sick, cleanse the lepers, raise the dead, cast out devils, transform individuals into new creatures as they were washed in the blood and became born of the Spirit.

Gospel to Whole World. There are records of Christian ministers of that time preaching in all the known countries of the world. Most biblical historians assume that the gospel went to all the known world at that time. However, the Holy Spirit is not limited to man's knowledge; He knew that the gospel had been preached in all the Earth. He inspired the Apostle Paul to state that the gospel (the death, burial, and resurrection of Christ) in Paul's generation "was preached to every creature under heaven" *(Col. 1:23)*. This means that the gospel was preached to every continent, tongue, and tribe of humanity, wherever there was a human creature and the sun shone.

Prerequisite for Spiritual Manifestations. It is good to know that spiritual manifestations of the supernatural power of God are not dependent upon the person's maturity, doctrinal correctness, or holy character. The only prerequisite for demonstrating the Holy Spirit power that Jesus gave to born-again, spirit-filled Christians was for them to believe and yield; and the supernatural gifts would operate. Because of this, the early Apostles and Christians were able to preach the gospel and demonstrate the power of God while the Holy Spirit was establishing the Church doctrinally in the dispensation of grace and truth in Christ Jesus. Peter preached the gospel, healed the sick, and raised the dead for years before he understood the truth that the Gentiles could become direct members of the Body of Christ without coming through Judaism.

5

The Church Separating From Judaism

An Unrecorded Period of Time. We know the least about the period of time from A.D. 68 to A.D. 100. The recordings of the Book of Acts stopped in the mid-60s and no author after that age "filled in the blank" of the historical records. It would be great to read of the later works by such helpers of Paul as Timothy, Apollos, Barnabas, and Titus, but all these and Paul's other friends drop out of the record at his death. For nearly 50 years after Paul's life a curtain hangs over the Church, and when at last it rises, about A.D. 120, with the writings of the earliest Church fathers, we find the Church in many aspects very different from that in the days of Peter and Paul.

The Great Distinction. The fall of Jerusalem in the year A.D. 70 made a great change in the relationship of Christians and Jews and the distinction between Christianity and Judaism. Among the many provinces under the rule of Rome, the land most discontented and disloyal was Judea. The Jews, by putting their own interpretation upon their prophetic writings, believed that they were destined to conquer and govern the world, and having that confident expectation submitted unwillingly to the yoke of the Roman emperors. About A.D. 66 the Jews broke into open rebellion, hopeless from its very beginning. What could one of the smallest provinces whose people were untrained in war accomplish against an empire of 120 million people, with a quarter of a million disciplined and seasoned soldiers? (The odds were no problem to God, but the Jews were in rebellion against God and under judgment, for Jesus has predicted that this destruction would come upon the Jews *(Mt. 24)*. Even the Jews themselves were broken into factions which fought and slaughtered each other as fiercely as did their common enemy Rome.

Jerusalem Destroyed. Vespasian, the leading Roman general, led a great army into Palestine. He was unexpectedly called to Rome to take the imperial throne and left the conduct of the war to his son, Titus. Following a terrible siege, made more terrible by starvation and civil strife within the walls, the city was taken and destroyed. Untold thousands of the Jews were put to death, and other thousands were enslaved. The Colosseum at Rome was built by the forced labor of Jewish captives, multitudes being literally worked to death. The Jewish state, after an existence of 13 centuries, was annihilated, and was not restored until 1948.

The fall of Jerusalem in A.D. 70 was a significant happening in light of the Jewish nation, the Church, and the fulfilled prophecy. The Christians who were inside Jerusalem accepted the prophetic utterances of Christ in Luke 21:20-24, Matthew 24:15-22, Luke 19:43,44, and Mark 13:14-20 as applicable to their situation. "It is very remarkable that not a single Christian perished in the destruction of Jerusalem, though there were many there when Cestius Gallus approached the city." (Clarke, p. 228.)

> Our Lord Jesus had ordered his followers to make their escape from Jerusalem when they should see it encompassed with armies; but how could this be done? God took care to amply provide for this. In the twelfth year of Nero, Cestius Gallus, the president of Syria, came against Jerusalem with a powerful army. He might, says Josephus, (War, b. ii c. 19,) have assaulted and taken the city; but contrary to the expectation of all, he raised the siege and departed. Josephus remarks that after Cestius Gallus had raised the siege, "many of the principal Jewish people forsook the city as men do a sinkng ship." (These were nearly all Christian Jews.) Vespasian was deputized in the room of Cestius Gallus, who, having subdued all the country prepared to besiege Jerusalem, and invested it on every side. But the news of Nero's death, and soon after that of Galba, the disturbances that followed, and the civil wars between Otho and Vitellius held Vespasian and his son, Titus, in suspense. Thus, the city was not actually besieged until after Vespasian was confirmed in the empire and Titus was appointed to command the forces in Judea. It was in those incidental delays that the Christians, and indeed several others, provided for their own safety, by flight. (Ibid., p. 230.)

Being Led by Prophecy. "Then let them which be in Judea flee into the mountains" *(Mt. 24:16).* This prophetic counsel evidently was wisely followed by the Christians. When God gave them that divine delay, all who believed in Christ left Jerusalem and fled to Pella and to other places beyond the river Jordan. Jesus told His followers to pray that their flight during that time be not in the winter or on the Sabbath. Someone must have taken Him seriously and prayed, for God answered that prayer. The destruction of Jerusalem was on August 10, A.D. 70, and the Christians did not have to make their escape on the Sabbath day. "Rabbi Tanchum observes that the favor of God was particularly manifested in the destruction of the first temple, in not obliging the Jews to go out in the winter, but in the summer." (Ibid, p. 230.) If the flight of the Christian Jews had been on the Sabbath, then the orthodox Jews could have risen up in religious indignation in the areas where the escapees traveled that day.

Horrors Beyond Comprehension. The horrors that took place before and after the fall of the city are beyond comprehension. There was murder, rape, and stealing each other's last morsel of food. Josephus relates a story that was typical of the things that happened to those in the siege who did not take Christ's words seriously and flee the city. "One Mary, the daughter of Eliezar, illustrious for her family and riches, who, being stripped and plundered of all her goods and provisions by the Jewish soldiers, in hunger, rage, and despair, killed and boiled her own suckling child, and had eaten one half of him before it was discovered." (Ibid, p. 230.)

Even the Roman General Titus acknowledged that God had helped him to execute God's judgment upon the Jews. When he was viewing the fortifications after the taking of the city, he could not help ascribing his success to God. He made the following statement, "We have fought with God on our side; and it is God who pulled the Jews out of these strongholds: for what could machines or the hands of men avail against such towers as these?" (Ibid, p. 231.)

Josephus calculates that 1,100,000 Jews perished in the city, that another 257,660 were killed in surrounding areas, and 97,000 were taken captive. Those above 17 years of age were sent to the works in Egypt; but most were distributed through the Roman provinces, to be destroyed by the sword and by wild beasts as they were forced to fight as gladiators in the amphitheatres. Titus, their conqueror, had 2,500 Jews murdered in honor of his brother's birthday, and had a greater number murdered in honor of his father's.

During the destruction of Jerusalem, the temple caught on fire causing the gold to run into the lower wall and between the blocks of the foundation. The soldiers took the temple apart stone by stone to retrieve the precious metals. There was not one stone left upon another, thus fulfilling the prophecy Jesus gave in Matthew 24:2, which more clearly manifested the fact that God's headquarters was no longer in the Law and Tabernacle of Moses, or in the Great Temple made of stone and precious metals. It was in the Church.

The Last of the 12 Apostles. By the year A.D. 100, the Church had been alive and active for 70 years. John was the only original Apostle still alive at that time. About the year A.D. 90 the cruel Emperor Domitian began a second imperial persecution of the Christians. Thousands of believers were slain, especially in Rome and Italy. At this time, John, who had been living in Ephesus, was imprisoned on the isle of Patmos, in the Aegean Sea, and there received the Revelation contained in the last book of the New Testament. It is assumed that John was in his late teens or early twenties when Christ called him to be one of the original 12 Apostles. General consensus is that he died at Ephesus about A.D. 100. If he had been 19 when called, he would have been 22 on the day of Pentecost, making his age at death approximately 92.

Three Generations of Christians. By the close of the first century there were families which for three generations had been Christian. The grandchildren of Peter and John could have been active ministers in the Church by this date. The Church could be found in every land and in almost every city from the Tiber to the Euphrates, from the Black Sea to Northern Africa, and, some scholars believe it extended as far west as Spain and Britain. Its membership included several million, and, over the next 200 years, tens of millions more would be added, and millions would be martyred for the cause of Christ. The well-known letter of Pliny to the Emperor Trafan, written about A.D. 112, states that in the provinces of Asia Minor bordering on the Black Sea, the temples of the heathen gods were almost forsaken, and the Christians were everywhere a multitude. When we study the later Epistles and the Book of Revelation we find that worldliness and false teaching were beginning to make inroads into the Churches. The standards of moral character were high, the supernatural power of God was being manifested by many, though the quality of spiritual life and purity of doctrine was less than it had been in the earlier apostolic days. Nevertheless, the church was strong, aggressive, growing, and rising to dominance throughout the world, especially throughout the Roman empire.

6

The Persecution Of The Church

"Suffering According to the Will of God" *(I Pet. 4:19).* It is a wonder to many why God allowed such a wholesale slaughter of His people during the first 300 years of the Church. It was not for judgment such as the Jews had suffered during the destruction of Jerusalem, for Stephen, the first martyr, was in the perfect will of God. The second martyr, James, the brother of John and pastor of the Jerusalem Church was beheaded by Herod. There is no indication in Scripture that this persecution came for any reason other than the wrath of the wicked against the righteous.

Why Church Persecution? To keep the Church pure for as long as possible is the most common reason given for God allowing this severe persecution. The persecutions kept hypocritical, dishonest, and insincere people purged from the Church. It separated the chaff from the wheat. No light decisions were made for Christ in those times, especially when acceptance of Christ meant possible loss of citizenship; imprisonment with daily starvation and torture until death;

crucifixion, and sometimes burning while still alive and hanging on the cross; being thrown into the arenas to be devoured by ravenous beasts; abduction and abuse of young women until their bodies gave way in death; the death of children ripped from parents who would not deny Christ. Every means of torture that the devil could inspire to the minds of wicked mortal men were used on the Christians during this time. These reveal only a few things that were done to the Christians. If one is interested in a complete coverage and detailed description of the various tortures and deaths of the persecuted Christians one should read *Foxe's Book of Martyrs.*

Rome's Reasons for Persecution

The most widespread and severe persecutions during this time were instigated by the Roman emperors to the Christians within the Roman empire. The Romans assumed that the Christians were just another sect among the Jewish religion, and they were tolerated as such until after the Destruction of Jerusalem. Then they were exposed as a separate group and made to stand alone with no laws to protect the Christian race from its enemies. There were several reasons why Christianity stirred antagonism and brought persecution from the Romans. Heathen worship was hospitable to new gods, and in order to promote business the Romans made places of worship for them. Christianity opposed all worship except to its own God; it rejected with scorn any business deals that involved other gods. Christians would not have their Christ recognized merely as one of many deities. Idol worship was a way of life and numerous images stood in every house, but the Christians would have none. Therefore, they were regarded by the unthinking as unsocial and morose, as atheists, having no visible gods, and as haters of their fellow men. One form of idolatry, emperor worship, was held as a test of loyalty. The Christians refused to render this worship, simple as it was to drop a handful of incense upon the altar, and because they sang hymns of praise and gave worship to "another King, one Jesus," they were looked upon by the multitude as disloyal and as plotters of a revolution. The secret meetings of the Christians for closed communion aroused suspicion, and were often made the grounds for accusation and persecution.

The practice of Christianity to look upon all men as equals was abhorrent to the Romans. Christianity made no distinction in membership and its services; a slave might be chosen as bishop in the Church. To the philosophic and ruling classes, the Christians were regarded as "levelers," anarchists, and subverters of the social order; hence, they were regarded as enemies of the state. The Second and Third Century Christians were still having the same problem Paul had when the gospel delivered people from idol worship and depleted the business interest of the idol makers. The heathens rose (as Demetrius the silversmith did in Paul's day) and demanded the destruction of Christianity.

Christianity Outlawed. During the years of persecution (A.D. 100 to A.D. 313) the Christian religion was forbidden and its followers were outlawed. They had no more citizenship rights than the slaves in the southern United States had before the Civil War. Persecution was not continuous, for only certain emperors brought severe persecution on the Christians during their reign. One such emperor was Septimius Severus. His spirit was so bitter and fierce that he was regarded by many Christian writers as the Antichrist. During this time some great Christian leaders were martyred. Such men were Simeon, bishop of the Church in Jerusalem, and Ignatius, bishop of Antioch in Syria, who were more than willing to be martyrs. On his way to Rome, Ignatius wrote letters to the churches hoping that he might not lose the honor of dying for his Lord. He was thrown to wild beasts in the Roman amphitheatre around A.D. 110. Polycarp, bishop of Smyrna in Asia Minor, died in A.D. 115. When brought before the governor and commanded to curse the name of Jesus Christ, he answered, "Eighty and six years have I served Christ and He has done me nothing but good; and how could I curse Him, my Lord and Savior?" He was burned to death.

Martyrdom vs. Translation. Such was the general attitude of the persecuted Church. They counted it a privilege to suffer martyrdom for Christ. They were the seed planting of the Church. *The early Christians were planted in martyrdom that the last generation Church may be harvested without death.* All of the last generation Church will not suffer martyrdom and death. A righteous remnant of multi-millions will overcome death, and instead of death conquering the Christians, death shall be conquered *(I Cor. 15:26,51,55).*

The Last Persecution. The last and most systematic and horrible persecution of all the series took place during the reign of Diocletian and his successors, from A.D. 303 to A.D. 310. In a series of edicts it was ordered that every copy of the Bible should be burned, that all churches throughout the Empire should be torn down, that all who would not renounce the Christian religion should lose their citizenship and be outside the protection of the law. (Many Roman officials and citizens had become Christians during the prior 50 years of rest from persecution.) In some places, while the Christians were assembled, their churches were set on fire and burned with all the worshippers within their walls. It is said that the Emperor Diocletian erected a pillar inscribed, "In honor of extirpation of the Christian superstition." Yet within 70 years Christianity became the official religion of the Emperor, the court, and the Empire.

Emperor Constantine. In A.D. 313 Emperor Constantine issued his memorable Edict of Toleration. By this law Christianity was sanctioned, its worship was made lawful, and all persecution ceased, not to be renewed while the Roman Empire endured. Thus, the Church passed from its period of preservation during the time of persecution to its political prosperity which brought about its decline and deterioration. The spiritual hidden Church fades into obscurity and the Structural Church begins to dominate until the beginning of the Reformation over 1,200 years later.

The

Deterioration

Of The

Church

1

The Church In Transition

Persecution's Purifying — Popularity's Polluting. Many things contributed to the deterioration of the Church into its apostate condition. To explain them all in detail would require a book in itself. The author will limit himself to those things which had a more direct bearing on the deterioration of the Spiritual Church. Most church historians agree that the Edict of Toleration was the most damaging to the *Spiritual Church* even though it brought life and liberty to the *Structural Church* which prospered greatly with its new-found social acceptance, political power, and material possessions.

The Transition of the Church From Spiritual to Structural

Constantine's Edict granted to "Christians and to all others full liberty of following that religion which each may choose," (Halley, p. 759) the first edict of its kind in history. It had as much effect in granting freedom to Christianity in its day as the Constitution of the United States did in our day.

Constantine's Vision. Christianity became favorable to Constantine because of a supernatural experience he received on the eve of the battle of Milvain Bridge, just outside Rome (October 27, A.D. 312). He saw in the sky, just above the setting sun, a vision of the Cross, and above it the words, "In This Sign Conquer." He decided to fight under the banner of Christianity, and won that crucial battle (Ibid., p. 759).

Constantine favored Christians in every way. He filled chief offices with them, exempted Christian ministers from taxes and military service, encouraged and helped in building Churches (there are no records of church buildings being erected until after the year A.D. 200, but after the Edict they began to be built everywhere. This was more because of persecution than divine principle). Constantine made Christianity the religion of his court, and he issued a general exhortation to all his subjects to embrace Christianity.

Because the aristocratic leaders of Rome refused to give up their pagan religions and adhere to his Christianity, Constantine moved his capital to Byzantium, and called it Constantinople after his name. It was the "New Rome," capital of the new Christian Empire. This was the seed of the eventual split in the organized church world. For centuries the struggle for the leadership and domination of Christendom was between Rome and Constantinople, which eventually resulted in the formation of the Eastern Orthodox Church and the Western Roman Catholic Church.

Christianity Made State Religion. Whereas Constantine encouraged his constituents to become Christians, Emperor Theodosius made it compulsory 70 years later, when he made Christianity the state religion of the Roman Empire. His decree forced all Roman Empire subjects to formally accept Christianity in order to maintain their citizenship, hold office, and carry on business. This was the final blow to the message of repentance, conviction of sin, spiritual rebirth, and the need for a transformed life in order to become a Christian. Christ had designed the Church to conquer by purely spiritual and supernatural means. Prior to this time conversion had been voluntary with a genuine change in heart and life.

Christianity Required. Theodosius not only demanded adherence to Christianity, but he undertook the forcible suppression of all other religions, and prohibited idol worship. Under his decrees, heathen temples were torn down and there was much blood shed among the heathen priests and worshipers. (What a reversal from less than a century before.) The military spirit of Imperial Rome had entered the Church. Christianity appeared to have conquered the whole empire, but by making the Church over into its own image the Roman Empire had conquered the Spiritual Church.

Must One Destroy the Other? When the writer speaks of the deterioration of the Church, reference is being made primarily to the Spiritual Church as revealed in the Book of Acts. The structural part of the Church was enhanced when Christians became politically dominant, and the world was blessed in its physical, moral, and social life. Slavery, gladiator fights, killing of unwelcome children, and crucifixion as a form of execution were abolished with the Christianization of the Roman Empire. Many humanitarian societies were established by the state through the influence of the Church. However, when the Spiritual Church was in control in apostolic days these humanitarian needs were met by the Church *without* state support or control.

Church Changes Its Nature. The Church had changed its nature, had entered its great apostasy, had become a political organization in the spirit and pattern of Imperial Rome, and had taken its nose dive into the millennium of dead works, formalism, and slavery to man-made religion. In other words, it had gone into slavery to a religious Pharoah and "Egypt" system as Israel had gone in her Egyptian bondage, treading the slime pit of self-works and building great edifices to house a dead religion with none of the life and reality of the Early Church.

Simplicity Lost. Worship in the *Early First Century Holy Ghost-filled Church* was in simplicity, in spirit and truth, with great exuberant praise and rejoicing. There were no elaborate churches or formal ceremonies, but they gathered together to bless and love one another, and to bless the name of the Lord with uplifted hands and joyful lips. They came together to be romanced by their heavenly Bridegroom in preparation for that great wedding day, the marriage supper of the Lamb, when they would eternally become His Bride and would sit down with Him in His heavenly throne to rule and reign with Him over God's vast domain. But now the worship had developed into elaborate, stately, imposing ceremonies which had all the outward splendor that had once belonged to heathen temples. Church worship was more like a sad funeral service than like a joyful wedding.

When the Goths, Vandals, and Huns overthrew the Roman Empire in A.D. 476, they generally received Christianity, but to a large extent their conversions were nominal and this further filled the Church with pagan practices. The Church continued to deteriorate and move into its dark age. The Church maintained its basic monotheistic faith, the Apostles' Creed, and its sacraments, but the heathens brought in religious paraphernalia and idol worship. They were outwardly forced into Christianity without a change of heart and without an understanding of its God and its way of life. These heathen, therefore, demanded that the Church give them physical replicas to represent the invisible Christian God, whom they did not know. They did not know how to worship Him in spirit and in truth as Jesus had said His followers would *(Jn. 4:23,24)*.

At Mercy of Clergy. There were very few copies of the Scriptures available for the everyday professing Christian to study. These people were at the mercy of the Church leaders concerning whether they received truth or error, life or death, reality or religion, and whether they were made a living stone in the living Spiritual Church or were made a cut-and-dried brick in the lifeless Structural Church.

Pagan Customs
and Christian Rituals

Just as the militant and political spirit of the emperor permeated Christianity, in like manner the pagan customs were converted to the rituals and observances of the Christian Church. The Christian Emperors forced the pagans into Christianity, and the pagans forced Christianity to transfer their own religious customs into the Church. For example, the sun worshipers observed the birthday of the Sun-god on the twenty-fifth day of December. To maintain this holiday for the pagans who were forced into Christianity, the celebration of Christ's birth was substituted. Likewise, Constantine officially recognized and named the weekly meeting day of the Christians "the venerable day of the Sun" (Sunday). This gave Christianity a national weekly holiday for service and worship to their God.

Veneration of Mary. The veneration of the virgin Mary was probably stimulated by the similarity of female deities in pagan religions. Some scholars believe that the worship of Artemis (Diana, the universal mother) was transferred to Mary. Pagan converts who formerly worshiped the Egyptian goddess, Isis, addressing her as "the Great Virgin" and "Mother of the God," naturally tended to look to Mary for comfort when their program of worship was outlawed and their temples were destroyed at the end of the Fourth Century. There are some surviving images of Isis holding her young child Horus in a pose remarkably similar to that of some early Christian *madonnas*. The only departed person that the Early Church deified or made any reference to in any form of worship, adoration, or prayer was the person of Jesus Christ. To make a statue replica of any saint, angel, or person of the Godhead and to use it as a part of Christian worship is a direct violation of the first commandment *(Ex. 20:3-6)*.

Petitioning Departed Saints. The "cult of departed saints and martyrs" grew rapidly in the Fourth Century. It arose among the people, but was approved by the great theologians of the age: Jerome, Ambrose, and Augustine. The Christian historian Theodoret boasts that in many places the statues of saints and martyrs took the place of pagan gods, and their shrines took the place of pagan temples. Entreating some saints and visiting certain shrines was claimed to cure barreness. Other saints protected travellers, detected perjury, foretold the future, and many healed the sick. It was never the teaching or intention of the Church leaders that the saints were to be worshipped. It was only suggested that they were in a special position to hear petitions and to present them directly to God.

During the deterioration time of the Church, many other pagan customs were incorporated into Christianity that complicated the simplicity of worship of the spiritual first-generation Church. Candles, incense, garlands, holy days, elaborate priestly robes and garments, signs and symbols, and many other things that were brought into the Church over the centuries of the Dark Ages were a combination of pagan custom and the old Jewish ceremonial religion which ceased with the coming of Christ and the Church Age.

The Deterioration of the Ministry

In apostolic days Early Church ministers were called apostles, prophets, evangelists, pastors, and teachers. There are also references to elders, bishops, and deacons. The bishops, elders, and pastors were men anointed by the Holy Spirit to have the oversight and the shepherding responsibility of the local flock of believers. The word "minister" was used more in describing a performance than in describing a person or position. (The title of priest was not given to ministers until after the Second Century.)

Jesus taught that he who would be the greatest among the Church was to be servant of all. Peter told the leaders not to "lord it" over the flock of God but to serve them. This was the spirit of the Early Church ministers. As the Spirit of Christ lessened in the

Church, the human desire for prestige and power increased.

Centralization of Control. At the close of the Apostolic Age churches were independent of each other, shepherded by a group of co-pastors. The main leader or senior pastor came to be called bishop. The others, later, were called presbyters. Gradually, the jurisdiction of bishop came to include neighboring towns. Bishop Calixtus (A.D. 220) was the first to base his claim on Matthew 16:18. The great Tertullian of Carthage called Calixtus an usurper in speaking as if he were Bishop of Bishops. When Constantine called the council of Nicea in A.D. 325 and presided over the First World Council of Churches, he accorded the Bishops of Alexandria and Antioch full jurisdiction over their provinces, as the Roman Bishop had over his. By the end of the Fourth Century the Bishops had come to be called Patriarchs. They were of equal authority, each having full control of his own province. The five Patriarchs who dominated Christendom were headquartered in Rome, Constantinople, Antioch, Jerusalem, and Alexandria. After the division of the Roman Empire into East and West, the struggle for the leadership of Christendom was between Rome and Constantinople.

Development of "Fathers." In the earlier centuries of the Church the bishops came to be affectionately addressed as "Papa" (Father), which comes from the word "Pope." About the year A.D. 500 "Papa" began to be restricted in use by the local bishops and became reserved for the Bishop of Rome. Over the centuries the word came to mean Universal Bishop. The idea that the Bishop of Rome should have authority over the whole Church grew slowly and was bitterly contested. It was the middle of Dark

Ages before the papal reign reached its greater power and jurisdiction.

Church Started Functioning on Satan's Kingdom Principles Instead of God's. The wickedness and corruption of humanity that was perpetrated during the years of the Dark Ages in the struggle for religious and political power is unbelievable. Christians should know the difference between Satan's kingdom principles and God's kingdom principles. In the spirit-world kingdom of Satan and his numerous angels and demons, there is a constant struggle for power and dominance. Each evil spirit wants to sit in the heavenlies and dominate and direct the other spirits to carry out works of evil. There is no voluntary submission or serving one another. There is forced servitude and obedience by the strongest and most cunning spirit who can gain control by any devilish means possible. Sad to say, this spirit and these Satanic principles dominated the church world the majority of the time during the Dark Ages. The history of the Universal Bishops (Popes) reads like the biblical record of the kings of Israel.

Follow God Not Man. Whether one is Catholic, Protestant, or Charismatic, the attitude should be the same concerning any religious leader who tries to dominate a person's Christian faith by his doctrine, fear tactics, threats of excommunication and damnation or submission without personal rights. Be assured that that religious man is not of the Spirit of Christ and the Lord is not backing him. Fear not, walk on and follow the meek and lowly Lamb of God.

2

Deterioration Through "Isms" and "Schisms"

Jesus Knew it Would Happen. The true Church started out in unity on the day of Pentecost and maintained oneness of doctrine, power, and purpose for several years. It gradually grew into many varied teachings, concepts, and practices concerning Christ and His Church, just as it has today in modern Christendom. Before listing the "isms" that developed in the first few centuries of the Church it is necessary to examine a few of the biblical accounts that predicted this development.

The Bible Speaks of the Dark Ages

"Now the Spirit speaketh expressly, that in the latter times some shall depart from the faith, giving heed to seducing spirits, and doctrines of devils; speaking lies in hypocrisy; having their conscience seared with a hot iron" *(I Tim. 4:1, 2)*. He then gives an example of "seducing spirits and doctrines of devils" in verse three, "Forbidding to marry, and commanding to abstain from meats, which God hath created to be received with thanksgiving of them which believe and know the truth." "For the time will come when they will not endure sound doctrine; but after their own lusts shall they turn away their ears from the truth, and shall be turned unto fables" *(II Tim. 4:3,4)*. "Take heed, brethren, lest there be in any of you an evil heart of unbelief, in departing from the living God" *(Heb. 3:12)*. ". . . there shall be false teachers among you, who privily shall bring in damnable heresies, even denying the Lord that brought them, and . . . many shall follow their pernicious ways; by reason of whom the way of truth shall be evil spoken of. And through covetousness shall they make merchandise of you" *(II Pet. 2:1-3)*. Peter also stated that men would arise who lacked spiritual understanding, and who would misinterpret Scripture and apply it wrongly ". . . our beloved brother Paul also according to the wisdom given him hath written unto you; as also in all his epistles, speaking in them of these things; in which are some things hard to be understood, which they that are unlearned and unstable wrest, as they do also the other Scriptures, unto their own destruction. Ye, therefore, beloved, seeing ye know these things before, beware lest ye also, being led away with the error of the wicked, fall from your own steadfastness." *(II Pet. 3:15-17)*. In II Thessalonians 2:3 and 10-12, Paul declared there would come a "falling away" first before the coming of the Lord took place; that a man would arise who would sit as God in the Temple of God. This system would lead them into strong delusion and cause them to believe a lie. God would allow this to happen "because they received not the love of the truth, that they might be saved." The great apostasy of the Dark Ages with its one-world church system fulfilled these Scriptures in a general way, but they may also be fulfilled in a personal and an intensified way at the end of the Church Age.

Falling Away Fulfilled. Thank God the true Spiritual Church, *the Body of Christ, has had its dark age, apostasy, and great falling away.* After this study on the *Deterioration of the Church,* the writer will advance to the section on the *Restoration of the Church,* and reveal that the Church has been on the move to full restoration during the last 500 years of this age. The Holy Spirit will not cease His work but will intensify His restorational work as the close of the Church Age nears, until Christ comes to be fully glorified in His saints, the people walking in fulness of truth.

The "Isms" of the Church

Scriptures Fulfilled. In the "Latter times" of the Early Church many began to "depart from the faith," and as they became dull of hearing and insensitive to the mind of Christ began to tune into seducing spirits. They began to propagate the "doctrine of devils" as Christian doctrine. The major universal church leaders were seeking higher offices and "making merchandise" of the Christians through their "covetousness." Throughout all the centuries of the Church there have been godly Christian leaders and saints who have loved the Lord with all their heart and have had but one desire, to glorify God and to bless His people. But they declined into a smaller and smaller remnant as the Church descended into the Dark Ages.

Human Understanding vs. Biblical Truth

Every generation seeks to interpret the Church in terms of its own thinking based on its past experiences in religion, culture, philosophy, and spiritual enlightenment. Christianity began to bring in converts from every race and every nation in the world. These converts began to interpret Christianity in the light of their past experiences and understanding of their own gods. Many segments of Christianity were integrated with Greek and Oriental philosophies and fables. The following "isms" are the ones that created the greatest controversies within the Church! Gnosticism, Manichaeism, Montanism, Monarchianism, Arianism, Apollinarianism, Nestorianism, Eutychianism, Monothelitism, Macedonianism, Patripassianism, Sabellianism, Pelagianism, and many other controversies raged in the Early Church. Most of these "isms" follow the name of a man who taught a particular doctrine that could not be accepted by the established Church system. Many of the Church Councils dealt with these teachings and made decisions concerning them. Most of them revolved around the "Mystery of the Godhead," and around the relationship between Jesus Christ in the Godhead and His nature(s).

"Ism" Relating to Godhead. The majority of the "ism" teachings of the Early Church concerning the Godhead are found today among the current Christian groups who believe in the "Jesus only," "One ness," "Twoness," "Trinity," or "Tritheist" concept of the Godhead: "Jesus Only" — Jesus is the Father, Son and Holy Ghost, one in one; "Oneness" — Three in One; "Twoness" — Three in Two; "Trinity" — One in Three; "Tritheist" — Three in Three. Although over simplified and somewhat comical, it would be good for each Christian to study the early "isms" and the full doctrinal meaning of these Godhead terms, and then refer to the Bible and determine his or her own personal belief. Some of the "isms" of the Early Church questioned the deity of Christ Jesus and described Him as being less than God. These "isms" were rightly condemned as heresy. All of the present Godhead beliefs mentioned in this paragraph acknowledge the deity of Jesus Christ and His equality with the Father. That's the reason the Holy Spirit can freely work with all the various groups holding different Godhead beliefs within mainline Christendom.

Modern Montanism and Gnosticism. Gnosticism has its modern day counterpart in some of the teachings of Jehovah's Witnesses, Christian Science, and Unitarianism. Montanism has its counterpart in the Pentecostal and Charismatic groups. It might be profitable for the reader to study the background of these groups to help understand and clarify his or her own beliefs. Church history books discuss some of these, but most can be found in *Baker's Dictionary of Theology.*

The Ebionites were different from the Apostolic Jewish Christians. They just added Christ to traditional Judaism, whereas main-line Christianity fully accepted Christ and the Church Age Truths and gradually separated from Judaism. (We have some Charismatics doing the same thing today with the Gift of the Holy Spirit. They just add the Holy Spirit to their old religious system. Some Messianic Jews are becoming modern day Ebionites.)

Development of Catholic. There is no "ism" name readily available to describe the Church's main body which was also developing doctrines and practices, sanctioned by its Councils and Bishops, that were adverse to the doctrines and practices of the Early Apostolic Church of the Book of Acts. The Church that existed between A.D. 300 to A.D. 500 is more closely identified with the modern historic Protestant churches in doctrine and practice. After the year A.D.

500 it correlates more to the present Roman Catholic Church. Many of the teachings and practices, such as penance as a sacrament, indulgences, purgatory, and the Papacy, were not in the Roman Church at that time. The word "catholic" means "throughout the whole, general, universal, all inclusive," etc. For this reason the word "catholic" was used when making reference to the Church throughout the world. "Wherever Jesus Christ is, there is the catholic Church" (*Baker's Dictionary of Theology*, p. 112). The churches were normally identified by saying "the church at Alexandria, or Antioch, or Rome," etc.

Through the centuries, the Bishops of Rome worked toward acquiring leadership of the Church and making their city the headquarters of the general, universal, assembly of believers. Therefore, the word "catholic" came to be identified with the world-wide church and during the Middle Ages developed into the Roman Catholic Church. "Historians refer to the Old Catholic Church as the phase of the development of Christianity which followed the apostolic and preceded the Roman Catholic." (Ibid., p. 112.)

"Isms" of State Church. Moving into the restoration of the Church the Catholic Church will be mentioned many times, since it was the ruling church system from which the Reformers evolved and against which they protested. Because of the Old Catholic Church's involvement with heathen customs, and its desire for political and materialistic gain, its "ism" problem was "paganism," "materialism," "ritualism," and "formalism." Therefore, the Christians of the first few centuries battled not only against a persecuting heathen world, but also against all the "Isms" and "Schisms" within their own fold. The Old Catholic

Church was becoming more formal, ritualistic, a religion of the mind, an intellectual faith, believing in a hard, fast system of doctrine. Emphasis was laid on correct belief and on obedience to the dogmas of the religious heirarchy, rather than on the inner, spiritual life.

Early Church Activities and Beliefs. The Spiritual Church of the Book of Acts practiced being justified by faith, cleansing from sin by the blood of Jesus, a personal relationship with Jesus Christ through a born-again, know-so salvation experience. Water baptism was more than a formality, it brought an identification with the death of Christ, a life of separation unto God in holy and virtuous living motivated by the love and grace of God. These Christians received the gift of the Holy Ghost and prayed often in their own supernatural prayer language of the spirit. Their ministers and leaders were not appointed by man for political reasons but were called, anointed, enabled, and appointed by the Holy Spirit. The minister did not "lord it" over the flock but ministered to them the living Word, supernatural healings, and miraculous deliverances by the gifts of the Spirit. They manifested the life and liberty in worship as portrayed in the Worship Book of the New Testament Church, the Book of Psalms. Communion was given without elaborate formal ceremonies. The presbytery laid hands on the Christians for healing, for the Holy Ghost, and for the revealing of their call and ministry in the Body of Christ. They lived in expectancy of the Second Coming of Christ in their day. They really believed that the wicked who died in their sins would suffer forever in Hell, while the righteous would be eternally rewarded. In the very beginning they had such love and unity that they had all things in common.

From New Born to Full Grown. They were not mature in all their doctrines and performances, but they were the "baby Church" which had all the elements and parts that would be a perfected part of the matured Church at the end of the Church Age. (Just as a baby boy has all that a grown man has, but he is not matured.) However, after 500 years of existence, the Church had lost all these experiential truths and had gone into Her winter season of sleep and darkness. Thank God, She was to be awakened a thousand years later and started on Her journey again. Nothing will stop Her until She is fully prepared as a Bride for Her Bridgreoom.

Restoration of Truth or Reactivation of Error. Progressing to the restoration of the Church, one should keep in mind that everything taught and manifested during each of the restoration periods is either a restoration of biblical truth or a reactivation of a false doctrine which developed during the deterioration of the Early Church. This is the reason that everything one hears and experiences must be examined in the light of the whole Bible, especially the New Testament which is the history, pattern, and instruction for the Universal Body of Christ. Everything new and different is not necessarily of the Holy Spirit. It must measure up to the Word of God, biblical hermeneutics (the science of biblical interpretation), Holy Ghost enlightenment, and divine wisdom (spiritual common sense). Stay in the Word and trust the Holy Spirit to lead you into all truth; be teachable, but not gullible; hunger and thirst after righteousness and maintain a love for the truth and you will go from glory to glory, and from faith to faith. The Holy Spirit will lead you into all truth until you are fully established in the present truth "and grow up in Him in all things which is the Head, even Christ" *(Eph. 4:15).*

3

The Effect
Of Islam On
Christendom

The Medieval Church of the Dark Ages. The period of the Dark Ages for the *Spiritual Church* was from its deterioration into an apostate church in the Fifth Century until the beginning of its restoration in the 15th Century. *Historically,* it was from the fall of Rome, A.D. 476, to the fall of Constantinople, A.D. 1453. *Culturally,* it was from the time when the civilized world was overrun by uneducated barbarians in the Fifth Century until the beginning of the Renaissance in the 15th Century.

The Church's Darkest Hour. The Church not only deteriorated doctrinally, but degenerated morally as well. The 200-year period just prior to and a little after the year 1,000 is called by historians the **"Midnight of the Dark Ages."** Bribery, corruption, simony, immorality, and bloodshed among the clergy and throughout Christendom make it just about the blackest chapter in the whole history of the Church. In the kingdoms of the world there were wars and rumors of wars. Entire nations were rising and falling to new conquerors. There was little justice and mercy in the world. The Christian Church was reduced to an empty form with virtually no life, love, or hope to offer suffering humanity. This apostate and idolatrous condition in the Church contributed to the birth of the Islam religion.

The Rise of the Islam Religion

The brief origination and history of Islam is as follows. It is reported that when Mohammed first came into contact with Christians in Syria, he was filled with horror at the amount of idols in the Church. It was recorded that when he was 40 years of age he went to a cave to think and pray. There, it is said, he had a vision. According to Mohammed's testimony the Angel Gabriel appeared to him and told him that God wanted him to go and teach all his fellow Arabs his revelation. Those outside his immediate family and friends rejected his new religion and tried to kill him. He fled to Medina, the same area where Moses fled just two millennia before. He started teaching his religion and building a following. The new religion was called "Islam," meaning submission and obedience to the will of God. Those who follow his teaching are called "Moslems," or "Muslims." Moslems looked to Mohammed as their prophet as the Jews looked to Moses.

He returned to Mecca with his militant followers and made converts of the whole area. His passion was to deliver mankind from the complicated idolatrous ways of worship the Church had imposed upon the people. He destroyed 360 idols in Mecca. A.D. 622 is recognized as the year of the birth of Islam.

Conversion from Mercy to Might. At first his followers tried to make converts by friendly persuasion. Soon they turned to the sword as a means of converting not only individuals but whole nations. With their fanatic zeal they conquered the whole of North Africa, Western Asia, and Jerusalem. The Moslems were taught that the highest realm of Heaven was reserved for those who died in military battle conquering "Unbelievers" for the Moslem religion. In contrast, the Early Church Christians believed that submissive, non-resistant suffering and martyrdom for Christ received the highest honor in Heaven.

Mohammed appeared at a time when the Church had become paganized with the worship of images, relics, martyrs, Mary, and the Saints. In a sense Islam was a revolt against the idolatry of the "Christian world." It delivered the people from certain bad conditions but put them into bondage of a worse nature *(Mt. 23:15).*

The Moslems Stopped. Within 110 years Moslems had swept nation after nation under their control until they tried to conquer Constantinople, the gateway to Europe. The Moslem march was stopped by the Christian army led by Emperor Leo II. The Moslems then tried to enter Europe through Spain and France but were stopped at Tours. They retreated to the Arabian-dominated world where the Moslem faith has been the controlling religion to the present day. Their barbarous treatment of Christians in Palestine led to the Crusades which lasted several hundred years during the Dark Ages.

The Religious Spirit. The Moslem faith produced a religious, hard, dominating spirit in its zealous followers. Followers were motivated more by a hate of the unbelievers of Islam than love for the souls of unbelievers. Their religion was propagated by the sword and encouraged slavery, harems, and the degradation of womanhood. Their greatest error, and proof that they were not a faith born of God, was the fact that they made Jesus no more than a Jewish prophet, inferior in every respect to Mohammed. The Moslems believe in the one true God (in Arabic *Allah)* of the Old Testament. Their concept of God is a fierce, relentless Oriental dictator, with no love for humanity outside the followers of the prophet.

Faith in God Insufficient. There are three great religions in the world today that accept the Old Testament Bible as the revelation of the true God of the universe: Judaism, Islam, and Christianity. However, there are no members of the Church of Jesus Christ in the Moslem or in the Jewish faith, for these faiths do not acknowledge Jesus as the Son of God and Savior of the world. Jesus is not looking to the Jews or the Moslems to fulfill His will and become His Bride. He is looking to the true Christian Church, the many-membered Corporate Body of Christ. Faith in God is insufficient.

Counterfeits Without Faith in Christ Jesus. Any religion, or so-called Christian denomination, that makes Jesus less than God, deletes the necessity of the redemptive work of Christ on Calvary for cleansing from sin and entry into Heaven, is a perversion, and counterfeit of God's true Church. They may preach and practice 90 percent of the Bible truths, but if Jesus Christ is not the only door and central figure of their faith, then they are "off" enough to cause their followers to miss God's plan for man. Rat poison is 90 percent good, edible, nutritious food, but has enough poison to kill the rats that eat it.

True members of the Body of Christ should not be swayed nor impressed by religious groups who contribute to the humanitarian needs of mankind but who are not Christ-centered. The world has benefited much from Moslem Arab scholars, especially in math, science, and geography. For instance, they invented and gave to the world the Arabic numeral system (1, 2, 3, 4) which eventually replaced the Roman numeral system (V, X, etc.).

Medieval Monasteries. In like manner, the Medieval Church of the Dark Ages developed four monastic orders between the 6th and 13th Centuries: the Benedictines, Cisterians, Franciscans, and Dominicans. The monks from these monasteries became the missionaries who took the story of Christianity to many heathen nations. One example is St. Patrick who evangelized Ireland in the Fifth Century. The monasteries gave hospitality to travelers, the sick, and the poor. Both the modern hotel and the modern hospital grew out of the hospice or monastery.

But as for the Church Jesus birthed and established, little remained of its original and experiential truths and supernatural demonstrations. It had deteriorated from a brilliant thousand-watt searchlight to a flickering one-watt candle.

4

The Mystery
Of The
Dark Ages

Where Was God?

There are some things that are very mysterious and very difficult for the natural mind to understand. The Dark Ages of the Church is one of these things.

Scripture shows that Jesus eternally ordained the Church. Then He died to redeem the Church. He sent the Holy Spirit to birth, empower, protect, and perfect the Church until She could be presented unto Himself, a glorious Church perfectly pure and mature.

Man's comprehension of love, concern, and wisdom is quite different from God's. God's ways are different from man's ways. His thoughts and methods of accomplishing His will are as far beyond man's as the Heavens are far above the Earth *(Isa. 55:8,9)*.

God's View of Time. God's concept and attitude toward time is also completely different. Time is so relevant, pressing, and trying to mortal man. Our beginning was at a certain time. Every day our lives are controlled by a 24-hour cycle of time. As a young person looks forward to each year of new recognition and opportunity, the years seem to take forever. After reaching his twenties, entering marriage, and beginning his ministry, the time begins to "normalize." Then the years speed up from the thirties to sixties until it seems as though they are passing by faster than the speeding box cars on a railroad track. But "Jesus Christ is the same yesterday, today, and forever" *(Heb. 13:8)*. Peter said that time to the Lord is different from man's concept of it, for "one day is with the Lord as a thousand years, and a thousand years as one day" *(II Pet. 3:8)*. According to God's time-table, Jesus has been gone from the Earth less than two days. Nonetheless, Hosea 6:2 says, "After two days will he revive us [full restoration]; in the third day he will raise us up, and we shall live in his sight" [resurrection and translation at the beginning of the third day].

Eternal Plan Takes Priority Over Process. Considering the many millions of saints who were· martyred in every diabolical, degrading, and humiliating method conceivable by men of demonized minds during the first 300 years of the Church, we must conclude that God considers suffering and death from a completely different perspective from mortal man. *God's eternal plan to bring forth His perfect man (Church) takes priority over the process and time period required to produce His Bride.*

The Psalmist declares that God who knows everything, even the beginning from the end, foreknows every member in His Corporate Body and that He has numbered all the days of the Church *(Ps. 139:15, 16)*. The Church is being "curiously wrought," formed, and put together, not in the higher realms of Heaven but in the lower parts of Earth. The Lord Jesus purchased the Church through suffering and death. His whole life and purpose is wrapped up in the Church. What purpose could He have then for allowing His precious Church to deteriorate into a 1,000-year apostate Dark Age? His divine love for the Church did not diminish with its decline. However, His fellowship and functioning with the Church was greatly hindered.

God's Sovereignity — Man's Will. Did Jesus leave the Church to its own ways for 1,000 years? Since God is sovereign why didn't He keep the Church doctrinally right, morally pure, and victorious over all Her enemies? We know that God made man and that He can do anything He will with man. Or can He? Could it be that God has decreed that He will never overrule mortal man's will in relation to service to Himself?

God did not stop Adam and Eve from sinning when they willed to eat of the forbidden fruit. He did not override the children of Israel when they set their will against God's will for them to enter into and conquer Canaan. He refused to fight their battle after they refused to obey His will and He left them to wander in the wilderness for 40 years. He started preparing a new generation and eventually had a people desirous and willing to fulfill His will.

Has God limited Himself in blessing mankind in willingness, faith, and receptivity to His grace and goodness? Why doesn't God make people do what is right? He convicts and constrains with His goodness and judgment, but if people will not yield He will not force them to be properly related to Himself against their will.

God Wants Mature Sons. God does not want a kingdom of subjects or slaves under forced servitude. He did not want robots or humanoids preprogrammed to act without any choice and without any initiative of their own. He created a being in His own image and likeness as a compatible creature capable of creative thoughts, a free spirit with a separate will of his own with the privilege of refusing or choosing to do God's will. He created a son, not a slave. Therefore, He desires *sons* not *subjects*. He desires intelligent, willful service from man. His joy is not to be an employer with employees, rather a Father with a family of children. He does not even want laborers as children working **for** Him but grown-up sons and daughters as co-laborers **with** Him. Jesus does not desire to rule and reign **over** His Church, but **with** His Church. He wants the Church to grow up to "the fulness of the stature of Christ" *(Eph. 4:11-15)* so that it can function on His level. An adult can come down to the level of a child and can be in fellowship with him, but a child cannot elevate himself to fellowship as an adult. He must grow to that level. God came down to man's level in the person of Jesus to translate the Church into His kingdom in the heavenly places in Christ Jesus. However, the Church cannot be *elevated* to maturity. It must *grow* to maturity. Growth requires submission and a willing participation in all that Christ is. God will settle for nothing less than a free-moral, fellow-being who chooses Him above all others and cooperates as a willing, loving companion. "Sons love because they choose to. Delight of heart to heart and mind to mind can occur only where *one freely chooses* to *cherish another.*" (Sandford, *The Elijah Task,* Plainfield, New Jersey, Logos International, 1977. p. 108.)

Therefore, if man is determined to go his own way then God does not sovereignly force him to walk by His side. Jesus fully revealed and demonstrated the character of God in His dealings with mankind here on Earth. Just as Jesus was God's perfect man, so the Church is to become Christ's perfected human race. The perfected Church-race of humanity will fully satisfy the original desire and plan that God had in His heart when He created the human race.

Jesus Limits Himself To Church. Jesus, by His foreknowledge, and the New Testament writers, by divine inspiration, declared that there would be a great falling away of the Church. The Church willfully went its own way and fell away from God's original pattern. Jesus did not bind or restrict Satan from leading the Church into deception and spiritual deterioration, nor did He sovereignly stop the Church from walking in Her own willful way. Jesus has limited Himself to the Church. He will enlighten and perform according to the hunger, receptivity, and response of His people to the moving of His Spirit, and to the cry of His ordained voices of reform.

Yet, it is a mistake to conclude that God has left Himself to the whim and fancy of man. God is still sovereign. Though I do not presently fully understand the "Why?" I believe the Dark Ages played a part in God's overall plan in purifying and perfecting His Eternal Church. God still rules in the affairs of man.

Church When Jesus Comes. There are many unanswered questions about the Dark Ages of the Church. Nonetheless, there is one thing that it definitely revealed and made perfectly clear: The Church that Jesus is coming back to receive unto Himself will not be like the Church of the Dark Ages. He is not coming for an apostate Church. It will not even be a malnourished, worn out, wrinkled, formal, lifeless, immature, retarded, lukewarm, falling away, or holding-on-till-Jesus-comes Church. If He had to prophetically wait until the "great falling away" took place before He could return for it, then He had no need to wait any longer, for the church of the Dark

Ages was in that condition. Thank God! He didn't even make a move toward coming for that church. He didn't come for it when the First Century Christians went through the tribulation of martyrdom, nor did He come for the church which had fallen away from the faith. He had 1,000 years in which He could have translated the remnant of the faithful few who were walking in truth. But He did not.

Rapture Not Back Door Escapism. When Jesus comes to translate His Church, it will not be God's heavenly helicopter coming to air-lift the saints out before they all backslide or before the devil has over-run their camp. When Jesus comes it will not be because the battle is too great for the Army of the Lord. Neither will it be to jerk the Church out before the antichrist system devours it; nor a retreat or an emergency rapture to preserve the Church from extinction. It is not "back door" escapism before the devil kicks down the front door.

Jesus Cannot Be Intimidated. God is not motivated by fear nor is He forced into action because of situations. Jesus has predestinated His Church to be perfect in purity and maturity, conformed to His image and likeness by the time He returns. All the devils in Hell or human rebels on Earth cannot stop Him from working on His building. He will not be threatened or intimidated by the "accuser of the brethren" into catching away His Church before He has put every living stone in place and has completed the building to **His** satisfaction. He will not literally come for the Church until She has gone through the "times of restoration." The Church-Bride has been retarded and restricted in Her growth for more than 1,000 years. He will now nourish Her during the "period of the great Restoration" until She is restored unto full beauty and performance, even as a mature Bride adorned for Her Husband, Christ Jesus.

The
Restoration
Of The
Church

1

Providential Preparation For Church Restoration

God's Methods. When God gets ready to do something new He makes preparation in certain areas. He prepares a **people,** a **product,** and a **place** to perpetuate His plan. The Lord then raises up a **man** with a **message** and a **ministry** which produces a **movement** that further fulfills His will by various **methods** and **means.**

People — Places — Products

In ages past when He was ready to actuate His "eternal purpose which He purposed in Christ Jesus" *(Eph. 3:11),* He made ready a *place,* planet Earth. He then brought forth His new creation, *Adam* and *Eve.* The *product* for man's use was all of Earth's creatures, elements, and atmosphere.

Man — Message — Method

In the destruction of the world by a flood, Noah was the *man.* The ark was the *means.* Repentance was the *message.* Water was the *method* by which the wicked were taken away. The *place* was on top of the water until planet Earth was ready for the migration of man again.

Deliverance From Egypt — Example. When God was ready to deliver the children of Israel out of their bondage and slavery in Egypt He made the same preparation. Moses was His man, and miracles in nature were His product. Canaan country was the place for perpetuating His plan. (Only God knew the time period of the journey and the day and hour when they would enter into Canaan and possess their promised place.) He stirred the Children of Israel's desire for deliverance by allowing their bondage to get worse, especially after Moses had given them hope of deliverance and a better life. Numerous details could be given concerning the same preparation that was made for the coming of Jesus, the Messiah, and the establishment of the Church.

Deliverance From The Dark Ages. According to God's consistent pattern, preparation was made for the deliverance of the Church from its bondage to a totalitarian religious system. Church members were slaves to religious rituals and to dead doctrines such as penance. They were whipped by the lashes of asceticism, thrown into solitary confinement by monasticism, and terrorized by the fires of purgatory, while living in constant fear of eternal damnation by a wrathful God. The church system that arose in the Dark Ages claimed to have power to open and shut the doors of Heaven to any human being. There was more paganism, superstition and unrest than there was pardon and peace.

The Church was in as much bondage spiritually as the children of Israel were physically. The Holy Spirit began to raise up voices of hope that proclaimed there was a better life in Christ. Men with a message arose, producing movements that prepared the way for the restoration of the Church. Products were produced which would help propagate the message. Old places were ready and a new country (America) was being prepared where the Holy Spirit would have freedom to continue His work of the restoration of truth to the Church until full restoration and maturity.

History Revolves Around the Church

The Renaissance, the rise and fall of nations, in fact, all of history revolves around the Church.

Thus the Church, and only the Church, is the key to and explanation of history. Therefore, history is only the handmaiden of the Church, and the nations of the world are but puppets manipulated by God for the purposes of His Church *(Acts 17:26)*. Creation has no other aim. History has no other goal (Billheimer, p. 26).

The Products That Produced

The Renaissance awakened Europeans to a new interest in literature, art, and science. This new knowledge stirred within them a desire to depart from ignorance, superstition, and religious domination of the mind and conscience. In Germany, England, and France, the movement was more religious, awakening a new interest in the Scriptures, Greek, Hebrew, and also awakening a search for the true foundations of faith, apart from the dogmas of Rome. The revival of learning helped produce the reformers of the great Reformation. The *Spirit of Truth* was arising in the

Church and the whole world was being enlightened in every area. The stage was being set for the greatest undertaking of the Holy Spirit since the original birth of the Church.

The Providential Product of Printing. The invention of the printing press provided the product that made the Protestant Movement possible. The discovery was made by Johannes Gutenberg in 1456. Before this invention, from the beginning of time, books had been circulated only as rapidly as they could be hand copied. Prior to this time it cost a working man his yearly wage to purchase a Bible. It is significant in showing the desire of that time that the first book printed by Gutenberg was the Bible. The press brought the Scriptures into common use, and led to their translation and circulation in all the languages of Europe. The people who read the New Testament soon realized that the papal church was far from the New Testament ideal. And the new teachings of the Reformers, as fast as they appeared, were set forth in books and pamphlets, which were circulated throughout Europe.

Inventions Of Travel And Communication For The Church. In each step of the restoration of the Church, natural inventions were brought into existence providing better methods of travel and communication. These new inventions were providentially brought forth for the purpose of propagating and proclaiming the new truths of each Restorational Movement: i.e., the printing press, locomotive, automobile, radio, airplane, television, etc. The more restorational truth and spiritual light the Church receives, the more natural enlightenment the world receives *(Prov. 4:18; Dan. 12:4).*

Practices That Provoked

The Church practice of selling indulgences caused the spark that ignited the fuel of the great Restoration. An "indulgence" is "defined by the *Catholic Encyclopedia,* VII, p. 783, as 'a remission of the temporal punishment due to sin, the guilt of which has been forgiven.'" *(Baker's Dictionary of Theology,* p. 283.)

Penance vs. Repentance. During the Dark Ages of the Church "penance" replaced "true repentance." Penance became the method whereby the Christian could atone for and remove the punishment due him for his sin by gifts to the church, good works, self-denial, mortifying the flesh by afflicting punishment upon himself, and by special decrees or requirements of the church. The first undisputed indulgences were granted in the 11th Century to induce men to go on the Crusades. All knights and soldiers who went on the journey would be granted an "indulgence" that would count in lieu of all penance. Just prior to the restoration, indulgences were being sold to lessen or eliminate one's time in Purgatory.

Purgatory is a doctrine of the Roman Catholic and the Greek Orthodox Churches. It teaches that there is a place where the dead go immediately after death to undergo purifying suffering. Only those believers who have attained a state of Christian perfection are said to go immediately to Heaven. The Roman Catholic Church had only acknowledged a few who had reached that stage. They are usually granted sainthood. Most of the Christians of the Dark Ages knew they would have to spend some time in Purgatory to atone for their sins. This time could vary from a few hours to millions of years. "Gifts or services rendered to the church, prayers by the priests, and masses provided by relatives or friends on behalf of the deceased can shorten, alleviate, or eliminate the sojourn of the soul in purgatory." (Ibid., p. 430.)

The supreme power and authority of the Pope in the affairs of the state as well as in the Church made the princes and kings of different countries more receptive to the message of the Reformers.

Men, Messages, And Movements

Forerunners of the "Period of the Great Restoration." There were several *men* and *movements,* forerunners of the Period of the Great Restoration, who sought to reform the Church from the 12th Century until the time of the Reformation. Many attempts were made to deliver the people from the bondage that the church system had heaped upon them. The voices from within the Church were suppressed and were placed in obscure places. Those who moved outside the state church were repressed and some were annihilated by bloody persecutions. These *men* and *movements* were seed plantings in the field of the Restoration of the Church. Others watered the plant as it grew, and the men of the Restoration period were reapers of the harvest. "I have planted, Apollos watered; but God gave the increase" *(I Cor. 3:6).*

Many *men* never see the fulfillment of their revelation and preaching, especially if they are ahead of their time. The Apostle Paul was such a man. His vision of the Church overcoming the sting of death and mortality was beyond his day. He gave us that promise from the Lord *(I Cor. 15:51-57; I Thess. 4:14-17).* But like the patriarchs of old who "died in faith having not yet received the promise" of the Messiah, Paul died in faith believing for physical immortality but, instead, was a seed planting and a forerunner to that day of deliverance for the Church. Paul spoke of himself as "one born out of due time" *(I Cor. 15:8)*. He was not born of God until after Christ's resurrection and departure from Earth, and he was not privileged to live to see His second coming, though he had divine insight concerning both. God is the one that determines what divine plan will be activated and fulfilled in our day. Our responsibility is to walk in the revelation He has given, be established in the present truth, and fulfill the will of God for our generation.

The forerunners of the great Reformation did the best they could with the revelation, ability and authority they had from the Lord.

The Albigenses Movement

During the 12th Century the Albigenses Movement grew to prominence in southern France. Members repudiated the authority of tradition, circulated the New Testament, and opposed the Church doctrines of purgatory, image worship, and priestly claims. They held some peculiar doctrines and rejected the Old Testament. To wipe out this nest of rebellion, Pope Innocent III declared them "heretic" and called for a crusade against them. The sect was extirpated by the slaughter of almost the entire population of the region, Catholic as well as Albigenses.

The Waldensians Movement

Peter Waldo, a rich merchant of Lyons was concerned with the brevity of life and sought counsel from a priest. Since the priest suggested that Waldo should sell his goods and give them to the poor, he did so in 1176. He turned his attention to the Scriptures and decided to follow the example of Christ. His followers called themselves the "Poor Men of Lyons." They went around preaching in simple garb, circulating the Scriptures, seeking to conform others to the Apostolic Church. They denied the efficacy of the mass and the existence of Purgatory. They revived the Donatist attitude (similar to the Baptist beliefs regarding separation of church and state and the Churches of Christ belief in baptismal regeneration) and adopted a pious view of life. In 1184 they were declared heretics by the Pope. They left France and spread into the Netherlands, Germany, and Bohemia, as well as Spain and Italy.

The John Wycliffe Movement

John Wycliffe (1329-84) was born and educated in England. He earned his doctorate in Theology and was greatly influenced by the writings of Augustine. He was the morning star that shined the brightest before the dawn of the Reformation. A high official in the affairs of England, Wycliffe provided England with a new proclamation of the pure gospel, acknowledging the Bible as the only source of truth. Declaring that Christ, not the Pope, was the head of the Church, he rejected the Doctrine of Infallibility of either pope or council, and held that papal decrees or pronouncements had authority only insofar as they were in harmony with Scripture. The clergy was not to be lords over the flock but were to serve and help the people. He attacked the mendicant friars, and the system of monasticism; wrote against the doctrine of "trans-substantiation" (i.e., that in the mass the bread and wine are transformed into the actual body and blood of Christ) regarding the elements as symbols;

and urged that the church service be made more simple, according to the New Testament pattern.

His greatest work was his translation of the Bible from the Vulgate, the Latin version, into English. It appeared in the year of his death, 1384. His followers were called Lollards, who at one time were numerous. After Wycliffe was declared to be a heretic by the Ecclesiastical system, his followers were severely persecuted and were virtually extinguished. John Wycliffe's strong influential preaching and his translation brought the plant of Restoration closer to harvest time. He added new life to the "babe in the womb" of the Structural Church that was soon to be birthed in Restoration and was soon to breathe and live on its own without the church body of the Dark Ages.

The John Huss Movement

John Huss (1369-1415), became the voice of reform in Bohemia as Wycliffe had been in England. He likewise was an educated man having earned his bachelor's and master's degrees at the University of Prague. By 1398 he was lecturing on theology at the university. He was ordained to the priesthood in 1401, and the next year became Rector of the University of Prague. Huss believed and preached all the teachings of Wycliffe. In his chief work, *On the Church,* Huss defined the Church as the **Body of Christ,** with Christ its only head. Although he defended the traditional authority of the clergy, he taught that only God can forgive sin. The clerical heirarchy of the world-dominating Roman Catholic Church branded him a heretic and his teachings as heresies. He was summoned to appear before the Council at Constance.

He agreed to go after safe conduct was guaranteed by King Wenceslaus, Emperor Sigismund, and by the Pope himself. But the pledge was violated upon the principle that "faith was not to be kept with heretics." He was condemned and burned at the stake, without a real opportunity to explain his views. However, his heroic death aroused the national feelings of the Czech people, who established the Hussite church in Bohemia until the Hapsburgs conquered Bohemia in 1620 and reestablished the Roman Catholic Church as the state religion.

According to tradition one of the most profound prophecies concerning the coming reformation was made by John Huss just before he was burned to death. "You are now roasting the goose, [Huss means goose in Bohemian] but in a hundred years there will rise up a swan whom you shall not roast nor scorch. Him men will hear sing and God will allow him to live" (Rev. David Huebert, "Outlined Study on Church Restoration," Chilliwack, B.C., Canada).

Girolamo Savonarola

Savonarola (1454-98) rose up as a voice of reform in Italy. He had no new revelation of Scripture to offer, but he preached against sin and corruption in commoners, government, clergy, and in the papal office. He gave some prophecies concerning the future development of Italy. There is one particularly interesting record of the results of his preaching. At the carnival in Florence in 1496, Savonarola inspired the burning of the vanities when the people made a great bonfire of cosmetics, false hair, pornographic books and gambling equipment. Savonarola suffered the same fate as the other reformers who dared question the authority of the pope, or the unscriptural doctrines and practices of the Dark Age Church.

A Changing World. There were many other contributions to the preparation necessary for the birth of the Reformation, such as the fall of Constantinople to Mohammed II in 1453. Most historians place that incident as the dividing point between medieval and modern times. It is hard to grasp what it would have been like to live in those days. The whole world was going through a revolutionary change and evolving into a new era. Printing marked the end of mass ignorance. Gunpowder ended the usefulness of knights and changed the whole strategy of warfare. The compass put an end to man's limited knowledge about unknown lands and seas. Man rediscovered that the world was not flat, but round. Without the fear of falling off the end of the world men began to explore the Earth. They began to advance learning and gain new understanding of the Earth, science, religion, and governments. Man slowly but steadily walked out of the shadow of the medieval Dark Ages and into the light of a new and modern world.

Eschatological Confusion. Theologians were at a loss concerning their eschatology. They did not know how to interpret what was happening in the light of biblical teaching concerning the end time. They did not want to make the same mistake as the theologians and people of the Tenth Century. Many were convinced that the world would come to an end in the year 1,000. From their understanding of Scripture most end-time prophecies had come to pass or were coming to pass. There had been a great falling away from the faith. It looked as though Islam was taking over the world and would be the antichrist system that would rule. There were wars and rumors of wars.

The people who lived in the Tenth Century thought the Bible said something that meant the world was coming to an end in the year 1000, which was called the 'millennium' from the Latin word meaning 1,000 years.

Some people were glad the world was coming to an end. They were so poor and miserable and unhappy that they were anxious to go to heaven, where everything would be fine and lovely — if they had been good. So they were particularly good and did everything they could to earn a place for themselves in heaven.

Others were not so anxious to have the world come to an end. But, they thought, if it were coming to an end so soon, they might as well hurry up and enjoy themselves here while they still had a chance.

The year 1000 came, and nothing happened. As time went on, without any change, people began to think the end was delayed for some reason they could not explain. (V. M. Hillyer and E. G. Huly, *The Medieval World,* Meredith Press, New York, New York, 1966. p. 54.)

Coming In Restoration First

The first millennium Christians were just as convinced that the coming of the Lord would take place by the year 1000 as present day Christians are convinced it will take place before the end of the second millennium. Those living in the 15th Century had no way of knowing what was about to break forth upon the world.

The "period of the Great Restoration" as proclaimed by Peter in Acts 3:21 was being ushered in. "Times of refreshing" will come from the "presence of the Lord" bringing more truth and more truth until the Church reaches God's standard, even if it takes 500 or more years. The properly prepared Bride is more important to Jesus than the time it takes to perfect His Bride-Church.

Let us now progress to the Restoration of the Church to determine the Men, Movements, Methods, Ministries, and Restorational truths God uses to bring His many-membered Corporate Body of Christ to the place where it is ready for presentation unto Himself.

2

The Scriptural Examination of Church Restoration

Jesus Must Be Kept In Heaven Until Acts 3:19-21!

This Scripture is at the core of this discourse and a key text on Restoration. It is expedient that this Scripture be given greater in-depth study than the other numerous Scriptures mentioned. The writer has used *Acts 3:19-21* in teaching the Restoration of the Church for 25 years. Nevertheless, before these things were put in writing, a thorough reexamination of this particular Scripture was made in the following areas: etymologically — to determine proper word usage; theologically — to evaluate the thinking of other theologians; exegetically — to derive the original Greek meaning, and topically throughout Scripture to be sure the interpretation given is in agreement with the teaching of the whole Word of God. After applying all the principles of biblical hermeneutics to this passage I am convinced its application to the Restoration of the Church is in divine order.

New Way and a New Day. In verse 19 Peter spoke to the Jews to repent and be converted, that their sins might be blotted out, for they had just crucified the "Prince of life," God's promised Messiah.

Jesus had recently fulfilled all the Scriptures concerning the suffering Savior. They missed the "day of their visitation" by not recognizing that the coming of the Messiah had taken place. There was now a new day and a new way, not by ancestoral descent as a Jew, but by being joined to Christ Jesus the Tree of Life in which there is neither "natural branch" by heritage, nor "wild branch" grafted in. But "both Jew and Gentile are all sinners in need of a Savior." All must repent and be converted. Those Jews who heeded his message of repentance were converted and became members of the Universal Body of Christ, the Eternal Church. The Early Church for the first 10 years was made up almost entirely of the natural descendents of Abraham. But finally, Peter and Paul received the revelation that natural descent has nothing to do with becoming a member in the Church of the Lord Jesus Christ. Peter's continuing message, with a promise of "times of refreshing" and a "second coming of Christ" was based on man's repentance and baptism into the Body of Christ. The whole New Testament was written for the benefit of the Church.

Prophetic Applications. Most prophetic Scriptures have two applications: natural and spiritual; individual and corporate. A prophetic Scripture can apply to natural Israel, the Messiah, and the Church, and not do injustice to the principle of biblical hermeneutics. It can have a natural fulfillment with Israel, personal fulfillment in Jesus, and then a spiritual corporate fulfillment in the Church. For instance, examine the Scripture in Hosea 11:1: "When Israel was a child, then I loved him, and called my son out of Egypt." The context of the Scripture definitely shows that the prophet is speaking of the time when God led the Nation of Israel out of Egypt. He showed His love by delivering them from their Egyptian bondage and slavery. However, Matthew, in his book *(2:15),* pulls one phrase from this Scripture to prove that it has a personal application to Jesus the Messiah. The Pharisee and Sadducee theologians could have argued with Matthew that he was taking the Scripture out of context. How could he use it to prove that this Jesus was the Messiah when it was clear that it was speaking of the Nation of Israel? Regardless of the seeming contradiction, the Holy Spirit did inspire Hosea to prophesy this concerning Israel, and also inspired Matthew to apply it to Jesus.

In the same manner, Hosea 11:1 can be applied personally to a sinner whom Jesus loved and called out of his Egyptian land of satanic bondage. It can also apply corporately to the Church which consists of many of God's sons. At the beginning of the Reformation, God called the Church out of its Egyptian land of religious slavery and dead works which existed during the Dark Ages. His call brought the Church out of Egypt as well as started it on its goal to ultimate restoration.

The Most Privileged People. Some theologians, especially those who get more excited about the restoration of the Jews and the land of Israel than they do about the Restoration of the Church, apply these Scriptures only to the Nation of Israel. They get more excited about the rebuilding of the temple in Jerusalem than they do about the Church being built as the Temple of God and the New Jerusalem. Christians today should get more excited about the Church and prophecies being fulfilled in it than about any other prophetic fulfillment. The Church is the highest realm, the most privileged people, and the greatest race of beings in God's eternal universe. Even Jews who become Christians are no longer Israelites in God's sight, but sons of God and members of the Body of Christ. "In Christ there is neither Jew nor Gentile" *(Gal. 3:28).*

Dispensational View. Other theologians, mainly dispensationalists, see no prophecies to be fulfilled in the Church between Jesus' first coming and second coming. They believe in the imminent return of Christ regardless of the condition of the Church. Their criteria for the coming of the Lord are what's taking place in the world and in Israel. However, the foremost and greatest criterion for the second coming of Jesus is that which is taking place in the Church. He is coming back for the Church, but our text states that Heaven cannot release Christ to return *until* the "times of refreshing, recovery, and revival" have restored all truth back to the Church, and until the "period of the great Restoration" has been accomplished in the Church. Notice, Peter says "times" of restitution or restoration indicating that there would come several restorational truth visitations to the Church "from the presence of the Lord." Jesus cannot be released from Heaven to return to Earth to set up His literal kingdom until His Church (His spiritual kingdom) has been fully established and perfected. Note how Acts 3:21 is rendered in different translations.

King James Version	*"Whom the heaven must receive until the times of restitution of all things,* which God hath spoken by the mouth of all his holy prophets since the world began."
The Living Bible	*"For he must remain in heaven until the final re-*

covery of all things from
sin, as prophesied from
ancient times."

Moffatt

"Christ must be kept in
heaven till the period of
the great Restoration.
Ages ago God spoke of
this by the lips of His
holy prophets."

**Revised Stand-
ard Version**

"Whom heaven must re-
ceive until the time for establishing all that God
spoke by the mouth of His
holy prophets of old."

**Amplified New
Testament**

"Whom heaven must re-
ceive (and retain) until the
time for the complete restoration of all that God
spoke by the mouth of His
holy prophets for ages
past from the most an-
cient time in the memory
of man."

Take note of the key word "until" or "till": "Heaven
must receive, keep, retain Jesus until . . ."; "the Holy
Spirit of promise is the earnest of our inheritance
until . . . ." These and many other Scriptures reveal
that certain things cannot happen "until" certain
other things are revealed and fulfilled. The key emphasis here is that Jesus cannot return from Heaven
to receive His Church unto Himself until it reaches
its scripturally predicted state of purity and maturity.
The Holy Spirit "presence of the Lord" has been
restoring truth after truth to the Church over the last

500 years and will continue to do so until the Church reaches the maturity He has pre-ordained.

Meaning Of "All Things". It is important that the words "all things" to be restored are restricted to "that which God hath spoken through the mouth of His prophets." There is no mention or prediction in the whole of God's book concerning the conversion and restoration of the wicked dead, fallen angels, or Satan himself. This devilish doctrine has been taught by different ones in Christendom from the time of Clement of Alexandria in the Second Century to the Universalist denomination of today. Universalism has no part in the Restoration of the Church. The Bible talks about the Church being restored, Israel being restored and the Earth being restored. But no mention is made of Satan, fallen angels, demons, or any wicked dead human soul being restored.

Of all the commentaries read, I feel the following comments give the best exposition of Acts 3:21.

> *(21)* Whom the heaven must receive. The words have a pregnant force; "must receive and keep."

> Until the times of restitution of all things. The "times" seem distinguished from the "seasons" as more permanent. This is the only passage in which the word translated "restitution" is found in the New Testament. Etymologically, it conveys the thought of *restoration to an earlier and better state,* rather than that of simple consummation or completion, which the immediate context seems, in some measure, to suggest. It finds an interesting parallel in the "new heavens and new earth" — involving, as they do, a restoration of all things to their true order — of 2 Peter

3:13. It does not necessarily involve, as some have thought, the final salvation of all men, but it does suggest a state in which "righteousness," and not "sin" shall have dominion over a redeemed and new-created world; and that idea suggests a wider scope as to the possibilities of growth in wisdom and holiness, or even of repentance and conversion, in the unseen world than that which Christendom has too often been content. The corresponding verb is found in the words, "Elias truly shall come first, and **restore** all things" (Charles John Ellicot, gen. ed., *Ellicot's Commentary on the Whole Bible,* 8 Volumes, Grand Rapids, Michigan, Zondervan Publishing House, 1954, Vol. 7; *The Acts of the Apostles,* E. H. Plumtree, DD., p. 19).

John the Baptist was the person who came in the spirit of Elijah. He was the instrument used to restore and prepare the way for the first coming of Jesus. The Church will be the instrument that will move in the power and spirit of Elijah, restoring all things which have been spoken by the mouth of all the holy prophets since the world began, releasing Jesus from the Heavens and bringing about the *Second* Coming of Christ.

A Prophet To Church Nation. As mentioned in the introduction of the book, the writer was not called and anointed to be a prophet concerning Israel or the world conditions, but a voice concerning the Church. He has no particular revelation on God's eternal plan concerning the Jews, Israel, or the Jewish Temple. He is not anti-Israel. He taught the book of Romans for four years in Bible college and emphasized.that chapters 9, 10, and 11 show the election, rejection, and restoration of Israel. Acts 3:19-21 evidently will have a natural fulfillment concerning God's chosen nation of Israel. "Natural" Israel and the Jews are having "times" of restoration that are gradually restoring them to all that the prophets predicted they would be and would have.

The Peak Of Fulfillment. There are three things that must dove-tail together in order for the coming of the Lord to take place: Old Testament prophecies and New Testament teachings concerning the Church, prophecies concerning the state of Israel and the Jews, prophecies concerning world conditions. *All three areas are reaching the peak of fulfillment, but the Church is the key to the fulfillment of prophecy for Israel and for the world.* Even the Christian prophets to Israel and extreme dispensationalists state that Jesus must finish His ministry to the Gentile Church and must call it out of the world before He can turn to the Jews as their Messiah King. This still puts the Church on God's priority list as the determining factor in the second coming of Christ Jesus.

Church In Driver's Seat. This fact puts Jesus and His Church in the driver's seat. Christians are to "redeem the time" and "occupy until He comes." This is not accomplished by getting excited about Israel or becoming discouraged over world conditions. The Church is *not* to sit around whining and pining for the coming of the Lord. If we are really serious about His coming, we should act upon St. Peter's words *(II Pet. 3:12)*, "to hasten the coming of the Lord," or as the Living Bible says to "hurry it along." This can be accomplished by us, the Church, going on to perfection in purity and maturity and becoming the last generation which overcomes all things, bringing about "the final recovery of all things from sin, as prophesied from ancient times."

None Saith Restore!!!

Through our study on the deterioration of the Church we saw where the Church was left spiritually deaf and blind. Most of the spiritual leaders of the Dark Ages had lost touch with the "Spirit of Truth" and the Spirit of revelation in the knowledge of the Son of God. The Church had not only lost original reality in the doctrines of Christ and the experiential truths of the Early Church, but they had also added man-made traditions, doctrines of devils, paganistic-type church buildings and ritualistic ways of worship. The Church was in the same condition before the days of the Restoration as Judaism was just prior to the coming of Christ Jesus. The pope and priests were "minoring in majors" and "majoring in minors" just as the Pharisees and Sadducees were in Jesus' day. The Scripture that most graphically describes the leaders of the medieval church is Isaiah 42:18-22. Of the leadership Isaiah says, "Who is blind, but my servant? or deaf, as my messengers that I sent?" The people are described as "a people robbed and spoiled; they are all of them snared in holes, and they are hid in prison houses; they are for a prey, and none delivereth; for a spoil, and **none saith, restore.**"

I Will Restore

The book of Joel contains one of the most encouraging Scriptures of Israel's natural hope and the Church's spiritual hope for Restoration.

> Be glad then, ye children of Zion, and rejoice in the Lord your God: for He hath given you the former rain moderately, and He will cause to come down for you the rain, the former rain, and the latter rain in the first month.

And the floors shall be full of wheat [Word of God], and the fats [Vats] shall overflow with wine [New Truth] and oil [anointing]. And I **will restore** to you the years that the locust hath eaten, the cankerworm, and the caterpillar, and the palmerworm, . . . ye shall eat in plenty, and be satisfied, and praise the name of the Lord your God, and none else: and My people shall never be ashamed. *(Joel 2:23-26)*

Last Day Church Will Be Greater. The end of the Church will be even greater than its beginning *(Eccl. 2:9)*. God promised that the glory of the latter house (Latter Church) will be greater than that of the former house (Early Church) *(Hag. 2:9)*. The Church flirted with the world and paganism as Samson did with Delilah. Samson's secret strength was discovered and taken away. His eyes were put out and he was put into prison. Blinded and chained to the grinding mill, he went in circles until his seven locks of hair began to grow. When Samson's hair was fully restored, God gave him back his ministry of destroying the enemy and delivering God's people. More was accomplished after his restoration than had been accomplished in all his former years. In like manner, the eyes of the Church were put out. The Body of Christ was bound at the grinding mill of doing penance and trying to earn peace with God by good works. It went in circles for 1,000 years, but its locks of hair began to grow, and will continue to grow until . . . . The last century Church will accomplish more in its generation than all that was done in former years.

Divine Desire For Spiritual Growth

The following Scriptures on progressive growth are included to clarify and amplify the fact that God desires and demands a going on and a growing up: Jn. 16:13; Acts 3:19-21; Eph. 4:12; Heb. 6:1,2; Eph. 5:27; Eph. 4:15; II Cor. 3:18; Heb. 5:14; I Jn. 3:1-3; Rom. 8:29; Heb. 2:10; Job 17:9; Ps. 84:7; Prov. 4:18; Is. 28:10; Ho. 6:3; Rom. 1:17: II Pet. 1:5; Phil. 3:14; Ps. 92:12; Ho. 14:5,7; Mal 4:2; II Th. 1:3; I Pet 2:2, II Pet. 2:2; Mk. 4:32; Eph. 2:21.

Scriptures Are Emphatic. From these numerous Scriptures it is evident that Christians who make up the Body of Christ, the Church, should be growing, increasing, and abounding continually. Christians are to go from "strength to strength," "faith to faith," "glory to glory"; to "follow on to know the Lord." Further, they must continue adding and growing in His grace and knowledge until they are "changed into His same image," and have "grown up into Christ in all things," "unto the measure of the stature of the fulness of Christ," becoming perfect in purity and maturity that Christ may present them unto Himself "a glorious Church not having spot or wrinkle or any such thing, but that they should be holy and without blemish."

"Sons of God it doth not yet appear what we shall be but we know that when He shall appear, we shall be like Him for we shall see Him as He is." "And every man that hath this hope within him purifieth himself, even as pure as Christ." "For whom He did foreknow He also did predestinate to be conformed to the image of His Son, that Jesus might be the first-born among many brethren." Christ Jesus suffered and died that He might bring "many sons unto glory" (that glory is Christ's image, likeness, and manifested presence and power). The Holy Spirit is commissioned to take Christians from "glory to glory" until the Church reaches Christ's perfect image, fulness, and maturity.

God's Predestinated Plan. When a person is born again he starts out as a babe in the Church. God's predestinated plan is for each one to grow until he becomes a fully mature son of God. The spirit is as pure and clean as it can ever be when it is cleansed by the blood of Jesus. We are perfect as newborn babies in God's sight. We no longer have any sinful past record, just a glorious future in Christ. Imputed righteousness is imparted instantaneously when Christ Jesus is received as Savior. However, it requires a process of time for redeemed human natures to appropriate all the attributes of the divine nature of which we have been made partakers. Christians have to be transformed in their thinking, attitudes, character, and emotions. In fact, they must be transformed in all areas of the soul, which includes the mind, emotions, and will. The spirit has been redeemed, the soul is being redeemed, and the body shall be redeemed. When Jesus returns, His Bride will be thinking His thoughts, manifesting His majesty, portraying His power and glorifying His grace. The Church will be a personification of His person, a replica of His reality, and a manifestation of His ministry.

Two Types Of Perfection

There are two types of perfection, progressive perfection and ultimate perfection. The Bible commands Christians to be perfect all their Christian lives. How is this possible? Christians can maintain a life that is pleasing and acceptable to God during each stage of their progressive growth. A normal healthy baby is perfect at the age of one month though he is not able to walk, or talk, has no teeth, and spends most of his day lying in bed sucking his bottle. This is all he is supposed to be and do at this stage of growth. To try to be more than he is capable of at that stage of growth would frustrate his spirit, confuse his mind, and disrupt his emotional peace and joy. The same principle applies throughout every stage of growth to manhood. If no disease comes into his body and he eats properly, drinks, rests, and exercises sufficiently, the child will grow to be as big, strong, and capable as any other healthy adult. If for some reason the child's growth stops before he reaches maturity, then he loses his progressive perfection and will never reach manhood until the hinderance to his growth is corrected.

Like a newborn babe, the Church was birthed on the day of Pentecost. It began to eat the Word, drink of the Spirit, exercise in the supernatural, and rest in the confidence of God's power to supply all its needs according to Christ's riches in glory. The Church continued to grow until its teachers began to feed it poisonous false doctrines, took away its diet of the Word and Spirit, stopped the Church from exercising itself in the supernatural manifestations of God, and allowed it no peace and rest, but kept it working with self-effort to become good enough to be acceptable to God.

Predestinated For Perfection. The growth of the Church was hindered for centuries. It maintained just enough truth to stay alive, but around the year 1500 A.D. God started the times of restoration and growth. He is determined to continue adding every truth and grace to the Church that is necessary for it to come to maturity and to be an ultimately perfected Bride, ready for proper presentation to the Bridegroom.

3

Heaven's Participation In Church Restoration

All Heavenly Beings Are Working With Christ's Church. There were many things taking place upon Earth around the year 1500. But that is not the only area where there was a lot of activity. All of the heavenly hosts under God's vast domain were created to work with Jesus in producing His eternal purpose. All of the host of Heaven is involved in the restoration of the Church.

Planet Earth — Lucifer's Headquarters. The Bible indicates that there are chief angels who have responsibilities greater than other angels, such as archangels Gabriel and Michael. Seemingly, Lucifer was at one time an archangel, but he and one-third of the angels rebelled against the rule of Jehovah God and were cast out of God's holy domain. Some theologians believe that planet Earth was Lucifer's headquarters before he fell. After his fall he was cast back down to Earth and all light was removed from him and from the Earth. Lucifer became a dark evil spirit and the Earth became a frozen mass along with all the gigantic historic creatures that roamed the Earth during the reign of Lucifer and his angelic beings. (The purpose of God's six successive days of creation was to restore the Earth to an inhabitable place for man's dwelling.) Lucifer and all his evil angelic host are still stationed around the Earth and have arrayed themselves against God's eternal plan for Jesus and His Church. Lucifer, who is called the devil, is recognized as the god of this present world system by the Apostle Paul *(II Cor. 4:4)*.

Dominion Transferred To Church. Jesus took away all the power of the devil and delivered it unto the Church. The devil refuses to acknowledge that he is defeated or to relinquish his dominion of this world to the Church. He has maintained his position, and restrained the Church by keeping it blinded to its rightful position. He continually convinces the Church that God's Word doesn't really mean what it says: that the Church cannot do all that Christ Jesus says we can do and that we don't really have what God's Word declares we have. As long as Satan can find professing preachers and teachers of Christianity who will work with him, he can keep the Church bound and restricted by doctrines of devils and man-made creeds. The devil knows that the Church has "power over all the power of the enemy" and that "all things are possible if the Church would only believe." Satan fears the Church as he fears Jesus. He knows the Church is a giant more powerful than all the devils in Hell. That's the reason he keeps the Church doped and lulled to sleep, for the Church is a sleeping giant.

An Announcement In Heaven. Let us go back now to the activities that were taking place in Heaven around the end of the Fifteenth Century. Imagine some of the activities and conversations that could have been going on in Heaven. Michael and Gabriel, under the leadership of Christ Jesus are directing the ministries of the angels in their heavenly affairs, and in their workings with mankind on Earth. Things had been progressing rather routinely until suddenly an unusual amount of divine presence began to emanate throughout the Kingdom of Heaven. Michael and Gabriel come before the Lord to find out what was causing this extra glory emanating from Jesus and prompting all of Heaven to be filled with unusual ecstacy. Jesus joyfully announces to them that the time for the "period of the great Restoration" of His beloved Church has arrived. This was activating His whole being with such anticipation that it was causing His beauty and brilliance to bathe Heaven with a greater abundance of His blessings. Michael and Gabriel immediately ask, "What can we and all the heavenly host do to hasten that day when you can be joined to your Church-Bride?"

The angels are also excited about that preordained event for they know that it will be the most festive celebration ever to be conducted in the eternal universe or on planet Earth.

The angels participated and rejoiced at the birth of Jesus on planet Earth. The death of Jesus upon the cross was the greatest revelation and demonstration that the heavenly host had ever beheld concerning their God's nature and character of love. When Jesus arose from the grave victorious over death, Satan and all the hordes of Hell, there was great rejoicing in Heaven. The birth of the Church was a joyous occasion creating a great celebration in Heaven.

Celebration of All Celebrations. The eternal Heavens have never witnessed anything like the celebration that will take place at the marriage of Jesus and His Bride. There will be millions of talented musician saints from all the ages playing thousands of different musical instruments, choirs of millions, and prophets and preachers proclaiming and portraying new revelations of God's glory and goodness in living realities. Mysteries of the ages will be made known. There will be special displays of God's creation and wonders of His universe. Whole star systems which were created and reserved for that day and hour will begin to explode in a fireworks display producing all the colors of the rainbow beyond the wildest imagination of man. There will be shouting, dancing, singing praises and rejoicing with joy sublime beyond compare as all tears are wiped away from the eyes of the Bride. The ring of unity and authority will be placed on Her hand and the crown of life upon Her head designating Her right to eternally co-reign with Her Lord and Bridegroom, Christ Jesus.

The Hour Is Not Known. The angels do not know the day or hour of this glorious event, but they do know that it is scheduled to happen in the near future. They are not a part of the Bride, but they are Her friends and helpers who are ministering spirits bringing Her unto this day of marriage. They know there has never been anything in all of Heaven to compare with this planned occasion. All of the heavenly host are excitedly looking forward to that day. They are doing all in their power to urge the saints on to fulfill all Scripture, reach maturity, and restore all things; then Jesus can be released from Heaven to receive His Bride unto Himself.

No Jealousy In Heaven. There is no sense of jealousy or competition within the heavenly host over the fact that blood-bought humanity has been chosen of God to be the Bride of the Lamb. There is no resentment that God has chosen the Church to sit down with Jesus in His Father's throne and to rule and reign with Him. The greatest joy of Heaven is to exalt Jesus and to bless others more than oneself.

The Angels' Pleasure. Whatever pleases Jesus gives the angels pleasure. They willfully and joyfully work with Him in the fulfilling of His purpose. The angels are happy about the fact that Jesus is activating and escalating the preparation of the Bride. But their joy has no comparison with the loving, longing, tingling excitement, and the joyful expectation of Jesus in His anticipation of the maturing of His Bride for marriage. Only His divine patience and knowledge that all Scripture must be fulfilled prior to receiving the Bride holds Him in Heaven. He cannot be released to come back physically, but He can start giving Himself to the Church as the way, the truth and the life. He can come as the rain to activate the seed of the Spiritual Church which has been lying dormant within the soil of the Structural Church. The Lord can send from His presence "times of refreshing" to His Church for the "time for the period of the great restoration" has come. Jesus will keep restoring His truth, His way, and His life to His Church until He is fully formed within Her. Then He will be released from Heaven to come in His personal resurrected human body and resurrect and translate the bodies of His redeemed humanity to meet Him in the air where they will enter into complete union with Him at the marriage supper of the Lamb.

Jesus Looking For a Man. To make a restoration a reality the business at hand was the need for a **man.** All Heaven knows that when God gets ready to do something on Earth He needs a mortal human to be His instrument for its fulfillment. Therefore, "the angels began to scatter around the earth in search of a man." *(Heb. 1:14).* The "eyes of the Lord began to run to and fro throughout the whole earth, seeking for a man . . ." *(I Chr. 16:9)*. "God sought for a man to stand in the gap and make up the hedge" *(Ez. 22:30)* to bring restoration to His Church.

The eyes of the Lord swept around the world. They came to Germany and zeroed in on a young man by the name of Martin Luther. The year was 1505. Jesus gave the command, "Start this man's preparation for his day of presentation for the liberation of my Church into its period of the great Restoration." Immediately all of Heaven began to concentrate on fulfilling God's will.

God Has His Own Methods Of Making His Man. God has several methods He uses in the making of a person for divine ministry. A few of these methods are dissatisfaction, frustration, conviction and consternation which lead a person to the place of desperation. At this point God brings a revelation which gives the person a deep appreciation of God's will for his or her life. This process makes that person willing to make God's truth known to the world regardless of the price.

Martin Luther, the Man. God put Martin Luther through this process until his day of presentation for the declaration of God's revelation of justification by faith. This truth established the Doctrine of Repentance from Dead Works, which is the initial truth to be restored during the Restoration of the Church.

Martin Luther had no idea what God had planned for him. He was only time and earth-conscious. He only knew that at that moment he and a friend were caught in an electrical storm. It looked as though his life could be ended momentarily. He thought over his last 22 years of life. He remembered his peasant parents' sacrificing and persisting until he had received a good education. He remembered attending the schools at Magdeburg and Eisenach and singing to support himself. Now he was enrolled as a law student at the University of Leipzig and would soon graduate to enter a law career.

Heaven's Choice Made God-Conscious. But Martin's thoughts were interrupted by the sudden clap of thunder and flash of lightening. The next moment his close friend was dead and he narrowly escaped death himself. Heaven had caught his attention. A consciousness of his sinful condition came upon him. He began to be motivated by a deep desire to find God. He started on his quest to find peace with God. He forsook his law career, and in 1505 entered the Erfurt monastery of the Augustinian Order.

Luther became dissatisfied with the condition of his soul through the fear of death and the convicting power of the Holy Spirit. In his day the surest road to salvation was the monastic life. He did everything his church order taught to make himself holy and at peace with God. He diligently practiced extreme asceticism, even to the extent of self-flagellation, endless fastings, and almost anything he could think of to inflict self-punishment upon his body. This type of self-denial and penance was guaranteed by the church to bring peace with God.

Luther became "frustrated" with a hard-hearted and tyrannical God, demanding so much and giving so little in return. The superior in his order suggested Luther give himself to the study of Scriptures and perhaps he could find his peace with God. It was the best advice he ever received from the church.

The Spirit Of Revelation. After two years in the monastery he was ordained in 1507 at the age of 24.

Four years later, Luther became a professor at the University of Wittenburg. It was during his years as a researcher and professor of biblical studies that the spirit of revelation came. Romans 1:17 became a living reality to him. "The just shall live by faith." He realized it was "not by works of righteousness which we have done but according to his mercy" and "by grace are you saved through faith, and that not of yourselves: it is the gift of God: Not of works lest any man should boast." *(Eph. 2:8,9).* In Martin Luther's words:

> I greatly longed to understand Paul's Epistle to the Romans, and nothing stood in the way but that one expression, 'the righteousness of God,' because I took it to mean that righteousness whereby God is righteous and deals righteously in punishing the unrighteous. Night and day I pondered until . . . I grasped the truth that the righteousness of God is that righteousness whereby, through grace and sheer mercy, he justifies us by faith. Thereupon *I felt myself to be reborn* and to have gone through open doors into paradise. The whole Scripture took on a new meaning, and whereas before 'the righteousness of God' had filled me with hate, now it became to me inexpressibly sweet in greater love. This passage of Paul became to me a gateway to heaven. (Dr. Tim Dowley, *Eerdman's Handbooks to The History of Christianity,* Grand Rapids, Wm. B. Eerdman's Publishing Co., 1977. *Reform,* by James Atkinson, p. 366.)

Luther Born Again. When Luther received his born-again experience through faith in the accomplished work of Christ on Calvary and received the imputed righteousness of God according to His mercy, it transformed his understanding of God and his teaching of the Gospels. He began to compare his Roman Catholic Church with the New Testament Church as revealed in the Book of Acts. He saw that many things were not biblical. Being a professor at Wittenberg University, he preached and lectured for more than four years after his revelation on justification. His convictions became stronger as he preached on this biblical truth and the errors of the Structured Church system.

Practices That Prompted. The degradation of the Structural Church agitated Luther into making a declaration of 95 theological arguments against its unscriptural practices. Luther rebelled in his born-again spirit against the sale and worship of supposedly holy relics. He renounced these assumptions and the religious, superstitious adoration and awe of these objects. The last straw was the issuance of a special indulgence by Rome. The reigning Pope, Leo X, needing large sums of money for the completion of St. Peter's church at Rome, permitted an agent named John Tetzel to go throughout Germany selling certificates signed by the Pope himself. These certificates purported to bestow the pardon of all sins, not only upon the holders of the certificates, but upon friends living or dead in whose behalf they were purchased, without confession, repentance, penance, or absolution by a priest. Tetzel told the people, "As soon as your coin clinks in the chest, the souls of your friends will rise out of Purgatory to Heaven." Luther vehemently preached against Tetzel and his selling of pardons, denouncing the Pope's authority to issue such indulgences. He also decided to take some definite action to rectify the situation.

The Reformation Began. All protestant historians make this memorable occasion the official day when the Reformation began. The hammer that caused an echo to be heard to the ends of the Earth was the one Luther used to nail his 95 declarations (Theses) to the Castle Church in Wittenberg, Germany. On the eve of All Souls' Day, October 31, 1517, Martin Luther's hammer sparked into flame the Restoration of the Church and brought about the Protestant Movement. News of his *Theses* spread like wildfire throughout Europe. Within a fortnight every university and religious center was agog with excitement. All marvelled that one obscure monk from an unknown university had stirred the whole of Europe.

They did not know that the God of Heaven had decreed that this man was the chosen instrument of the Lord to loose that rock (Church) that was hewn out of the mountain (Christ) and start it rolling. It would gain speed and size as it progressed like a snowball rolling down a snow-covered mountain. When it reached its objective it would become judgment to the nations and bring the great giant image crumbling to the ground, putting all things fully under the feet of Jesus and His Church.

Religion Tries to Stop Restoration. The devil and the religious system tried to stop this voice of Reformation as they tried to stop the reformers of the past. But this man was the swan that Huss had predicted would arise 100 years later and who God would not allow to be martyred but would cause to live. He would be the singing prophet who would open the door for the Spiritual Church to emerge from the Structural Church as a butterfly emerges from its cocoon and starts on its flight to full restoration. Luther was the man God used to lead the Church out of its religious Egyptian bondage 1,500 years *after* the coming of Christ, as Moses was the man who led the Children of Israel out of their literal Egyptian bondage 1,500 years *before* the coming of the Messiah.

You will notice from the beginning of the record of man that great changes take place in cycles and in multiples of 500 years. Even the Church has had similar experiences. It was birthed in A.D. 30 and around 500 years later had gone into apostasy. By the year 1,000 it had degraded to its depths, and 500 years later the period of the Great Restoration started. Hopefully, within another 500 years the "restoration of all things" will have taken place releasing Jesus from Heaven to return for His Bride, bind the devil in the bottomless pit, and set up the Kingdom of God on Earth.

Luther's Objective. Martin Luther's only objective in making a public notice of 95 arguments against the church's abuse and use of indulgences, relics, etc. was simply to help delete some of these unscriptural practices from the Church. The *95 Theses* were not intended as a call to reformation. Luther had no idea of breaking away from his beloved Catholic Church and starting another movement which would emerge into a whole new Christian era. Luther did not have this in mind, but it was in the mind of Jesus. Luther stood for reform within the Roman Catholic Church; nevertheless he was excommunicated three year later, in 1520. He was commanded to recant, as were all his followers. They were given 60 days, and if they didn't recant from their so-called heresies, the penalty would be death.

Luther Excommunicated. Luther dared to defy the Pope and his councils who claimed "authority to shut the gates of Hell and open the door to Paradise." The Roman Catholic Church made a decree that all of the faithful to the church were to burn all of Luther's writings. Luther met the excommunication with defiance and called it "the execrable bull of Antichrist." He publicly burned it December 10, 1520, at the gates of Wittenberg, before an assembly of university professors, students and common people. This constituted Martin Luther's final separation and denunciation of the Roman Catholic Church. Luther's dramatic stand against both Pope and Emperor fired the imagination of Europe. He started a chain reaction that swept around the world. Other men in other countries arose to propagate the same truth: Ulrich Zwingli, John Calvin, John Tyndale, John Knox, Philip Melanchthon and Martin Bucer. These are the men best known for their contributions to the great Protestant Movement.

Structured Church Shaken. The Roman Catholic and Eastern Orthodox churches went through a great shaking. The Protestant Movement sparked wars between nations in the separation and ensuing battle between Catholicism and Protestantism. Halley states, "The number of martyrs under Papal Persecutions far out-numbered the Early Christian Martyrs under Pagan Rome." (Halley, p. 793.) Confusion and chaos temporarily reigned in different countries until the lines were drawn between Catholic countries and Protestant countries. "The Reformation was followed by a hundred years of religious wars." (Ibid., p. 792.)

Can Truth Cause Problems? Could all this confusion, war, persecution, hatred, and division be the result of a Restoration of Truth? Yes! Consider what happened to God's chosen people Israel and to the religion of Judaism when Jesus came bringing the revelation of Grace and Truth! The revelation of Jesus Christ made provision for the restoration of man back to God, but it also brought riots, revolution, and a revolt of His followers against the established religious system. The Protestant Movement likewise created a world-wide revolution. One will notice in studying the Restoration of the Church that each of the Doctrines of Christ bring about the same responses. Every Restorational revelation brings a revolution. New wine cannot be contained in old-dried-and-set-in-their-ways wineskins; it will burst forth every time. New wineskins must be prepared to hold the new wine (truth). "In every nation where Protestantism triumphed a National Church arose: Lutheran in Germany; Episcopal in England; Presbyterian in Scotland; etc." (Ibid., p. 794.)

Regardless of the upset of religion, men, and nations, Heaven was thrilled. For the Spiritual Church, the Body of Christ, had taken the first step in its journey to full Restoration — the formation of the Bride unto perfect beauty and maturity in quantity and quality.

4

Chart On Restoration Of Church Explained

Explanation of the Headings on the Chart

Approximate Date. These dates are designed to give only the general time of each particular movement. For example, the preparation for restoration transpired over a several hundred year period. The actual birth of the "period of the great Restoration" which became known as the "Protestant Movement" is recognized by historians as the day Martin Luther nailed his 95 theses to the door of the Church in Wittenberg, Germany on October 31, 1517. Since the chart gives a general overview of the period of the great Restoration of the Church, a round-figure date is more easily grasped and remembered.

Spiritual Experiences. This heading indicates the spiritual blessings which accompanied that particular restoration movement. These spiritual experiences are not the Doctrines of Christ. Yet they are a vital part of the function of the Church. They are scriptural ways for members of the Church to have fellowship with God. They are attributes of God and methods

RESTORATION OF THE CHURCH

Approx. Date	Spiritual Experiences	Doctrines of Christ Hebrews 6:1,2 Acts 3:21	Three Baptisms	Three Witnesses	Restoration Movements
1500	**Justification** Study of Word Prayer Peace	1+† **Repentance From Dead Works** Grace of God Eph. 2:8,9	1. Repentance (unto Christ) Spirit	1. Blood	**Protestant** Lutheran Episcopal Presbyterian
1800	**Sanctification** Conviction Faith, hymns Joy, Singing	2+† **Faith Toward God** Divine Faith Healing James 5:14,15	2. Water (into Christ) Soul	2. Water	**Holiness** Baptist Methodist (All Evangelicals) Church of God C & M Alliance
1900	**Manifestation** Other Tongues Hand clapping Shouting, Fasting Dancing in Spirit Musical Instruments	3+† **Doctrine of Baptisms** Gifts:1 Cor. 12:7-11 Message in Tongues Interpretation of Tongues	3. Spirit (Christ into) Body	3. Spirit	**Pentecostal** Assembly of God Pent. Holiness Foursquare Pent. Ch. of God United Pent. Ch.
1950	**Ministration** Singing Praise Spiritual Songs Worship, Psalms Body Ministry Praise in Dance Acts of Faith	4+† **Laying on of Hands** Gifts: Prophecy, Healing, Faith Word of Knowledge, Word of Wisdom Laying on of Hands for: Healing, Deliverance, Holy Ghost Revealing Place in Body of Christ Impartation of Gifts by Holy Spirit	teaching on	Body of Christ	**Charismatic** (Orig. L.R.) Fellowships Independents

Dr. W. S. "Bill" Hamon, P. O. Box 27398, Phoenix, Arizona, 85061 © Christian International Publishers whereby mortal man can express his love and worship to God. You will notice that each Restoration Movement involves more of man's whole being in his worship to God with his spirit, soul, and body.

The spiritual experiences placed within each movement are the ones that remained an acceptable way of worship and of teaching within the Christian denominations established at that time. For example, the Holiness Movement had incidents where all of the spiritual experiences and manifestations listed under the Pentecostal Movement took place in their meetings. However, when the sovereign move of the Spirit had finished His work of revelation and demonstration, the churches failed to maintain those spiritual experiences by faith, teaching, and practice. Every time a new restorational truth is to be restored the Holy Spirit supernaturally opens the mind of man to new understanding and ways of worship. That truth has been in the Word of God all the time, but until the time of revelation and refreshing comes from the presence of the Lord, man does not grasp its meaning.

Doctrines Of Christ

There are two hermeneutically acceptable interpretations to Hebrews 6:1,2.

> Therefore leaving the principles of the doctrine of Christ, let us go on unto perfection, not laying again the foundation of repentance from dead works, and of faith toward God, of the doctrine of baptisms, and of laying on of hands, and of resurrection of the dead, and of eternal judgment.

1. Repentance from Dead Works
2. Faith toward God
3. Doctrine of Baptisms
4. Laying on of Hands
5. Resurrection of the Dead
6. Eternal Judgment

Concept Number One: Foundational Personal Application. This is the Christian concept that Hebrews 6:1,2 contains the general doctrines of the Christian Faith. When one has an understanding of these foundation truths, one can progress to more advanced teachings and maturity. Some theologians look upon these Doctrines of Christ as being similar to the Apostles' Creed which was the initial confession of a person in the Fourth Century being baptized into the Christian Church.

The Apostles' Creed

I believe in God, the Father Almighty, Creator of heaven and earth; and in Jesus Christ, His only Son, Our Lord; Who was conceived by the Holy Ghost, was crucified, died, and was buried. He descended into hell; the third day He arose again from the dead; He ascended into heaven, sitteth at the right hand of God, the Father Almighty; from thence He shall come to judge the living and the dead. I believe in the Holy Ghost, the holy catholic [universal] Church; The communion of saints, the forgiveness of sins; The resurrection of the body; and the life everlasting; Amen. (Eerdman's *Handbook to the History of Christianity,* p. 145 and *The World Book Encyclopedia,* Vol. 1, p. 526.)

Personal Fulfillment. With the basic concept of Hebrews 6:1,2 a person simply repents from his dead works, expresses his faith in a living God, acknowledges his faith in Christ Jesus by baptism in water, and in the Holy Spirit, receives the laying on of hands and confesses his belief in the general resurrection of the dead, and eternal judgment of the wicked at the great day of Judgment. By going through this process of Christian initiation into the Doctrines of Christ one would be brought to a place of perfect standing with God.

These six doctrines are looked upon as the foundation stones of the Christian faith which are to be established in our lives. We then are to "go on unto perfection," not continually laying over and over again these same basic truths of the Christian faith. The Christian walk is not in a circle but it is a straight and narrow way that is always going onward and upward.

Concept Number Two: Restorational Corporate Application. This is the interpretation which we want to emphasize in our study on the Restoration of the Church.

The six principles of the Doctrines of Christ were lost during the Dark Ages of the Church. They have been and are being restored to the Church in the chronological order in which they are listed in Hebrews 6:1,2. Their arrangement was not coincidental. It was divinely inspired by the Holy Spirit.

Our study will reveal that the first four doctrines have already been restored. The reader does not have to take this statement by faith for it has been recorded in the annals of Christianity during the last 500 years. It is not a wild concoction of some preacher with an active imagination. It is an historical fact.

The restoration of each of the Doctrines of Christ will bring about a major restorational movement and the establishment of new experiential truth to the Eternal Church. The first four already have. The context of Hebrews 6:1-3 indicates that, when these six are fully operating in the Church again, a seventh Doctrine of Christ which is seen in the biblical teaching on perfection will result. The writer discussed in an earlier chapter the difference between progressive perfection and ultimate perfection. The seventh Doctrine of Christ will be Ultimate Perfection. The six Doctrines of Christ with their end result are:

1. Repentance from Dead Works
2. Faith Toward God
3. Doctrine of Baptisms
4. Laying on of Hands
5. Resurrection of the Dead
6. Eternal Judgment
7. Ultimate Perfection

Lost Doctrines Reestablished. When the writer to the Hebrews speaks of "leaving" the principles of the Doctrines of Christ, it is important to understand that in a restorational aspect, one cannot leave something until it has been established, or in this case, reestablished. The Church that went into the Dark Ages lost these truths one at a time until the experiential realities of the six Doctrines of Christ were no longer in existence. The Church cannot go on to full maturity until the Holy Spirit reestablishes the foundation upon which the Early Church was built. For example, Solomon built a beautiful temple for the habitation of God. For years it was a praise to the glory of God, but Israel began to fall away from the faith and finally became an apostate nation. The Babylonians came and destroyed the temple completely. When the

Jews, led by Zerubbabel, returned from their Babylonian captivity, they had to start again with the basics. They had to relay the foundation before the remaining part of the temple could be built.

The same truth could be expressed in the analogy of a person travelling by automobile across the United States. If a person wished to travel by automobile from California to Florida he or she must enter and journey through six states (Arizona, New Mexico, Texas, Louisiana, Mississippi and Alabama) before arriving at the Florida state line. Florida would be the ultimate objective, but there is no way to arrive in Florida until that person leaves California. He or she could not even enter Arizona before leaving California, and by the same token, could not enter New Mexico before having travelled through Arizona. The same pattern would have to be followed state by state in the continuous journey from California to Florida.

Same in Spiritual. There is no way for a person to travel from an unregenerate state to maturity without incorporating each of the six doctrines of Christ into his life. One must first repent of dead works, leaving behind these dead works when entering into the state of faith toward God, and then going on into all the other Christian truths until the state of Ultimate Perfection is reached. The six Doctrines of Christ laid down in Hebrews 6:1,2 reveal the chronological order in which God has and is restoring the Church back to divine order and fulness.

Three Baptisms — Three Witnesses. The information under this chart heading is an illustration of how the "Three witnesses in earth" *(I Jn. 5:8)* are correlated with the three basic baptisms in Christianity. The writer is not trying to convey that a person is not saved or does not have the witness of the Holy

Spirit until baptized with the Holy Ghost. However, there is a difference in the experience of being birthed into the kingdom, the Church, by the Holy Spirit, and that of being baptized with the Holy Spirit. The reader is advised to avoid getting involved in "splitting doctrinal hairs" or trying to "tag" the author with some doctrinal belief. The whole purpose of this correlation is to give a general view of the emphasis and main teaching of that particular "Restorational Movement." If this little side thought becomes more bone than meat, it should be laid aside. Do not let it disturb you. The reader should "eat" all the good meat (truths) that is on the platter (the Book) and lay the bone (the author's idea about Scripture which may differ from the reader's) aside. That which witnesses to each should be absorbed by each. That which does not, should be regarded later when further study can be made on it.

Brief Explanation of Number One:

1. Repentance 1. Blood
(unto Christ)
Spirit

"Baptism of Repentance," "Blood," "Unto Christ," "Spirit." The main baptism emphasis of the Protestant Movement was "repentance." The word repent means to turn about. The main emphasis of Martin Luther and the other Protestant reformers was for man to turn from his dead, religious works and trust wholly in the accomplished work of Christ. By grace man is saved through faith, not by works of any kind, neither humanistic nor religious. The "baptism of repentance" brings humanity "unto Christ" who remits their sins by His precious "blood." I John 5:8 states that "there are three that bear witness in earth: the Spirit, and the water, and the blood; and these three agree in one." (Christ Jesus is the one.) When a person biblically repents he receives the witnessing agent of the "blood." He comes "unto Christ" and receives the redemption of his "spirit." He receives a new heart and a new spirit, born again, old things pass away, all things become new; he becomes a new creation in Christ Jesus. In conclusion, the "baptism of repentance" brings a person "unto Christ" where he is justified by faith and receives the "witness of the blood." This is a ministry mainly to his "spirit." His spirit has been redeemed.

2. Water   2. Water
(into Christ)
Soul

Correlation Number Two

"Into Christ," "Soul." Water Baptism by immersion was one of the main emphases of the Holiness Movement. Although there had been groups for centuries who had contested baptism by sprinkling and the baptism of infants, it was not until during the restoration of the "Faith Toward God" doctrine that baptism by immersion became a world-wide accepted and established truth in the Church. Water baptism is the experiential truth that buries the "old man" and immerses the new creature "into" Christ. Water baptism is where the Christian receives the "witness of the water" in his relationship with Christ. The sanctification of the "Soul" was another emphasis of the Holiness movement. The soul of man is identified as emotions, mind, and will. The soul is sanctified, but will continue to go through a process of transformation until it is conformed to the image of Christ Jesus in thought, attitude, and dedication.

3. Spirit   3. Spirit
(Christ into)
Body

Correlation Number Three

"Christ" "into" "Body." The restoration of the "Doctrine of Baptisms" climaxed the three basic Christian baptisms (of repentance, water, and Holy

Spirit). The baptism of the Holy Ghost is what makes the body of man the Temple of God. The Bible does not speak of man's spirit as being the temple of the Holy Ghost but it describes his body as the temple. The Pentecostal Movement emphasized Baptism of the Holy Ghost with the physical evidence of speaking in other tongues. For a person to have the full three-fold witness that God established in the Church he needs to receive all three baptisms.

Summary. The baptism of repentance brings one unto Christ where the redemption of the spirit is received and the blood of Jesus witnesses to the reality of the born-again experience: the person is identified with Christ's *death* on the cross. Water baptism buries the old man and puts a person into Christ, sanctifying the soul and setting it apart to serve the Lord: the person is identified with Christ Jesus in His *burial*. The baptism of the Holy Spirit makes the flesh-and-bone body the temple of the Holy Ghost and puts Christ (anointing) into the Christian. He then dwells not only in the spirit and in the soul but also in the body. The Christian is enabled to function more fully in the heavenly realm and manifest the supernatural gifts of the Holy Spirit: the Christian is then identified with Christ in His *resurrection*.

Meaning of Great Commission. The "gospel" is more than "Christ *died* for our sins." It is the death, burial, and resurrection of Jesus Christ (I Cor. 15:1-5). Christianity is more than justification, it also includes sanctification and glorification. Jesus could have had more in mind when He commanded the Apostles to "go ye therefore, and teach all nations, baptizing them in the name of the Father, and of the Son, and of the Holy Ghost" than just words to say over a person when baptizing them in water. He could have had all three basic baptisms in mind. There is no record in the Scriptures that anyone in the New Testament or Early Church ever used those words when baptizing a person. Neither Peter, Paul or any of the New Testament writers ever commanded anyone to be water baptized "in the name of the Father, and of the Son, and of the Holy Ghost." Did Peter and Paul fail to obey Christ's command or did they have a deeper understanding of that command than the one theologians have given it? God the Father has commanded all men to repent (baptism of repentance). Jesus the Son is the Bridegroom of the Church-Bride and Christians take on His name at the ceremony of water baptism. When a Christian is baptized into the Holy Ghost he or she receives the "anointing" and the Holy Ghost's personal gift, giving the Christian his or her own prayer and praise language in the spirit. These three basic baptisms do not give the Christian perfection or maturity, but they do grant all three witnesses God established on the Earth. It moves the Christian one step closer to maturity, and endows him with the right and power to function as a lively member in the many-membered Corporate Body of Christ. With these, Christians have the potential and the power for full performance.

Restoration Movements

Under this heading are listed the major Christian denominations established from the truth which that movement restored. Only those Churches are listed which are well known today and had their origination in that restoration truth. The main purpose of this section of the chart is not to give degrees of importance to any particular church denomination, but to show the origination of the mainline Christian denominations. The chart reveals only the highlights of the progression of the Church during the period of the Great Restoration. It started around 1500 and it is assumed, will climax around the year 2000. Still, God has not revealed the day, hour, or year to anyone except Jesus *(Rev. 1:1)*. Assumptions can only be made based on His pattern of performance in times past. It should be kept in mind that the restorational work of the Holy Spirit is not to produce church denominations but to perfect the Church, which is the **One Many-Membered Universal Corporate Body of Christ.**

5

The Protestant Movement

Libraries of Information Available. Because of the vast amount of information available on the Protestant Movement, a limited amount will be given in this book. "More books have been written about Luther, the great German Reformer, than about any other figure in history, except Christ." *(Eerdman's Handbook,* p. 360.) Only information needed to reveal to the reader how the first Doctrine of Christ was restored, and which of the present Christian denominations originated from the Protestant Movement is given. Different writers over a 400-year period have contributed volumes on the men, doctrines, and history of the great Reformation. To keep from writing endless pages on interesting but not directly pertinent information, I will restrict my comments to that which will give explanation, clarification, and amplification to those major points which are on the "Restoration of the Church" chart.

Explanation of "Protestant Movement" and Restoration of "Repentance From Dead Works" Doctrine

Approximate Date A.D. 1500
(left-hand margin of chart)

The year A.D. 1500 is used to indicate the general time when the Protestant Movement began. Those unfamiliar with the details of Church history will be able to look in this column and determine the century in which each restorational truth was restored. The Repentance from Dead Works doctrine was restored in the 16th Century. Historians recognize October 31, 1517 as the exact date of its birth.

**Spiritual
Experiences**

Justification
  Study of Word
  Prayer
  Peace
. . . .

Justification

Under the major heading (Spiritual Experiences) is a sub-heading which describes the main spiritual emphasis of each restorational movement. There are seven such words, one by each of the seven Doctrines of Christ. For example, "Justification" was the spiritual experience the Church received when the First Doctrine of Christ was restored. "Sanctification" was the spiritual experience restored to the Church with the restoration of the Second Doctrine of Christ during the Holiness Movement, etc.

Study of Word

During the Dark Ages of the Structural Church, there was very little Bible reading even among the priesthood. The writings and decrees of popes and councils were read, studied, and accepted as divine instructions as much as the Scriptures. In most countries, Christians were discouraged from reading Scripture and in some areas Bible reading was forbidden. Amos 8:11 describes the condition of the Church for several centuries: "a famine in the land . . . of hearing the words of the Lord." Few Bibles were available beyond the walls of churches, universities, and monasteries. The average person had no way of checking the Bible to determine the truth of what was being propagated. One had to accept whatever the church system said was necessary to escape purgatory and eternal damnation.

Making God's Word Available. The providential discovery of the printing press enabled the ministers of the Protestant Movement to make the Word of God available to the people in their own language, at a price they could afford. It allowed the Bible to be circulated more widely than ever before. The Latin Vulgate edition had been the Bible of the Roman Catholic Church for over a thousand years. When all the other translations began to be produced by the Protestants, the Vulgate translation was confirmed by the Council of Trent in A.D. 1546 as the official Bible of Roman Catholicism. Latin had become the sacred language of the Roman Catholic Church. Regardless of the national language of the people, the mass was normally conducted in Latin.

Numerous Bible Translations. Each restorational Protestant man of God received the divine desire to make the Word of God available in the language of the native people. Within the first half of the 16th Century every major European nation had a Bible translated into its own language. Luther translated the Bible into German, which not only enlightened Germans but contributed greatly to the growth of European languages. Tyndale produced the first English Bible from the original Greek and Hebrew. The Bible was translated into other languages including French, Dutch, Italian, Spanish, Swedish, and Danish.

The men of the Protestant Movement were filled with divine zeal to make every Christian as knowledgeable in the Scriptures as the clergy. William Tyndale made this emphatic statement to a Roman Catholic clergyman: "If God spares my life, ere many years pass, I will cause a boy that driveth the plow shall know more of Scripture than thou dost." *(Eerdman's Handbook,* p. 370). The Protestant Movement reestablished the spiritual experience of studying the Word of God by the ministers *and* individual Christians. Every true restorational movement lifts up Christ Jesus and reestablishes the Body of Christ in the Word of God. Each truth-restoring movement rekindles a burning desire within Church members to read the Word, study the Word and listen to the preaching of the Word of God.

Prayer

The truths taught in the Protestant Movement put the Body of Christ members back into a true, personal, and direct prayer relationship with God. Jesus was magnified as the only God-ordained and acceptable mediator between God and men. "For there is one God, and one mediator between God and men, the man Christ Jesus" *(I Tim. 2:5).* This eliminated the need for the Virgin Mary as mediator, the clergy as pardoning priests, and the departed saints as intercessors. Jesus said, "Whatsoever you ask the Father in **My Name** that will I do" *(Jn. 14:13)*. These truths restored biblical *prayer* to the true *Ecclesia,* the called out Church. Every restorational movement brings clarification and magnification to the purpose and power of prayer.

Peace

When the Church is established upon the Word of God, when it prays directly to God on the merits of Christ's accomplished work and not on its own works, then there is peace. But there was no peace for the Church of the Dark Ages. However, when the Restorational brethren presented the true grace of God, justification by faith and true repentance, the believers were delivered from "doing penance," "asceticism," and the fear of "purgatory." It gave them the assurance of right standing with God and direct access to Heaven at death. They quoted Romans 5:1,2 with great peace and joy: "Therefore being **Justified** by **Faith** we have **Peace** with God through our Lord Jesus Christ: By whom also we have access by **Faith** into this **Grace** wherein we stand, and rejoice in hope of the glory of God." They became knowledgeable of the truth and the truth made them free and full of peace *(Jn. 3:35)*.

There were manifestations of other spiritual experiences during the Protestant Movement but the ones that became established practices and teachings of the Protestant churches were: study of the Word, prayer, and peace. Church liturgy took on new freedom and new liberty when it was stripped of all the formal religious ceremony accumulated during the deterioration of the Church.

Doctrine of Christ, Repentance From Dead Works

Grace of God, Ephesians 2:8,9. Repentance from dead works and deliverance from tradition of the elders which made the "Word of God of none effect" (Mk. 7:13) was the cry of the Holy Spirit in the restoration of this Doctrine of Christ. The primary ministry of the Protestant preachers was lifting the Church out of the "miry clay" of dead works and setting its feet on the solid rock, Christ Jesus. The main purpose of this restorational truth was to separate the Body of Christ from the dead works, paraphernalia, tradition, bondages, and the non-biblical religious practices that were heaped upon the Church during its deterioration.

The Protestant Movement delivered the Church from:

> the authority of the pope, the merit of good works, indulgences, the mediation of the Virgin Mary and the saints, and all sacraments which had not been instituted by Christ. They rejected the doctrine of transubstantiation (the teaching that the bread and wine of communion became the body and blood of Christ when the priest consecrated them), the view of the mass as a sacrifice, purgatory and prayers for the dead, private confession of sin to a priest, celibacy of the clergy, and the use of Latin in the services. They also rejected all the paraphernalia that expressed these ideas — such as holy water, shrines,

chantries, wonderworking images, rosaries, paternoster stones, images, and candles. *(Eerdman's Handbook,* pp. 372, 373.)

Justification by Faith Only. "For by grace are ye saved through faith; and that not of yourselves: *it is* the gift of God: Not of works, lest any man should boast" *(Eph. 2:8,9).*

Ephesians 2:8,9 basically summarizes the teachings of Luther, Calvin, Knox, and other leaders concerning the doctrine of Repentance from Dead Works. One of the great principles of the Reformation was salvation by the free and undeserved grace of Christ, that is "justification by faith only." "The Protestant believed that by the action of God alone, in the death and resurrection of Christ, he was called from sin to a new life in Christ. From this proceeded the fruits of the Spirit in loving acts." *(Eerdman's Handbook, p. 373.)* Works were to follow faith instead of justification by works.

Five great principles were established by the Protestant preachers:

1. True Christianity is founded upon the Scriptures.
2. Christianity should be rational and intelligent.
3. Christianity should be a personal, direct relationship with God without man-appointed intermediaries.
4. Christianity should be spiritual in the simplicity of the Gospel without ritualistic ceremonies.
5. The local and national church concept instead of the one worldwide church with the pope as supreme.

Luther's teachings of justification by faith and of the universal priesthood of believers might be called the cornerstone of Protestantism.

Hundreds of Scriptures could be given and volumes of books have been written on the doctrine of Repentance from Dead Works, being justified and made righteous by faith, the blood of Jesus, and the unmerited grace of God. The information given is sufficient to portray the restoration of the first Doctrine of Christ and the activation of the Period of the Great Restoration. The Church had taken its first step of restoration and has six more to take to obtain its Ultimate Perfection.

**Restoration
Movements**
Protestant

The Name "Protestant."   In A.D. 1529 there was a legislative meeting of the hierarchy of Church and State (Diet of Spires) with representatives from the Holy Roman Empire (which at that time included Germany, Spain, The Netherlands, and Austria). They gathered to make a decision concerning the growing conflict in Germany between the followers of the Reformers and the followers of Catholicism. The northern and southern German states were divided between the Roman Catholics and the Reformers. The southern princes, led by Austria, adhered to Rome, while those of the North were mainly followers of Luther. At this Diet, the Catholic rulers were in the majority, and they condemned the Lutheran doctrines. The majority ruled that Catholics could teach their religion in Lutheran states, but forbade Lutheran teachings in Catholics states. To this unequal ruling the Lutheran princes made a formal "protest." From that time they were known as "Protestants," and their doctrine as the *"Protestant religion."* All churches that have arisen since the beginning of the Reformation are normally classified as "Protestant." The world normally only divides Christianity into two groups, Catholic and Protestant. These are the only two world religions that recognize Jesus Christ as the Son of God and a co-equal with God.

Protestant Movement Churches

Lutheran
Episcopal
Presbyterian

These three churches are best known today as the Christian denominations which emerged because of the Protestant Movement. They originally were established separately more from national origin than from doctrinal differences. All of the Protestant ministers agreed upon the doctrines of "Repentance from Dead Works," Justification by Faith, salvation by the grace of God, and the individual priesthood of the believer. However, as each denomination began to formulate its own creeds, doctrines, and forms of church government, certain differences developed which made each unique. These three denominations are more often recognized by historians because each became a national church within the 16th Century. The Lutheran Church became the Christian religion in Germany; Episcopalian in England, and Presbyterian in Scotland. Each was governed by Christian leaders of their own nation without any connection or control from the pope in Rome or other Protestant denominations. They established the local and national church concept. (America was established by Protestants who fled to America to escape persecution from Catholicism and from the Church of England. However, America never developed a national church system, allowing "freedom of worship" for all Christian faiths and eventually, for non-Christian religions. The individual states in the United States never developed a state church. America still professes to be a "Christian" nation, neither Catholic nor Protestant.)

The Lutheran Church

The name "Lutheran" was a nickname fastened upon the followers of Martin Luther by their enemies during the Protestant Reformation. To the Roman Catholic Church, which had been the only government-recognized church for over 1,000 years, the word "Lutheran" was spoken with great disdain, ridicule, and contempt. Lutherans were called heretics, of the devil, a false cult, fanatics, and rebels of the Church as Lucifer was a rebel against God. This same attitude was taken toward all Protestants, especially during the 16th and 17th Centuries. There was no compatibility, compromise, friendly confrontation, or cooperation such as occurs in 20th Century America. Protestants for several centuries after the Reformation believed the Roman papacy to be the Antichrist and the fulfillment of Revelation 17, "Babylon the Great Harlot, Seated on the Seven-Headed-Ten-Horned Beast." The Catholics believed all Protestants to be the Judas church system which forsook the truth, and had fallen away from the faith, thus becoming "anathema," the cursed apostate church.

Historically, the Lutheran Church came into existence because Martin Luther broke away from the Catholic Church and his followers fought for the right to be a church separate from Catholicism.

Spiritually, it came into existence because a man of God received a revelation of truth that made it impossible for him to continue in the same religious system which he felt was contrary to the Word of God. He would have had to deny his knowledge of the Word of God, his conscience and his newly received spiritual experience in order to remain a priest who promoted the doctrines and practices of the Roman Catholic Church.

Restorationally, it came into existence because the Holy Spirit initiated the period of the Restoration of the Church. The Lutheran Church became one of the Protestant Christian denominational churches which helped establish and maintain the first restorational doctrine of Christ — Repentance from Dead Works.

One Three-Fold Summary Only. The historical, spiritual, and restorational aspects of each man, movement, and denomination in the following Restorational movements will not be summarized. But the same principles and aspects could be applied to each one that the Holy Spirit uses to restore another doctrine of Christ in the Church, thereby bringing the Body of Christ one step closer to Ultimate Perfection.

The Presbyterian Church

John Knox is recognized as the founding father of the Presbyterian Church. He was born in Scotland, went to the University of Glasgow and was ordained a priest. After his conversion to Protestantism, he was involved with John Calvin at Geneva. In 1559, he assumed the leadership of the Reformation Movement in Scotland. "By his radical and uncompromising views, his unbending determination, and his resistless energy, even against the opposition of the abilities and fascinations of his Romanist sovereign, Mary, Queen of Scots, he was able to sweep away every vestige of the old religion, and to carry the reform far beyond that in England. The Presbyterian Church as planned by Knox became the established church in Scotland." (Jesse Lyman Hurlbut, *The Story of The Christian Church,* Grand Rapids, Michigan, Zondervan Publishing House, 1970. p. 125.) Because of John Knox' close association with the teachings of Calvin, his Presbyterian church doctrines were strongly Calvinistic, expressing forcefully his "sovereignity of God" and "predestination" doctrines more so than any other Protestant group.

The Episcopal Church

The Episcopal Church evolved from the Church of England and is an extension of many of its doctrines and practices. "It is stated in the preface of the *Book of Common Prayer* of the Protestant Episcopal Church (today known generally as the Episcopal Church) that 'this Church is far from intending to depart from the Church of England in any essential point of doctrine, discipline, or worship.' The Protestant Episcopal Church constitutes the 'self-governing American branch of the Anglican Communion.' " (Frank S. Mead, *Handbook on Denominations,* Nashville, Tennessee, Abingdon, 1975. p. 130.) It bore the name of the Church of England for 150 years after it reached the shores of America. Sir Francis Drake brought the church to the shores of what later became California in 1578. Sir Walter Raleigh, in charge of colonists, brought the church to the East Coast of America a few years later.

The Church of England originated in the Fourth Century when Christian missionaries came to the British Isles. It was always more British than Roman though it was under the supremacy of the pope until the Reformation. Henry VIII became King of England about the time Martin Luther broke with the Roman Catholic Church. He wanted Reformation more for political than spiritual reasons. He did not want the kind of Reformation that Luther, Zwingli, Calvin, and Knox sought. In 1534, he secured independence from Rome and established the Church of England as the national church with himself as "the only supreme head on Earth of the Church of England."

Archbishop Thomas Cranmer piloted the Reformation through the reign of King Edward VI and wrote most of the doctrines of the church in the Prayer Books of 1549 and 1552. Cranmer believed in most of Luther's and Calvin's doctrines and incorporated them into the Articles of Faith of the Church of England. The Church of England was more Catholic in its liturgy but more Protestant in its doctrine. For that reason the Episcopal Church retained more of the ritual of Catholicism, and its church services are conducted with more pomp and ceremony than other Protestant churches.

Other Groups That Made Preparation For The Next Major Restoration

While the Historic Protestant churches were becoming nationally recognized, and denominationally established, other groups were receiving new scriptural insights which would make them the forerunners of the Holiness (Evangelical, Fundamentalist) Movement.

The Puritans

The Puritans and the Anabaptists were the two main groups to prepare the way for the next move of God. Those who worked to purify the Church of England from the Catholic religious ceremonies were called "Puritans" (Separatists, Independents). Thomas Cartwright was the greatest leader of the Puritan Movement. Puritanism never did become a separate Christian denomination but it did help promote Protestantism. It was the platform from which Thomas Cartwright championed the cause of Presbyterianism in England. Puritanism laid the foundation from which several churches were built during the century: Congregational, Quaker, and the "Particular" and "General" Baptists.

The Anabaptist

The Anabaptists (meaning "rebaptizers") are the best known for their definite teaching that infant baptism has no saving grace any more than adult baptism without a prior confession of faith. They would rebaptize any Lutheran, Anglican, Presbyterian, or Catholic who had only received baptism by sprinkling as an infant. In addition, they had four other strong teachings which were not acceptable to the national Protestant churches or Catholicism.

Doctrines That Divided

1. Discipleship: Christianity was more than mental faith and verbal confession, it must produce a transformed life and a daily walk with God.
2. Brotherly Love: mutual aid and redistribution of wealth, having all things common. Among

Moravian Anabaptists it even led to Christian communal living.

3. Restoration of the Church: "They were not interested in simply reforming the Church; they were committed to *restoring* it to the vigor and faithfulness of its earliest centuries." (Eerdman's *Handbook* pp. 400, 401.)

4. Separation: With strong conviction they insisted upon separation of church and state. All the established Protestant churches still retained the Catholic concept of Church and State integration.

Cooperation For Extermination. Protestant and Catholic joined forces to exterminate Anabaptism. To them "the Anabaptist seemed not only to be dangerous heretics; they also seem to threaten the religious and social stability of Christian Europe." (Ibid., p. 402.) In the carnage of the next quarter of a century, thousands of Anabaptist Christians were put to death (by fire in the Catholic territories, by drowning and sword in the Protestant regimes). Only three groups were able to survive in Europe beyond the 16th Century as ordered communities: the "Brethren" in Switzerland and south Germany, the Mennonites in the Netherlands and north Germany, and the Hutterites in Moravia.

The Mennonites. Menno Simons was one of the strongest personalities to promote and preserve the best teachings of the Anabaptists. Although Menno was not the founder of the movement, most of the 20th Century descendants of the Anabaptists are called "Mennonite." The Baptist churches of the coming centuries would become the greatest promoters of the Anabaptist teachings.

Controversial Theology of the Protestants: Arminianism vs. Calvinism

John Calvin's *Institutes of the Christian Religion* published in 1536 became the basic doctrines and guide for most Protestant Churches. However "when the United Netherlands (Dutch Republic) was declared independent in 1609, Calvinism was declared the official state religion. But some of the ministers of Holland did not accept the full import of the Calvinistic doctrine of predestination and grace. Resulting discussions brought to the fore Jacob Arminus, a Doctor of Theology of Leyden, who could not accept the ultrapredestination viewpoint." (Elgin S. Moyer, *Who Was Who in Church History*, Chicago, Illinois, Moody Press, 1962. p. 18.) Calvinism (C) and Arminianism (A) are presented in five main points.

C. 1. Election is determined solely by the sovereign will of God.

A. 1. Before the foundation of the world God determined to save, through Christ, those who believe in Christ and preserve in the faith unto the end, and to leave the unbelieving under condemnation.

C. 2. Christ died for the elect only.

A. 2. Christ died for all and redemption is for all, but only those who believe will be saved.

C. 3. Man's whole nature is affected by the fall, and he is without any merit to attain salvation.

A. 3. Man is in a state of apostasy and sin, and has no saving grace of himself; it is needful that he be born again and renewed in Christ that he may rightly understand, think, will, and do what is truly good.

C. 4. All the elect will be saved. God's grace is irresistible.

A. 4. Without the grace of God man can do nothing; but this grace is not irresistible.

C. 5. God's elect are eternally secure. (Once saved, always saved.)

A. 5. Those who have become partakers of Christ are given sufficient grace to win the victory over all sin, and all who are actively willing and ready to accept Christ's help will be kept by him from falling into the hands of Satan. (Ibid., p. 18.)

All mainline Protestant churches are either Arminianist, or Calvinist or a combination of both, in their doctrines. In the coming Restoration Movements, the Wesleyans in the Holiness Movement and most in the later Pentecostal Movement are more Arminian in doctrine than Calvinist, although at the Synod of Dort in 1618 Arminianism was condemned, and the Arminians deposed. It is interesting to note that throughout Church history and the restoration of the Church, many teachings and practices that the councils of the ruling Christian religions condemned as heresy were later established as truth, and some practices and doctrines that they sanctioned were later proven *wrong* by Scripture.

Protestant Movement Summarized

By using the key words of the chapter on God's providential preparation for restoration, a summary of the Protestant Movement is possible:

Its **purpose** was to activate the period of the Great Restoration of the Church. Europe was the **place** of its birth and growth. The priest and **people** that came out of the Catholic Church were the ones that propagated it. The **product** that publicized the Protestant Movement restorational truths was the printing press. The key **man** God used was Martin Luther. The **message** was Repentance from Dead Works — justified by faith, by the mercy and grace of Jesus Christ, and nothing else. The **ministry** was the preaching of the Word. The **method** was by faith in God and by the use of every means available. The **result** was the Corporate Body of Christ, His Church, awakened from Her lethargy and apostasy, taking the first of seven steps to Ultimate Perfection.

6

The Holiness Movement

Restoration of the Faith Toward God-Doctrine of Christ. The Holy Spirit was commissioned to lead the Church into all truth. Since the experiential truths of the six Doctrines of Christ were lost in the deterioration of the Church during the Dark Ages, it was necessary for the Holy Spirit to activate the "Period of the Great Restoration." The Protestant Movement was the first of the Restorational "times of refreshing" to come "from the presence of the Lord." The time for the restoration of more truth to the Church had arrived. An insight into what those truths might be can be obtained by studying some of the Old Testament "types and shadows" concerning the Church.

The History of Israel. The history of the Children of Israel was written for typological illustrations of what would happen to the Church, I Corinthians 10:11. Their origination and deterioration in Egypt, and their journey to full restoration in Canaan portrays the Church in its origination, deterioration, restoration, and ultimate destination. A more detailed presentation will be given in a later chapter. At this point let us look at Israel's historical happenings which correlate with the first two restorational movements of the Church.

The *Passover* typifies the truths restored during the Protestant Movement. The children of Israel passing through the Red Sea, standing on the banks of Jordan, and drinking the waters of Marah typify the three truths restored during the Holiness Movement: Water Baptism, Sanctification, and Divine Healing. These three truths of the Holiness Movement were restored in the same sequence as Israel's journey. After participating in the Passover and being delivered from Egyptian slavery, the Children of Israel crossed the Red Sea after God rolled back the water. When they reached the other side Jehovah brought the water together and drowned the Egyptian army. Their Red Sea experience separated them from Egypt. They then sang, danced, and rejoiced with a great emotional frenzy. Journeying on they reached the bitter water of Marah. There God made with them the covenant of healing and delivered them from all their sicknesses and diseases.

Church Making Same Journey Spiritually. The three phases of the "Faith toward God" doctrine were restored in the same sequential order. Water baptism for "born again believers only" was restored during the 16th and 17th Centuries. Baptism by immersion became the doctrine of all Holiness churches (except Methodist). The Anabaptist and later Baptist organizations were the main groups God used to restore the truth of *believer's baptism by immersion.* The truth of holiness was restored during the 18th and 19th Centuries. John Wesley and the Methodist preachers were used to restore the "holiness" part of the Faith toward God Doctrine which includes "separation from the world," "Christlike character," and "sanctification of the soul." The truth concerning divine faith healing was restored during the middle part of the 19th Century. A.B. Simpson and his Christian Missionary Alliance church was used to restore the truth of faith healing.

Tabernacle of Moses Portrays the Same. The same sequential order of the restoration of truth to the Church can be seen in the Tabernacle of Moses. The arrangement of its seven major pieces of furniture reveal the seven Doctrines of Christ and the chronological order in which they will be restored. Only those that typify the truths restored thus far in our study are listed:

Protestant Movement: The Brazen Altar - Justification.
Holiness Movement: Laver - Water Baptism and
Sanctification
Table of Shewbread - Divine Healing

With this introduction, the writer will now explain the second restorational truth portrayed on the chart.

Explanation of Information on the Chart

Approximate Date

The three truths restored during the restoration of the "Faith toward God" Doctrine of Christ cover a 300-year period from the 17th Century to the end of the 19th Century. However, the Holiness Movement was burning the brightest between 1750 and 1850 with the apex about 1800. The year 1800 is selected as the round figure date most accurately portraying the time of the Holiness Movement and restoration of the Faith toward God Doctrine of Christ.

Sanctification

Sanctification was a major restorational truth of the Holiness Movement. Though it was taught during the Protestant Movement, it was not the main issue. The words saint, sanctify, and holy come from the same Greek root *(hag-)* which means set apart, separate, holy. John Wesley is recognized as the great exponent of the sanctification message. The Methodist Church became representative of the sanctification phase of the Holiness Movement in the same way as the Baptist churches became representative of the water baptism phase of the "Faith toward God" restorational doctrine. Many books have been written on the Holiness Movement and its leaders. One of the best and most recent written accounts is *The Holiness Pentecostal Movement in the United States* by Vinson Synan. On page 17, he gives this description of holiness doctrine.

> By 1740, Wesley's ideas on theology were fairly well cast in the permanent mold that would shape the Methodist Movement. Succinctly stated, they involved two separate phases of experience for the believer: the first, conversion, or justification; and the second, Christian perfection, or sanctification. In the first experience the penitent was forgiven for his actual sins of commission, becoming a Christian but retaining a "residue of sin within." This remaining "inbred sin" was the result of Adam's fall and had to be dealt

with by a "second blessing, properly so-called." This experience purified the believer of inward sin and gave him "perfect love" toward God and man. The perfection which Wesley taught was a perfection of motives and desires. "Sinless perfection" would come only after death. In the meantime the sancti-fied soul, through careful self-examination, godly discipline, and methodical devotion and avoidance of worldly pleasures, could live a life of victory over sin. This perfection could be attained instantly as a "second work of grace" although it was usually preceded and followed by a gradual "growth in grace." (Vinson Synan, *The Holiness Pentecostal Movement in the United States,* Grand Rapids, Michigan, William B. Eerdmans, 1971, pp. 18, 19.)

The *Holiness* teachings had two emphases. The first included the inward work of sanctification, an en-duement of power for holy living, witness of the pres-ence of the Lord within the soul, as well as within the spirit, and a daily God-consciousness of the real-ity of Jesus Christ. The second emphasis was "world-liness," the rights and wrongs for Christians. Most Holiness sermons in the 1800s were filled with zeal-ous instructions "on the evils of drinking, dancing, theater-going, card playing, swearing, and 'even wine on the family tables.' " (Ibid., p. 44.)

Conviction

The previous *Protestant Movement* established the Doctrine of Repentance from Dead Works. The em-phasis was against the use of religious works as a means of justification. There was very little teaching on holy living, personal sins, or worldliness. In the *Holiness Movement* sin was made exceedingly sinful. Great conviction came upon the sinners when the gospel was preached. Numerous reports tell of men shaking under conviction until they came screaming to the altar asking forgiveness. Conviction concerning the participation of saints in worldly amusements came from the strong preaching of the Holiness preachers. Sanctification of the soul and separation from the world was the Holiness message that established convictions which are still practiced among some Holiness churches and have also carried over into the Pentecostal Movement.

Faith, Joy, Hymns, Singing

There are three levels of *faith:* saving faith, the fruit of faith, and the gift of faith. Saving faith was restored in the Protestant Movement but the fruit of faith was restored in the Holiness Movement. "Faith without works is dead" (*Jas. 2:26*), and "Faith worketh by love" (*Gal. 5:6*). Faith is more than a mental acknowledgement of a scriptural truth. It produces corresponding attitudes and actions in thought and living.

Joy, Hymns, Singing. The Holiness Movement added joy and singing to the "peace" and "prayer" that the Protestant Movement restored to the Church. Martin Luther and the Protestant reformers wrote many great hymns but nothing in comparison with the thousands of songs written and sung by John and Charles Wesley and other Holiness preachers. Singing became a part of the gospel message and worship service. Every restorational truth is accompanied by Holy Spirit inspired songs and hymns that express the truth and life giving experiences being received by the Church members.

Release of the Soul. Restorationally speaking, the Protestant Movement dealt with *justification* of the *spirit*. The Holiness Movement dealt with *sanctification* of the *soul*. It gave the soul its release in expressing love, worship, praise, and prayer to God. The soul is defined as the mind, emotions, and will of man. The emotional part of the soul of born-again believers became quite demonstrative during the Holiness meetings.

Divine Restorations Bring Emotional Fervor. Numerous historical periodicals relate some of the emotional expressions of the "heart religion" Holiness groups. One Anglican minister who observed a meeting stated,

> Many were "panting and groaning for pardon" while others were "entreating God, with strong cries and tears to save them from the remains of inbred sin, to sanctify them throughout . . ." Numbers testified to having been sanctified, instantaneously, and by simple faith.

> At times the emotions of the sanctified Methodists would exceed the limits of control. "Some would be seized with a trembling, and in a few moments drop on the floor as if they were dead; while others were embracing each other with streaming eyes, and all were lost in wonder, love, and praise," wrote one observer. Another noted that some wept with grief while others shouted for joy so that it was hard to distinguish one from the other. [These are the same emotions manifest by

the Israelis during the restoration of the Jewish Temple. Every time a new truth is restored to the Church-Temple there is great rejoicing over the new truth and some grieve over the fact that it is not the same as they have known in times past.] At times the congregations would raise a great shout that could be heard for miles around. The same Anglican minister (Jarrah) later observed that *"as the emotional element abated, the work of conviction and conversion abated too."* (*Ibid, p. 21.*)

Peoples' Reactions to Holy Spirit Power Peculiar to Natural Mind.

Most historians of Holiness Movement history record the great Cane-Ridge camp meeting in Logan County, Kentucky in 1800 as being the most demonstrative. The skeptics called it "godly hysteria" or "emotional fanaticism," but the participants called it "the blessing," "conviction," "being saved," "receiving sanctification," or "baptism of Holy Ghost." The Holiness believer's emotional experiences included such phenomena as falling under the power, jerking, barking like dogs, falling into trances, the holy laugh, and such wild dances as King David performed before the Ark of the Lord.

In August, 1801, the Cane-Ridge revival reached its peak when crowds variously estimated at from 10,000 to 25,000 gathered. In the light of blazing campfires hundreds of sinners would fall "like dead men in mighty battle." Others would get the "jerks" and shake helplessly in every joint. Peter Cartwright, a Presbyterian minister, reported that he once saw five hundred jerking at once in one service. The unconverted were as subject to the "jerks" as were the saints. One minister reported that "the wicked are much more afraid of it than of small pox or yellow fever." After "praying through" some would fall into trances for hours, awakening to claim salvation or sanctification. In some services entire congregations would be seized by the "holy laugh," and ecstasy which could hardly be controlled. A responsible student of these phenomena has estimated that by 1805 over half of all the Christians of Kentucky had exhibited these "motor phenomena." (*Ibid, p. 24.*)

Because of their falling to the floor while sometimes jerking and rolling, they were tagged *"holy rollers."*

The Cane-Ridge Camp Meeting was activated when Methodist minister John McGee preached in the Red River Presbyterian Church. The zeal of the Lord was within and the anointing came upon him until he "shouted and exhorted with all possible energy." Soon the floor of the church was "covered with the slain" of the Lord while "their screams for mercy pierced the heavens." The ministers in charge of the Camp meeting were Presbyterian and Methodist. Because these emotional experiences were more often in Methodist meetings they were tagged "Methodist fits." In the revival that hit the University of Georgia in 1800-1801, students visited nearby campgrounds and were themselves smitten with the "jerks" and "talking in unknown tongues." By 1830 the Holiness camp meetings had become more institutionalized. The more frenzied aspects of the revival had become little more than a memory, while primary concern turned from religious experience to doctrine. The Holiness Movement in the South retained more of the emotional and demonstrative aspects of the movement than the northeastern area.

Doctrine Without the Doing. The Early Church went into its Dark Ages because men became more interested in doctrine than experience. Man does not like to be subjected to the "foolishness of God" even though it is wiser than the wisdom of man *(I Cor. 1:25)*. The natural man tries to know God by intellectualism, human reasoning, and theological discourse. The proud, sophisticated, conservative religious person was appalled at the demonstrative emotionalism of Holiness saints. Remember that the original Church, the Body of Christ, was birthed not in doctrine but in supernatural experience, accompanied by such physical and emotional demonstrations that onlookers thought they were drunk. What dead Christian religious denominations call dignified, God calls petrified and sometimes putrefied. Doctrine and order is necessary and scriptural, but not to the exclusion of experiential and emotional worship. Doctrine is the wood of the Church, but divine emotion and zeal is the fire. Doctrine is the mind of the Church, but experience is its heart. When Christian denominations relegate all emotion and demonstration from the church service they retain "a form of godliness but deny the power thereof." *(I Tim. 3:5)* Sad to say, every Christian denomination established during the last 450 years of the Church's restoration lost the life and reality in which it was birthed by the second and third generation of descendants.

Faith Toward God — Doctrine of Christ #2

Faith toward God is the second Doctrine of Christ to be reestablished in the Church as a functioning truth. **"Faith** which worketh by Love," *(Gal. 5:16)* is the basic and ultimate essence of Christianity. "Without **faith** it is impossible to please God" *(Heb. 11:6)*. Every blessing derived from Heaven by humanity is by **faith.** "God is no respecter of persons" *(Acts 10:34)*. His blessings are dispensed on the basis of faith and obedience to His truth. **Faith** is the medium of exchange for heavenly blessings as money is the medium of exchange for earthly things.

Every restorational truth will be established in the Church and received by members as they have **faith.** Each Doctrine of Christ will be restored as the Church has **faith** for it. However, God is the "author and the finisher of our **faith"** *(Heb. 12:2)*. The Holy Spirit inspires **faith** to believe and receive when it is time for the fulfillment of another truth. The responsibility of members of the Body of Christ is to respond to the Holy Spirit: to be teachable and changeable but not gullible or unstable; to be open to new truth, yet proving all things with Scripture and holding fast to that which is good — believing and receiving new truth, but not being deceived, proud, or presumptuous.

True Movements Also Spawn Counterfeits. Every restorational movement has had its preachers who have gone into erroneous teachings. Every movement has established mainline churches who maintain the truth which the Holy Spirit restored to the Church. Each movement also spawns false cults, a diversion of the truth sufficient to destroy its members' true spiritual life. The onlookers are discouraged from participating in the restored truth because of those who have perverted it. "In every genuine move of God, Satan has sought to pervert what God was doing to make the truth unpalatable to the true people of God." (Dick Iverson, *Present Day Truths,* Portland, Oregon, Bible Press, 1975, p. 59.) There can be no such thing as a counterfeit, unless there is a genuine article. A person who has been discouraged by a counterfeit will find there has to be the real from which the counterfeit was produced.

Truth Becomes Neutralized. History has proven that the mainline restorational churches who retain the truth do not usually go into error. They do allow the truth to become neutralized by denominational tradition. They formalize the truth into creeds without the life-giving flow of the Holy Spirit. Retaining the doctrine they forget the doing. The verbal expression is there without the heart experience; a form of godliness but not the power of God which originally accompanied that restoration of truth. The same original principle of performance that caused the Early Church to deteriorate into the formal and lifeless church of the Dark Ages is seen in this fact.

Such became the condition of many of the Lutheran, Episcopal, and Presbyterian churches. They had fought so hard to be separated from all religious dead works and paraphernalia that they eventually went to extremes in "faith only." After Luther and the other original Protestant reformers had gone to Heaven, second and third generation church leaders were trained in their denominational colleges. They were taught the doctrines without the original restorational reality. By the time the Holiness Movement came into full force, the historic Protestant churches had deteriorated to a mental faith without a heart and life change.

Restoration of a Faith-Experience Reality. The **Faith Toward God** doctrine not only restored new faith, (true faith produces a living experience, not just a mental acknowledgement of a scriptural truth), but reactivated the justification by faith truth back to its original reality. "Faith Toward God" restored the faith-experience of believers, baptism by immersion; the faith-experience of sanctification of the soul, victorious living over worldly and fleshly things; the faith-experience of a baptism in Christ's presence, love, and reality; the faith-experience of discipleship and of the Lordship of Christ Jesus; the faith-experience of divine healing for all the physical health needs of the body.

It was essential that these faith-experiences be restored and reestablished in the Church. Just as a building must have a foundation and walls before it can be completed, the restoration of truth was necessary before greater growth, maturity and full restoration could be obtained for the one eternal Body of Christ which is predestinated for Ultimate Perfection.

Holiness Movement Churches

There were literally hundreds of separate church groups established during the Holiness Movement. Most of them became Christian denominations. Some developed into mainline Restorational churches. Some went into fanaticism, others into cults. Brief histories of the "Baptist" denomination will be given to represent the Christian denominations that originated from "believer's baptism by immersion"; of the Methodist denomination to represent the churches established from "sanctification"; and of the Missionary Alliance to represent the churches established from teachings on "divine faith healing."

Baptist

Baptists are first mentioned because they represent the first phase of the Holiness Movement: believer's baptism by immersion. There are 10 major Baptist denominations in the United States, as well as numerous others. *The Handbook of Denominations* by Frank S. Mead uses 25 pages to briefly mention some of the major and minor Baptist groups.

Present day Baptist groups evolved from the Puritan and Anabaptist movements in Europe; to the "Separatists" and "Independents" of England; to the "General" and "Particular" Baptists. The first Particular (British) Church dates back to 1638. The Particular Baptists were more fundamental, holding strongly to Calvinistic views. The General Baptists were more liberal in their doctrine and a portion of the group evolved into the "Unitarian" church. Roger Williams came to America in 1631 and became the champion for the cause of Baptist beliefs in the early days of colonial America, especially those of "separation of church and state." Roger Williams and John Clarke established the first Baptist churches in America at Providence and Newport, Rhode Island, in the late 1630s.

There were many debates among the Baptists concerning Calvinism and Arminianism. Calvinism prevailed and became the theological standard of many, if not most, Baptists in America today. In the mid-1700s, during the revivals of George Whitefield and John Wesley, another controversy arose among the Baptists. The division was between the Old Lights, or Regulars, who distrusted revivals and emotionalism, and the New Lights, or Separates, who demanded a reborn membership in their churches.

Most Baptists are evangelical and very missionary minded. "It will be remembered that the Baptists in England formed the earliest modern missionary society in 1792 and sent out William Carey to India. The adoption of Baptist views by Adoniram Judson and Luther Rice, while on the way to Burma, led to the organization of the Baptist General Missionary Convention in 1814." (Hurlbut, p. 159.)

There was another major separation in 1845 when the Southerners "seceded" from the Northern Baptists to form their own Southern Baptist Convention. The primary issues were over slavery and denominational structure rather than doctrine.

Baptists established strong fundamental doctrines but were not involved in the Holiness part of the movement as the Methodists were. Their general beliefs are given because they are the basic truths upon which the majority of the Holiness and Pentecostal churches were built.

"While Baptist groups differ in certain minor details, they are generally agreed upon the following principles of faith: the inspiration and trustworthiness of the Bible as the sole rule of life; the lordship of Jesus Christ; the inherent freedom of the individual to approach God for himself; the granting of salvation through faith by way of grace and contact with the Holy Spirit; 2 ordinances — the Lord's Supper and baptism of believers by immersion; the independence of the local church; the church as a group of regenerated believers baptized upon confession of faith; infant baptism as unscriptural and not to be practiced; complete separation of church and state; the immortality of the soul; the brotherhood of man; the royal law of God; the need of redemption from sin; and the ultimate triumph of God's kingdom." (Mead, p. 38.)

Methodist

John Wesley is recognized as the founder of Methodism. Methodism was an extension of Philip Jakob Spener's teaching (in his *Pia Desideria,* 1675) which became known as "pietism." (Moyer, p. 384) Spener taught that a genuine Christian life begins with conscious awareness of forgiveness of sins and a 'witness of the Spirit' that one is adopted into God's family. He believed that the experience of *justification by faith* must be balanced by a dedicated and obedient life. To maintain purity of motive the believer should refrain from any activities that might lead into sinful acts. Influenced by the Puritans of Strassburg, he recommended abstaining from popular amusements and moderation in both food and dress.

The "pietist" truths sparked the "Moravian" revival of 1727. In Great Britain this revival was preceded by three weeks of constant group prayer. Three weeks after the revival began, a prayer chain was started which lasted 100 years. People were filled with the Spirit, and spontaneous prophecy and spiritual song became common. Within 25 years, 100 Moravian missionaries had been sent to foreign countries, more than all Protestantism had produced in two centuries. Moravian missionaries were instrumental in the conversion of John and Charles Wesley. Wesley inherited his doctrinal emphases from the "Pietists" and "Moravians."

John Wesley studied in his earlier years at Christ Church, Oxford. While there he helped form the "Holy Club" of which George Whitefield was a fellow member. Because of their habit of being methodical in Bible study, prayer, and Christian religious practices, they came to be known as the "Methodists." John graduated from Oxford and was ordained to the

Anglican ministry. However, according to John and Charles Wesley, they did not receive their born-again experience until May, 1738. It occurred in a Moravian society meeting on Aldersgate Street in London.

Lay-Preachers and Gospel Singing. The unique doctrines of John Wesley and Methodism have already been presented. However, two additional contributions of Methodism should be mentioned. First, John Wesley was one of the first to use *lay preachers* to promote the gospel. Previously the only men ordained to the ministry were those with seminary and university degrees. It was the lay preachers who took the Protestant-Holiness gospel into the wild frontiers of America. Many Holiness groups and denominations were eventually established during the next 150 years by these men. That is the reason some Holiness groups developed an attitude of anti-education for the ministry. There are still groups who feel formal Bible college training would hinder the flow of the Spirit for anointed preaching. Second, there was gospel singing. John was the vibrant preacher but Charles was the singer. He wrote over 6,000 hymns, 4,000 of which were published. What John preached, Charles put to song. Singing became a co-laborer with preaching for the salvation of souls and the building up of the Church.

The numerous and various brands of present 20th Century Methodism vary from the very liberal in doctrine and living to the old-time Holiness doctrine.

Christian & Missionary Alliance

Albert Benjamin Simpson founded the alliance church. He was a Canadian of Scottish background, educated at Knox College, Toronto.

Fresh out of college, called in 1865 to become pastor of the Knox Presbyterian Church, Hamilton, Ontario. During nine years in this church, 750 members were received into the communion. Near the close of the year 1873, he entered upon a new charge, the Chestnut Street Presbyterian Church in Louisville, Kentucky. Here he promoted a revival and the building of a new church. During the revival under the ministry of Major D. W. Whittle and the singing of P. P. Bliss, A. B. Simpson came into a new Christian experience, the fulness of the blessing of Christ, or sanctification through faith in the provision of the atonement, served the church in Louisville with success until 1880, when he resigned to accept a call to the Thirteenth Street Presbyterian Church, New York City. (Moyer, p. 374.)

Truth Illuminated to the Mind of Man. His new experience revolutionalized his Christian life. With his tremendous zeal for the Lord, he soon overworked himself causing his already unhealthy body to give out completely. The doctors gave him only a few months to live. It was during this time that he searched the Scriptures in regard to the nature of man, the nature of sin, and our position as believers in Christ. He saw man as consisting of a two-fold nature. He saw him as being both a material and a spiritual being. Both areas had been equally affected by the fall, his body was corrupted by disease and his soul was corrupted by sin. Through his intensified study of the Scripture, the Holy Spirit illuminated his mind with the reality that Jesus had made provision for the divine healing of our bodily ailments as He had for the forgiveness of our sins. With that revelation and conviction, his faith laid hold of the promise of God. He had been taught that "by whose stripes ye were healed" *(I Pet. 2:24)* and other such Scriptures were only for the healing of man's sinful soul. But now he realized it was also for the healing of the body. God confirmed his revelation and faith by supernaturally healing his body and by extending his ministry for another 35 years.

Simpson edited the *Alliance Weekly* and wrote more than 70 books. His principles of Divine Healing are contained in his book *The Gospel of Healing*. The basic doctrines of the Missionary Alliance Church are summarized in what he called the "four-fold Gospel"; Jesus Christ as "Saviour, Sanctifier, Healer, and Coming King."

Church Moves On. The Holy Spirit brought forth a man with a message that caused a restorational movement. It restored another truth to the Body of Christ which brought more of Christ's complete redemption into the Church and took the Eternal Church one step closer to its ultimate redemption of spirit, soul, and body. Every restorational truth raises the faith level of the Body of Christ. The last truth to be restored to the mortal Church will raise its faith to the level of overcoming the last enemy of the Eternal Church.

Other Mighty Men of the Movement

The most prominent men of the Holiness Movement were Jonathan Edwards, George Whitefield, Philip Jakob Spener, A. G. Spangenberg, Count Von Zinzendorf, Howell Harris, George Fox, Blaise Pascal, Charles G. Finney, Charles H. Spurgeon, Billy Sunday, Dwight L. Moody, Frances Jane (Fanny) Crosby, and William Booth. There were hundreds and thousands of others who only Heaven has properly recorded and can give the just recognition and rewards.

They have joined the great cloud of witnesses who have finished their race and fulfilled the will of God for their generation. They are waiting for us to fulfill the restored truth for our generation. The last day Church will fulfill the final details and will restore the last truth, thereby activating the Second Coming of Jesus, uniting all members of the Body of Christ throughout the Church Age. All Heaven is depending on each generation to fulfill its work of restoration. Nothing thrills Heaven more than for the members of Christ's Body to be established in all restored truth and to fulfill the present truth for their generation (II Pet. 1:12; Rev. 6:10,11).

Other Mainline Holiness Churches. Literally hundreds of churches originated in the years between 1600 and 1900. Every mainline restorational church developed doctrinal statements based on the old Catholic "Apostles' Creed" and the doctrines of the Protestant Movement, plus whatever phase of the Holiness Movement it accepted. Some groups developed unique traits. For instance, the Churches of Christ opposed the use of any instrumental music in church worship. They also originated the statement "speak where the Bible speaks and be silent where the Bible is silent."

Each Faith Feels it is God's Favorite. Most Holiness groups, the same as virtually all Christian denominations, disclaim being a denomination. Each group normally developed some minor doctrinal definition of truth and some practices that made them feel they were the "True Church"; God's elected, selected, called-out, faithful followers, the Bride of

Christ. Many claim apostolic succession or claim that their heritage goes back to the Early Church and the Apostles. Some Baptists go all the way back to John the Baptist. Nearly every group tried to pick what it believed to be the most authentic biblical name. The name "Church of God" is mentioned several times in Scripture, for that reason over 200 independent Holiness groups chose the name Church of God in one form or another.

Non-Mainline Churches

(Normally classified as cults)

The major groups originating during this time were the Unitarian, Universalist, Christian Science, Seventh Day Adventist, Mormons, Jehovah Witnesses, Swendenborg Church, Spiritualist, and some other groups. Most were started by Protestant and Holiness preachers adding some supposedly scriptural practices or teachings to their Holiness truths. These additions were erroneous enough to separate them from the main stream of restorational truth. The author does not classify them as restorational churches. They branched off and cut away from the main stream and became spiritual "bayoux" and "miry" places."

Isms and World Events

The main "isms" outside the Holiness Movement that affected Christendom were Deism, Rationalism, Modernism, Intellectualism, Humanism, Atheism, Communism, and Darwinism, which are still a curse within our public schools.

Some world events during this time were: America was colonized mainly by Christians seeking religious freedom; the American Revolution and its independence in 1776 as a self-governing nation; the French Revolution; the European Wars; the American Civil War; abolishment of slavery; and other significant events.

The inventions which affected communications and travel were the stagecoach, James Watt's steam engine, steam ships, railroads, electricity, the telegraph, the telephone, and newspapers.

Holiness Movement Summarized

Its **purpose** was to restore the Second Doctrine of Christ, Faith toward God, to the Eternal Church. It was conceived in Europe, but America became the **place** of its birth and growth to maturity. The **men** were numerous. John Wesley is the **man** most noted for promoting Holiness. The **people** who participated and the ministers who propagated the truth came from Protestant Movement churches. The **message** was three-fold; believer's baptism by immersion, sanctification, and divine healing. The **ministry** was preaching of the Word accompanied by special singers, great conviction, blessings, and physical manifestations of emotions and healings. The **products** that carried its message to the ends of the Earth were the steamship and railroad. (Christ came in Holiness truth to take the world out of the Church in preparation for His personal coming to take the Church out of the world.) The **result** was that the Eternal Church crossed its Red Sea of water baptism, became sanctified and separated from the world, journeyed on to receive Christ's redemptive work of divine healing. The second great giant step was taken by the Church in its restorational walk to its "Canaan" of full maturity in Christ Jesus.

7

The Pentecostal Movement

Preliminary Preparation for the Pentecostal Movement. To gain a full knowledge and appreciation of the preparation and activation of the Pentecostal Movement, one should read Dr. Vinson Synan's book, *The Holiness-Pentecostal Movement in the United States.* Over 220 pages of historical accounts and quotations are verified and authenticated by hundreds of research sources. Another good book on the Pentecostal Movement which was also written from a doctoral dissertation with numerous research sources is *The Pentecostals,* by John T. Nichol. Sufficiently detailed references are given to lead one into an almost endless research project on the Pentecostal Movement.

These two books have been used as primary sources to verify the author's personal knowledge of the Pentecostal Movement. To offer in this particular book the details of people, places, experiences, teachings, and happenings would require hundreds of pages and would be repetitious of work which has already been done by capable men. The purpose of this section is to reveal the fact that there was a Third Restorational Movement called the Pentecostal Movement. The presentation is the same for this movement as the two preceding sections. The Pentecostal Movement came into being because the Holy Spirit was continuing His commissioned work of restoring all truth to the Eternal Church. This third world-wide movement restored the revelation and reality of the third Doctrine of Christ: "The Doctrine of Baptisms."

People, Problems, and Preaching that Provoked and Prepared

It would be over-simplified and abbreviated to say the Holy Spirit desired to restore a truth and did it. But God never does anything on Earth without mankind, and He normally follows the pattern presented previously in the preparation and activation of the Protestant Movement.

After the Civil War, the older major Holiness churches were affected by the changing times. Many ministers in the Holiness Movement became concerned that the movement was becoming worldly. They were concerned that the Church was becoming modernistic and was on the verge of substituting "social works" for "saving grace." The conservatives in the Holiness Movement were not as concerned about "social reform" (women's rights, the abolition of slavery, antimasonry, and prohibition) as they were the "social sins" about church members. "Rather than trying to reform society, they rejected it. In the holiness system of values the greatest social sins were not poverty, inequality, or unequal distribution of the wealth, but rather the evil effects of the theater, ball games, dancing, lipstick, cigarettes, and liquor" (Synan, p.68).

Differences that Divided. The Methodists took a stand against what they felt was an over-emphasis on sanctification in the latter part of the 19th Century. "A measure of the intensity of the conflict over sanctification is the fact that 23 holiness denominations began in the relatively short period of seven years between 1893-1900." (Ibid, p. 53.)

Many of the churches formed during that time accepted the truths of the Pentecostal Movement such as the Church of God, the Pentecostal Holiness Church, the Fire-Baptized Holiness Church, and the Church of God in Christ. The Pentecostal Church of the Nazarene denomination rejected the Pentecostal Movement and in the General Assembly of 1919 the denomination voted to drop the word "Pentecostal" from the name to avoid being identified with the new Pentecostal or "tongues" Movement.

In many of the Holiness pulpits and publications, ministers were propagating the need for a restoration of the Early Church's pentecostal power. Numerous prayer meetings were held beseeching the Lord to send another Pentecost. He did! But not quite the way they expected or the way most men would have chosen.

Evolvement of the Pentecostal Movement

Church historians have given evidence of times of "tongues speaking" occurring in different areas and in different times since the birth of the Church on the day of Pentecost. The Holiness Movement was no exception. There were occasions of "tongue speaking" in the Rev. Edward Irving's services in his Presbyterian Church, London, 1831; in a Dwight L. Moody meeting in 1875; and in many of the Holiness camp meetings as well as during the Welsh revival.

Though "tongues speaking" was manifested at times, no one had a revelation or understanding of it. No one was taught to seek for the experience as they were taught to seek and believe for justification and sanctification. The first time someone sought the experience was in Topeka, Kansas.

Topeka, Kansas. It was at the Rev. Charles Fox Parham's Bible School during a watchnight prayer service December 31, 1900. Parham had previously challenged his students to diligently search the Scriptures to determine the consistent biblical evidence for the reception of the "Baptism of the Holy Ghost" or the "gift of the Holy Ghost" *(Mt. 3:11; Acts 1:5; 2:4,38,39).* When he asked the students to state the conclusion of their study, to his "astonishment," they all answered unanimously that the evidence was "speaking with other tongues." They were convinced from their thorough scriptural study that the only consistent manifestation immediately following the Holy Spirit Baptism was "speaking with other tongues." However, none of the students nor Parham had received any such manifestation prior to this watchnight prayer meeting. In this service a student named Agnes N. Ozman requested Parham to lay hands on her head and pray for her to be baptized with the Holy Ghost with the evidence of speaking in tongues. Miss Ozman received and began to speak in a language unknown to her. Some understood that she was "speaking in the Chinese language" while a "halo seemed to surround her head and face." (Sarah E. Parham, *The Life of Charles F. Parham, Founder of the Apostolic Faith Movement,* Joplin, Missouri, The Tri-State Printing Company, 1930. pp. 52-53.) Following this experience, Ozman was unable to speak in English for three days, and when she tried to communicate by writing, she invariably wrote in Chinese characters. After she experienced "tongues" the rest of the students sought and received the same experience. Somewhat later Parham himself received the experience and began to preach it in all his services. This event is commonly regarded as the beginning of the Pentecostal Movement in America.

Azusa Street Revival in Los Angeles. Six years later, 1906, the Movement was launched to the world at the Azusa Street Revival in Los Angeles. A former student of Parham's, who had been a Baptist minister and was now a southern Negro Holiness preacher, was the instrument God used to escalate this truth. During the three years of the continuous Pentecostal revival at Azusa Street people came from all over the world to discover what new things God had wrought. It was carried by the news media and brought to the attention of the world. The Pentecostal Movement started as a spark of fire ridiculed by the press and rejected by most religious organizations. But 50 years later it was a roaring fire recognized by some of the same news media and national magazines as a "Third Force" in Christendom, equivalent in many aspects to the "Protestant Movement."

The third section in the "Restoration of the Church" chart reveals the Third Doctrine of Christ, the major truths, spiritual experiences, and churches that were established during the Pentecostal Movement.

Approximate Date

As mentioned earlier there were many reports of "tongues speaking" prior to 1900. But 1900 is when the revelation and faith came forth from God for the

Body of Christ to understand and receive the gift of the Holy Ghost. The "Tongues Movement" and the "Pentecostal Movement" are synonomous. The year 1900 is the round figure date used to indicate the beginning of the restoration of the *Third Doctrine of Christ,* the *Doctrine of Baptisms.*

Doctrine of Baptisms (Doctrine of Christ #3)

It is interesting to note that this is not the doctrine of "Baptism" singular. It is the doctrine of "Baptisms" plural. Ephesians 4:5 states there is "one Lord, one faith, one baptism." But there are several characteristics of our one Lord, many experiences in the one Christian faith, and several different types of Christian baptisms. Paul was promoting unification, not limitation.

The Third Step. It is significant that this is the **third** Doctrine of Christ to be restored. The **third** of the three basic baptisms is the *Holy Spirit;* the other two being repentance and water. Emphasis is now on the **third** of the three witnesses: blood, water and the *Spirit.* It is fulfillment of the **third** baptism of the great commission into the name of the Father, and of the Son, and now the name (character, power) of the *Holy Ghost.* First justification, then sanctification, and now *manifestation* of the gift and gifts of the Holy Spirit are to be emphasized.

The unique character of the Pentecostal Movement which separated it from the Holiness Movement was the "Baptism of the Holy Ghost with speaking in other tongues." The Holiness Movement believed in the baptism of the Holy Ghost and encouraged people to seek it. But there was no consistent manifestation agreed upon as the evidence. Various experiences were accepted: sanctification, immersion in love, great joy, shouting, falling in trance, the holy dance, victory over worldly habits, and baptism of fire. Many other manifestations and experiences were recognized as evidence that a person had received the baptism.

The Pentecostals called it the **third** experience. First, Justification cleanses the spirit of man from all sin. Second, Sanctification cleanses the self-life (soul) of the believer and sets him apart for holy living. Third, the Baptism of the Holy Ghost brings great power for service and lifts the believer into the heavenly realms to function with the supernatural gifts of the Holy Spirit. To restore the Church to the heavenly supernatural *manifestations* of the Spirit *(I Cor. 12:7-11)*, symbolically speaking, the Holy Spirit used a three-stage rocket. The Protestant Movement launched the Church into restoration. The Holiness Movement thrust it beyond Earth's gravitational hold, and the Pentecostal Movement put the Church into orbit in the heavenly realms.

Establishment of Tongues Speaking. The Pentecostal Movement established "Tongues speaking" as the only scriptural evidence that one had received the "Gift" or "Baptism" of the Holy Ghost. The *gift* of the *Father* was *Jesus* and He was given to the *World* that whosoever believes in Him should not perish but have everlasting life. The *gift* of *Jesus* was the *Holy Ghost* and He was given to the *Church* to take it from birth to maturity. The *gift* of the Holy Ghost was a new *spirit language "other tongues,"* and that ability was given to the *individual believer.*

Based on the testimony of those who have experienced "tongues speaking" in the 20th Century, and that of the Apostle Paul in I Corinthians 14:14,15, the following definition is given concerning the *gift* of the Holy Ghost: *The Holy Spirit enablement of the redeemed human spirit to direct the vocal organs to pray and praise in a language not known or understood by the natural mind of the person making the vocal expression.* Pentecostals did not teach that a person was not saved or did not have any of the Holy Spirit before speaking in tongues; rather that one had not yet received the "gift" or "baptism" of the Holy Ghost. The blood cleanses from sin, the water and Word cleanse from carnal and selfish soulishness, and the Spirit empowers for supernatural service. (One Pentecostal organization did develop the doctrine of "Holy Ghost or Hell," i.e., one was not truly saved until one had spoken in tongues which was evidence of the Holy Spirit.)

Pentecostal Additions. Basically, the only new major teaching that the Pentecostal Movement added beyond what the Protestant-Holiness Movement had already established in the Church was the *gift:* (tongues) of the Holy Ghost and the activation of the nine gifts of the Spirit. It also revived and re-emphasized all the truths that had been restored in the Protestant and Holiness Movements. Every *true* restorational movement incorporates all truth that the Holy Spirit has previously restored and adds new enlightenment and involvement in those truths. Prayer, faith, worship, etc., take on new dimensions with each *restoration movement.*

Progressive Restoration of Water Baptism. One Pentecostal group took water baptism one step further. The Holiness Movement took it from ceremonial infant baptism to believer's baptism, from sprinkling to immersion. All Pentecostals practice water baptism by immersion. The Holiness took it from a ceremonial Christian ordinance to the experiential reality of being buried in the likeness of Jesus' death. This Pentecostal group then took it from identification — from using titles of the Godhead — to using the proper name of Jesus in the water baptismal formula.

One Restorational Step Closer. The third Doctrine of Christ was restored to the Church and moved the Body of Christ one step closer to maturity and full restoration.

Gifts of the Spirit
(I Cor 12:7-11)

The supernatural manifestations of the Holy Spirit are classified into nine categories called by Pentecostals the "nine gifts of the Spirit." They are divided into three groups:

1. The gifts of utterance; tongues, interpretation of tongues, and prophecy.
2. The gifts of revelation; word of knowledge, word of wisdom, and discerning of spirits.
3. The gifts of power; faith, gifts of healing, and working of miracles.

All nine gifts of the Spirit were demonstrated in the early days of the Pentecostal Movement. Ministries such as Aimee Semple McPherson exemplified the doctrine of divine healing and the gifts of healing. It would take volumes to relate all of the signs and wonders that were wrought in the Pentecostal Movement. However, by the third and fourth decade of the Movement, just a few churches around the world were moving in the original glory. As a whole, the only two gifts that were being manifested within the local church services on a regular basis were the gifts of tongues and interpretation of tongues.

Same Holy Spirit but Different Operations. The "tongues" evidenced at the Baptism of the Holy Ghost were considered a different operation of the Spirit than the "gift of tongues" exercised during a church service. A brief explanation: Tongues used in private prayer and praise are for the edification of the individual and require no interpretation *(I Cor 14:2,4)*. It is the individual's personal communication with God. Tongues spoken in a church service are called a "message in tongues" or a manifestation of the "gift of tongues" and require an interpretation *(I Cor. 14:5,27,28)*. The operation of the gift of tongues followed immediately by the gift of interpretation of tongues produces the same results as the gift of prophecy: "edification, exhortation, and comfort" to the church members present *(I Cor. 14:4)*. The different use of "tongues" for private edification and for church edification is the criterion for a proper understanding of I Corinthians 14. Paul was not condemning the Corinthians, but recommending for them the proper use of the gifts of tongues, interpretation of tongues, and prophecy to avoid disorder and confusion. "For God is not the author of confusion, but of peace, as in all churches of the saints." "Let all things be done unto edifying" *(I Cor. 14:26,33)*. The Apostle Paul's conclusion and summation of the chapter was not "tongues have ceased, dispensationally depleted, of the devil, unscriptural, or not for the whole church age" but "brethren, covet to prophesy and *forbid not to speak with tongues*." The "Love Chapter" *(I Cor. 13)* is the meat between the sandwich bread of the gift-ministry chapters, 12 and 14. It takes all three to make a balanced spiritual sandwich.

Manifestation

Much thought and theological evaluation was given to the choice of the word *manifestation* to flow with the other headings in this column. I would have preferred to make one, two, and three "Spiritual Experience" sub-headings: Justification, Sanctification, Glorification. Because many Christians think of translation and glorified bodies when the word glorification is mentioned, it was moved to the fifth doctrine. The words *invigoration* and *jubilation* were considered as they had significant meanings concerning the experiential truths established in the Church during the Pentecostal Movement. The word **manifestation** was chosen since the main topic of the Pentecostal Movement and the Doctrine of Baptisms is "manifestation" of tongues when baptized with the Holy Ghost. There were also "manifestations" of the gifts of the Spirit (I Cor. 12:7-11), and pentecostals expressed their praise with various physical "manifestations" such as raising their hands, "dancing in the Spirit," etc.

Other Tongues:

Hundreds of books have been written by participants in the tongues movement on the value and purpose of "speaking in tongues" by the Holy Spirit. They all agree that it is a "Spiritual Experience" which brings divine blessing into their lives, making Jesus more real and precious. The author has not been able to find anyone who has received the experience testifying that it made them feel negative toward God or that it motivated a desire for fleshly lusts. There have been reports of some unorthodox actions performed by the tongues talkers during worship and prayer services.

Reasons For Speaking In Tongues. Some books list over 50 scriptural reasons for speaking in tongues. Some books go into word studies in Hebrew and Greek to show the scriptural validity of a 20th Century Pentecostal experience of "speaking in tongues." Here are a few of the reasons given for a favorable and positive attitude: God is the author of the "other tongues." He, through the Holy Spirit, motivated the 120 to speak in tongues on the day of Pentecost *(Acts 1:5; 2:4)*. Tongues seemed to have been the established evidence that the early Apostles recognized. Peter, 10 years after the day of Pentecost, preached the gospel to Cornelius' gentile household, and they received the gift of the Holy Ghost while he was preaching. Peter based his assurance that they had received the same experience as the Jewish Christians upon the fact that "he heard them speak with tongues." He then commanded them to be baptized in water in the name of the Lord *(Acts 10:44-48; 11:13-17)*.

New Testament Written by Tongues Talkers. It is a historical fact that 22 of the 27 books of the New Testament were written by "tongues talkers" and it is very probable that the other five were also. More than *20 years* after the day of Pentecost Paul established the Corinthian Church on his missionary journey. He evidently made the baptism of the Holy Ghost a part of his gospel message. Approximately three years later he wrote in his first Corinthian letter instructions for the proper use of tongues in private and public worship *(I Cor. 14)*. There is not one Scripture in the Bible which states or implies that anyone ever spoke in tongues "of the devil," "from psychological self-inducement," "hypnosis," "catalepsy," "hysteria," or "emotionalism." There is no scriptural evidence that tongues have ceased or will cease before the end of the Church Age. The Church came into the world talking in "other tongues" and it will go out "talking in tongues." The gift of the Holy Ghost gave the Church the power to preach the gospel with supernatural signs and reach the world in its generation. The same Holy Ghost power will give the last day generation power to preach the Gospel with supernatural signs and wonders and reach the world with the Gospel of the Kingdom in their day.

Pentecostal Purposes for Speaking in Tongues. A select few of the numerous reasons given by Pentecostals concerning the value and purpose of speaking in tongues are as follows:

1. Speaking in tongues edifies (encourages, builds-up) a Christian like an electrical battery-charger recharges a battery *(I Cor. 14:2)*.

2. Speaking in tongues generates the power of God within the Christian like the Hoover Dam generates electricity. The reservoir of water is typical of man's innermost being filled with Holy Spirit; turning of the turbine as water flows over it is typical of the believer talking in tongues, as rivers of living waters flow out of his innermost being; turbines turn a dynamo down inside the dam which generates electricity; talking in tongues is to the believer what turbines are to a dam, turbines generate electricity in the dynamo—talking in tongues generates the power of God within the inner man. "Ye shall receive power [*dynamo*] after the Holy Ghost is come upon you" *(Jn. 7:38,39; Acts 4:8)*.The Baptism of the Holy Ghost with speak-

ing in tongues gives the Christian a built-in power-producing plant, but it only generates more power as the "water flows over the turbine."

3. Speaking in tongues was not given just for an evidence, but it is to be a daily part of the believer's prayer and praise to God. The greatest gift Jesus ever gave the Church besides Himself was the gift of the Holy Ghost. He is Comforter, Enlightener, Teacher, Enabler, and Divine Guide of the Church with the divine commission to take the called members of the Body of Christ through conviction, conversion, sanctification, empowerment, ministry, and from glory to glory until the Church is conformed to the image of Jesus Christ. The Holy Ghost **talking in tongues** played a vital role in the **origination** of the Church, and will fulfill even a greater role in the full **restoration** of the Church.

Manifestation:
Pentecostal Ways of Worship

The "Spiritual Experiences" listed with this restorational movement are those which became acceptable Pentecostal practices and ways of worship. Those manifestations which could not be backed by Scripture were not encouraged, nor did they become a regular part of the church service. Some of the manifestations were not necessarily directly inspired by God or by the devil, but were normal reactions of the individual to the joy, love, exciting, and overwhelming presence of the Lord. They were responding as any normal human being responds in various ways to extreme joy, happiness, and excitement by laughing, jumping, screaming, running, or dancing wildly for a few moments. (These emotions are demonstrated daily on 20th Century television game shows and sports events.) When Pentecostal Christians began to respond in Church with such manifestations, it was highly criticized and ridiculed by the secular and religious world. Even the Holiness Churches, who a century before had most of these manifestations in their churches, now condemned them.

The following are the "Spiritual Experiences" that Pentecostals retained after the Holy Ghost had done His sovereign work of restoration.

Lifting of the Hands in Worship

Probably the most distinctive manifestation recognized as Pentecostal worship is that of lifting up the hands in worship to God. Lifting of the hands carries a universal language. It shows allegiance and respect for a higher power. If the heart is right with God the lifting of the hands is an expression of worship to God even without the accompaniment of verbal expression. The worshipper is symbolically saying "I need," "I surrender," "I pledge allegiance," "I exalt and honor," and "I worship." Some key scriptures are Psalms 134, I Timothy 2:8, Psalms 28:2, 88:9, 119:48, 14:2, 143:6, and Hebrews 12:12.

Hand Clapping

The Pentecostal Movement produced many special manifestations. After a supernatural time of praise and prayer the whole audience would start clapping simultaneously as if a great victory had been won. It was not normal Pentecostal policy to clap after a special song, miraculous healing, prophecy, or a good point in a sermon. Such was felt to be the world's way of responding. They did not want to give the glory to the human vessel, rather to the God who had blessed them through the vessel. Therefore, they responded with hearty "amens," "hallelujahs," or with the lifting of hands and voices in praise to God for a few moments. However, a practice that has remained a Pentecostal practice unto the present is that of clapping the hands in rhythm to the fast church hymns and choruses of praise. The exhortation to "clap your hands" is found in the New Testament Church worship and song book, The Book of Psalms *(Ps. 47:1; 98:8; and Is. 55:12).*

Shouting Praises

The old time Holiness "shouting Methodists" and "praying Baptists" were able to adjust to the "Pentecostal shout of praise" more than other groups. The praise service resounded with shouts of "Praise the Lord," "Hallelujah," "Glory, glory, glory," "I love you Jesus," "Glory to God," and with many other expressions, plus bursts of praise in "other tongues." The Bible describes shouting not as carnal emotion but as a characteristic of the righteous. All those who "trust in the Lord" will **shout** for joy *(Ps. 32:11).* Those who "favor the righteous cause" will **shout** for joy and be glad *(Ps. 35:27);* for God hath clothed them with salvation and that is cause enough for any Christian to **shout** and rejoice. The Pentecostals felt they were the "Zion" of the church world. Therefore, they had a right to fulfill Isaiah 12:6, "Cry out and **shout,** thou inhabitants of Zion: for great is the Holy One in the midst of thee."

When King David was restoring the ark of the covenant to its rightful place, its restoration brought much "shouting." Shouting for joy was a restorational spiritual experience of the Pentecostal Movement.

Fasting

Since the days of the Holiness Movement, more and more enlightenment has been received regarding fasting. Several books are now in print on the purpose and power of fasting. Joel 2:12-17 is the foundation upon which great blessings and restoration are received. It is when God's people humble themselves with *fasting* and turn from their own ways that their prayers are answered with restoration of truth and blessings *(II Chr. 7:14; Mt. 4:2, 17:21; Acts 13:2,3; II Cor. 6:5, 11:27).*

Dancing In The Spirit

The Pentecostal Movement emphasized Jesus' first commandment, "Thou shalt love the Lord thy God with all thy heart, with all thy soul, with all thy mind and with all thy strength" *(Mk. 12:30).* Sometimes when the Pentecostals began to praise God with all their *heart, mind* wholly on the Lord, and *soul* (emotions) fully excited, they would dance before the Lord with all *their strength.* This dance was done with eyes closed and supposedly under direct control of the Holy Spirit. It was believed by most Pentecostals that the participant was "in the flesh" if he or she was in control or deliberately directing any of the actions. "Dancing in the Spirit" was a common practice among Pentecostals for decades, especially the churches in the southern part of the United States and in the Black Pentecostal churches.

Musical Instruments

Prior to the Pentecostal Movement, the use of musical instruments was very limited in the Christian Church service. The organ was about the only instrument ascribed sacred sanction sufficient for use in the holy house of worship. This attitude was developed during the Dark Ages when singing and worship were more like a funeral service than a wedding or jubilee celebration.

Salvation Army Music. William Booth and his Salvation Army introduced the use of drums, trumpets, and other instruments in their mission and street evangelism. The Pentecostals took Psalm 150 to be applicable to New Testament worship and incorporated almost anything that could make a tune into their worship and singing. The use of guitars, accordions, violins, trumpets, drums, etc., plus piano and organ can be found in most all Pentecostal churches, even to this present day. Psalm 150 says that saints are to praise God in His sanctuary with "sound of the trumpet," "Psaltery and harp," "timbrel and dance," "stringed instruments," "organs," "loud cymbals," and "upon the high sounding cymbals." King David, the authority on music and worship declares that the music could be loud but must be played skillfully *(Ps. 33:3)*. It requires only a scriptural study in Psalms and the Book of Revelation to realize God loves noise, loudness, and volume in praise, even in Heaven itself. How much more does He desire these ways of worship within the Church as it is being restored *(Ps. 98:4, Ezr. 3:13; Rev. 5:12, 7:10)?*

Pentecostal Movement Churches

Every new restorational movement results in the establishment of many new church denominations.

Neither Martin Luther, John Wesley, nor W. J. Seymour had any intention of starting a new movement or of breaking away from his church organization. New truth must be poured into new wineskins. New church groups must be raised up to hold the new truths being restored to the Church. This does not mean that God forsakes the prior movement. God works with every person and group on whatever level of faith and receptivity they will function. The Lutheran and Presbyterian organizations were still getting people justified by faith while at the same time they were persecuting, opposing, and condemning the Baptist and Holiness churches. The Baptists were still getting people saved and baptized in water and the Methodists were getting people saved and sanctified while they both were at the same time condemning, rejecting, and making outcasts of the Pentecostals.

The Persecuted Become the Persecutors. It is one of the ironies of church history that the persecuted participants of the former restorational movement became the primary persecutors of the next restored truth. The Jews persecuted Jesus, Judaism persecuted the Christians, the Catholics were the main persecutors of the Protestants, the historic Protestant churches persecuted the Holiness Movement, the Holiness Movement persecuted the Pentecostals, and the Pentecostals initially resisted and rejected the next restorational truth movement. Rejection of a new move comes when the previous truth participants form denominations with set creeds and doctrines. The "wineskin" of denominationalism becomes set in its ways and has no flexibility to new truth. The wineskin bursts open and many people pour out and start a new church group which will normally end up being another church organization.

The Unexpected Source. Also, rejection of a new truth occurs when the desired revival and restoration comes through an unexpected source, person, or at an undesirable place. Preachers of the National Holiness Movement had for years called for a "new Pentecost" that would shake the world and user in the 20th Century with "Early Church" apostolic power. Preachers who proclaim the need for a new move, revival, or restoration of truth many times reject that truth when it is restored, especially when it begins with someone outside their Christian denomination or fellowship. It is very hard for the preacher to accept it when the restoration is accompanied with spiritual experiences, manifestations, and teachings different from or beyond his present Christian experience or doctrine.

Rebellion Against Restorational Truth Causes Division. Pentecostal denominations went through the same process that the Protestant and Holiness Movement denominations did in their day. Initially they were rejected, persecuted, and made total outcasts from the established Christian religion of their time. They gradually gained a status of suspicious toleration and eventually were accepted by the community and general Church world. A divine restoration of truth brings about a "hot war" between those who "accept" and those who "reject." After the battle is over and almost everyone has either "stayed with the old" or "gone with the new," the two groups evolve into a "cold war" relationship and practice tolerance of each other without accepting the other group as being fellow members of the Body of Christ worthy of their love and fellowship.

Reasons for Different Denominations. If division over restoration of truth were the only cause for the formation of different Christian denominations, then we should only have five major groups: Catholic, Protestant, Holiness, Pentecostal, and Charismatic. However, there are hundreds of separate denominations even among mainline restorational churches. Each new movement has produced a greater number of independent organizations. Many divisions came from different understandings and applications of the same truth; some from personality clashes; some from carnal ambitions of religious men; some from petty doctrines and practices; and some from major issues upon which those within that restorational movement could not agree.

Doctrines That Divided. There were two basic major issues and a few minor differences which caused the formation of the numerous Pentecostal organizations. First, when does an individual receive **Sanctification**: at conversion, or during an additional instantaneous second work of grace, or through progressive sanctification unto ultimate perfection? The Methodistic Holiness churches such as the Pentecostal Holiness Church became advocates of the "second work" sanctification. The "Baptistic" type of Pentecostal churches such as Assembly of God advocated the "finished work," which promoted sanctification as initially received at conversion, but that entire sanctification should be pursued as a "progressive" rather than as an "instantaneous" experience.

Secondly, **Water Baptism:** in the name of the Father, Son, and Holy Ghost, or in the name of the Lord Jesus Christ? Those who used Matthew 28:19 as the authority and instruction for their water baptism formula became known as the "trinity" or "three God people." Those who used Acts 2:38 as the Biblical instructions for their water baptism formula were called "Jesus Only," or "Oneness" Pentecostals.

Pentecostals Believe in Divine Healing. All Pentecostals believe in supernatural healings through faith in God. They accept the teachings of A. B. Simpson on divine healing and the operation of the Holy Spirit gift of healing. However, the same argument that arose in the previous healing movement became an issue among the Pentecostals. Some propagated the teaching that doctors and medicine of all kinds were of the devil. Others who professed to believe in divine healing but consulted doctors or used medicine were accused of backsliding, denying the faith, leaning on the arm of flesh, or sinning. Other Pentecostal groups practiced divine faith healing, but did not believe it to be sinful or unscriptural to also use doctors and medicine.

Some disagreed concerning whether a divorced or remarried person could scripturally function as an ordained minister. Most Pentecostals agree that women have the right to teach and preach, though there are varying beliefs concerning the qualifications for ministerial ordination.

Arguments Over Godhead. There were also endless arguments and debates over the Godhead doctrines: "Onenessism," "Twonessism," "Trinitarianism," and "Tritheism." The two different Godhead groups condemned and rejected each other, broke fellowship and started different Pentecostal organizations. Interestingly, the Holy Spirit did not take sides in the issue. The Holy Spirit baptized the "trinity" and the "oneness" alike, just as He did the "second work" and "finished work" Pentecostal believers. Those who were justified by faith in Christ Jesus having all their sins washed away by the blood of Jesus, and asked and believed for the Holy Ghost baptism received the same Holy Spirit manifestation of speaking in "other tongues" regardless of their Pentecostal camp.

Holy Spirit Not Involved in Doctrinal Differences. It is comforting to know that the Holy Spirit does not lower or limit Himself to man's doctrinal differences. Whether it is historic Protestant Christians differing over Arminianism and Calvinism, or Holiness and Pentecostals breaking fellowship over water baptism modes and formulas, practice of divine healing, sanctification or manifestations of the Holy Spirit, the Holy Spirit and heavenly angels do not become involved. Truth is truth and error is error. However, a person can be doctrinally right (scripturally correct) but spiritually wrong (un-Christlike attitude and actions, as referred to in Romans 1:18). One can also be spiritually right but doctrinally wrong concerning doctrine beyond the basics of Christianity. Some day each Christian will realize that God works with all members of His Body even though they are not perfect in doctrine and living.

General Pentecostal Beliefs. All major Pentecostal organizations believe in the truth of the Apostles' Creed which was preserved during the Dark Ages of the Church. They also believe all the restorational truths and spiritual experiences which were restored during the Protestant and Holiness Movements. All true Pentecostal denominations accept "other tongues" as the evidence (consequent manifestation) of the gift or baptism of (in, with) the Holy Spirit. Most are premillennial and pre-tribulation rapture in their eschatology and are Arminian in their theology. The basic doctrines of all Pentecostals are based on this restorational Christian Heritage. Additional comments concerning each Pentecostal denomination's stands on major controversial issues in the movement follow.

Although scores of organizations arose, only a select few will be listed in order to represent the different aspects of the Pentecostal Movement.

Pentecostal Movement Denominations

Pentecostal Holiness Church

This denomination is the result of a merger of three separate Holiness organizations which originated in the 1890s. All three *(the Fire-Baptized Holiness Church, Pentecostal Holiness Church, and the Tabernacle Pentecostal Church)* embraced the Pentecostal Movement and finalized their merger by 1915. This group was an extension of Methodist Holiness and "second work" sanctification. It was Trinitarian and practiced divine healing, but not to the exclusion of all doctors and all medicine.

Assemblies of God

This organization was the result of a national conference of independent Pentecostal ministers, meeting in Hot Springs, Arkansas in 1913. The conference was called for a five-fold purpose: (1) to achieve better understanding and unity of doctrine, (2) to know how to conserve God's work at home and abroad, (3) to consult on protection of funds for missionary endeavors, (4) to explore the possibilities of chartering churches under a legal name, and (5) to consider the establishment of a Bible training school with a literary division.

By the fall of 1918, the Assemblies of God Pentecostal denomination had evolved with headquarters in Springfield, Missouri. This largest of the Pentecostal groups stands for "finished work" and progressive sanctification. They are Trinitarian, but some propagate tritheism because of a conflict with "Onenessism." Divine healing combined with both pro and con attitudes concerning medicine, a strong missions thrust, and a Christian education program are the denomination's special tenets.

International Church of the Foursquare Gospel

This church organization was founded by Aimee Semple McPherson, one of the greatest evangelists of her day. Healings and miracles accompanied her preaching. Her foursquare gospel was based on Ezekiel's vision *(Ez. 1:4-10)* of the four faces: those of a man, a lion, an ox, and an eagle. To Miss McPherson the faces and the corners of the square represented the four main truths of the Pentecostal gospel: Salvation, Baptism of the Holy Spirit, Divine Healing, and the Second Coming of Christ. In 1923, she built the Angelus Temple in Los Angeles, California. With a seating capacity of 5,000, the church was filled at every service. The Temple became headquarters for the organization when it was incorporated in 1927.

The Foursquare Church incorporated "finished work" sanctification, Trinitarianism, divine healing, and miracles. Originally, it was more against than for medicine.

United Pentecostal Church

Both Oneness and Trinity brethren attended the Hot Springs, Arkansas, national convention in 1913. The Oneness brethren had hoped that the oneness doctrine and baptismal formula would be accepted as part of the statement of faith. The majority voted for the trinitarian doctrine and trinity baptismal formula. In order to practice their own beliefs, the oneness ministers separated and started their own group. Approximately one-fourth of the oneness ministers separated from the convention that formed the Assembly of God organization and that same percentage remains today.

Originally an interracial body, Pentecostal Assemblies of the World Church was splintered when White ministers separated and began the Pentecostal Church, Inc. Another group, also White, formed the Pentecostal Assemblies of Jesus Christ. In 1945, the two churches merged forming the United Pentecostal Church. This group interprets sanctification more as anti-worldliness. They are oneness and Jesus Only in their Godhead doctrine and water baptism formula. Divine healing is practiced.

Black Race Churches

The Church of God in Christ, founded by Elder Mason, is typical of the scores of Pentecostal Black churches throughout the United States. The Black ministers were very instrumental in promoting the Pentecostal Movement. The baptism of Holy Ghost and fire melted prejudices, making Pentecostal services meeting places of love and acceptance for all, regardless of racial origin. Black Pentecostal churches are more numerous in the South and in the New England states. Most of them are Oneness in their doctrine and baptismal formula.

There are many Black and White Pentecostal organizations who used the name "Church of God" in their denominational title. The Church of God, Cleveland, Tennessee, and the Pentecostal Church of God of America, Joplin, Missouri, are two of these. The Pentecostal Church of God of America allows those who have been divorced for the cause of fornication to be admitted to the ministry. Some of the smaller organizations practiced the Pentecostal ordinance of "foot washing" more often.

Pentecostal Legalisms. Both the larger and smaller Pentecostal groups originally taught that almost everything not directly glorifying God was a sin and could cause backsliding.

> "Included in the catalog of 'social sins' were: tobacco in all its forms, secret societies, life insurance, doctors, medicine, liquor, dance halls, theaters, movies, Coca Cola, public swimming, all competitive sports, beauty parlors, jewelry, church bazaars, and facial makeup." (Synan, p. 190.)

The Oneness groups also added the teaching that it was a sin for a woman ever to cut her hair. Many groups were made more conscious of the things they should not do rather than what they should do.

Related Events During The Pentecostal Movement

The "**isms**" that opposed and diluted the Holiness Movement were still actively opposing the restoration of the Church. The world's evolvement into secularism and materialism was affecting Christendom. Communism was causing the Church to go underground in northern Europe. Millions of Christians were tortured and martyred behind the Iron Curtain. Nazism arose to become one of the most barbaric, cruel, and destructive systems ever perpetrated upon the human race. Nazis murdered six million Jews and thousands of Christians. Hitler seemed to be so demonized that many theologians declared him to be the Antichrist. Others thought Mussolini was the Antichrist.

The Fundamentalists arose to oppose the "Liberalism" theology that was being propagated throughout Christendom. They preserved the inerrancy of Scripture and many other fundamental truths essential to biblical Christianity. Unfortunately, while they were preserving scriptural truths with one hand, they were persecuting a restoration of truth in the Pentecostal Movement with the other hand.

The most significant world-changing events during this time were World War I and World War II; communism's takeover of Russia; realignment and development of new nations through wars and colonial expansion; establishment of the League of Nations; a "boom" of prosperous good times after World War I followed by the great "Depression."

The **inventions** that affected communication and travel were the automobile and gas engines, the airplane used for commercial travel, radio broadcasting, the phonograph, wire recorder, the camera, and the movie projector.

The Pentecostal Movement Summarized

Its **purpose** was to restore the Holy Spirit to His powerful performance in the Church. By gifting the individual believer with "other tongues" and by releasing the gifts of the Holy Spirit to the Church, He restored the third doctrine of Christ to the Church, the Doctrine of Baptisms. The **place** of its birth was the United States, after which it spread to the world with its greatest percentage of growth among Christendom in South America. The Pentecostal Movement claims no single person as its founder. However, W. H. Seymour comes as close as any **man** to qualifying for the role. The **people** who participated and the ministers who propagated the Pentecostal truths came from the Holiness Movement churches. The **message** was the baptism of the Holy Ghost evidenced by speaking in "other tongues." The **ministry** was preaching of the Word accompanied by healings, miracles, speaking with new tongues, and gifts of the Holy Spirit. All types of musical instruments and singing were used to promote the gospel and to worship God. The **products** used to spread this restorational truth to the ends of the Earth were the automobile and the radio. The Church advanced in its restorational journey to its "water from the Rock" experience. The **result** was more powerful performances, greater evangelism, and the "rivers of living water" flowing out of the saints' innermost being in **other tongues**. The Pentecostal Movement was another progressive step in the walk of the Eternal Church, to Her promised Canaan Land.

8

The Charismatic Movement, An Expansion Of The Latter Rain Movement

Fourth Doctrine Restored. Restoration of the fourth Doctrine of Christ, **"The Laying on of Hands,"** produced another major movement. This movement started in the late 1940s and infiltrated into every Pentecostal group in the 1950s. During this time, it was known as the "Latter Rain" and "Revival" Movement. By the early 1960s, very few Christians were knowledgeable of the movement except the Pentecostal churches which had been affected by it. However, in the mid-1960s, the Holy Spirit had spread the "truths" and "spiritual experiences" of the restorational doctrine into every church group within Christendom. The move of the Holy Spirit which took the four restorational doctrines of Hebrews 6:1,2 and made them known to all Christian denominations and independent church groups became known as the **"Charismatic Movement."**

The "Catch-up" Move of the Holy Spirit. As you have noted in this study on the "Restoration of the Church," the restoration of each Doctrine of Christ has produced a major world-wide movement.

1. Repentance from dead works, *The Protestant Movement*
2. Faith Toward God, *The Holiness Movement*
3. Doctrine of Baptisms, *The Pentecostal Movement*
4. Laying on of Hands, *The Latter Rain Movement*

The Charismatic Movement was a *"catch-up" move* of the Holy Spirit. It was the time Jesus knocked at the door of the Church and gave every person within Christendom a chance to "catch up" with the Holy Spirit in His work of restoring all truth to the Church. It was the sounding of the trumpet for every Christian to come to the front line of all presently restored truth.

Protestant and Holiness Historians. Church history books written by Protestant and Holiness writers give many details concerning the Protestant and Holiness Movement churches and Reformers such as Martin Luther, John Knox, John Wesley, Whitfield, and many others. They show how their different denominations developed. Most of these *church history* books reveal the Christian denominations established by the end of the 19th Century. If one only read their history of the Church, one would assume that nothing new has happened in the Church since these churches were established. If mention is made of the Pentecostal Movement, it is usually treated in a derogatory manner or as hardly worthy of note.

Pentecostal Historians. The writers of church history from Pentecostal circles do the same thing with their history of the Holiness-Pentecostal Movement. If the Latter Rain Movement is mentioned, it is only given a few paragraphs and the impression given is that "Latter Rain" was just a small branch of Pentecostals who preached and practiced a little differently than the main Pentecostal body. Surely, it will not be offensive to some Pentecostals to face the fact that there was a truth-restoring move of the Holy Spirit called the Latter Rain Movement. This movement was just as major and vital in the steps of restoration of the Church as were the three prior major truth-restoring movements.

God is Building His House. The Protestant Movement was built upon the Apostles' Creed and upon basic truths that remained within the Catholic Church. The Holiness Movement was built upon the truths and practices of the Protestant Movement. The Pentecostal Movement was built upon the Holiness Movement. The Latter Rain Movement was built upon the Pentecostal Movement, and the Charismatic Movement was built upon the Latter Rain Movement. As an illustration, the Catholic Apostles' Creed is the basic foundation of God's house, the Church. The Protestant Movement was the floor, the Holiness Movement the walls, the Pentecostal Movement the ceiling, the Latter Rain Movement the roof, and the Charismatic Movement the windows and doors. In other words, a complete Charismatic believes and practices all of the biblical truths that were maintained by the Catholics during the Dark Ages. He also believes and practices all of the truths and spiritual blessings that have been restored since the days of the Reformation to the present time.

An Up-to-date Account. Since the Charismatic Movement was built upon the Latter Rain Movement, it is essential that study be given to the Latter Rain Movement as it was to the Pentecostal, Holiness, and Protestant Movements. How the Charismatic Movement evolved, its unique characteristics, and the part it played in the Holy Spirit's work of Church Restoration will be discussed. To be an honest witness of "those things which I have seen and heard" and to give an accurate up-to-date account of the progress of the Holy Spirit in His Restoration of the Church, the Latter Rain and Charismatic Movements must be presented.

Holy Spirit Motivation. The writer believes his convictions and motivation are close to the same concerning the *Restoration of the Church* as Luke's were when he began writing and putting in order the events in the *life of Christ.*

> "Several biographies of Christ have already been written using as their source of material the reports circulating among us from the early disciples and other eyewitnesses. However, it occurred to me that it would be well to recheck all these accounts from first to last and after thorough investigation, to pass this summary on to you, to assure you of the truth of all you were taught" *(Lk. 1:1-4 LB).*

Blessed Assurance. May this account of the Restoration of the Church help *"Present-truth"* Christians to be assured of the truth of all they are believing and experiencing in accordance with God's Word.

9

Restoration Of Laying On Of Hands Doctrine

Preparation for Outpouring. During the late 1930s and early 1940s, many of the Pentecostal organizations were conducting conferences with endless discussions over controversial doctrines. Second and third generation Pentecostals arose who did not know the former glory. Much of the original supernatural manifestation had disappeared from the average congregation. A church with supernatural gifts in operation and with manifestations of supernatural worship was the exception rather than the general rule. Many old-timers in the church were testifying about the good old days. The newer ministers and younger generation saints became hungry for a new visitation of God. Joel 2:15-17, Hosea 6:3, and Hosea 10:1 became the sermon topics for many Pentecostals, that is, "call a fast, let the ministers weep between the porch and the altar, saying spare thy people . . . break up your fallow ground . . . ask for rain in time of latter rain . . . then shall you know if you follow on to know the Lord . . . He shall come unto us as the rain — as latter rain upon the Earth."

Latter Rain Made
Preparation for Charismatic Harvest

The Lord Jesus heard the cry of those Pentecostal ministers and saints, and in 1947 and 1948 the latter rains in Israel fell in the fall season and brought the crops to maturity in preparation for harvest time. The spiritual Latter Rain Movement brought greater growth and maturity, preparing the Church for the great harvest of souls brought into present truth by the Charismatic Movement of the 1960s and 1970s.

Charismatic Christian Heritage. One of the purposes of this book is to reveal to *"Present-truth"* believers how their present Charismatic Christian heritage evolved into its present state of doctrines, principles, and spiritual blessings. Most Charismatic Christians do not know there was a truth-restoring movement beyond the Pentecostal Movement which was tagged by its opponents the "Latter Rain Movement." For this reason, a constant comparison will be made between Pentecostal and Latter Rain doctrine and ways of worship.

Approximate Date
(Explanation from chart)

The Laying on of Hands Doctrine was restored in two major groups. They are the "Deliverance Evangelism" group which was birthed in 1947, and the "Latter Rain" group which began in 1948. The Charismatic Movement began approximately 15 years later, in the mid-1960s. The year 1950 was chosen as the round figure date signifying the time when the fourth Doctrine of Christ was restored to the Church.

Laying on of Hands
(Fourth Doctrine of Christ)

The "Deliverance Evangelism" group of ministers manifested laying on of hands for *healing* and *deliverance.* The "Latter Rain" group manifested and restored the experiential truth of *laying on of hands and prophecy for revealing one's place in the Body of Christ* and for the *impartation and activation of the gifts of the Holy Spirit.* Both groups received and practiced the *laying on of hands for receiving the Holy Ghost.*

Introducing Primary Methods of Receiving. In the Pentecostal Movement, the primary method used to pray people through to the baptism of the Holy Ghost was "tarrying." Some would tarry before the Lord in travailing prayer for hours before receiving. Some tarried and sought for the "baptism" for years before receiving. The Laying on of Hands Doctrine taught that the Christians were to receive "other tongues" immediately when hands were laid upon them. Some ministers went to extremes and refused to pray for an individual beyond the first touch. They taught that the only time the disciples of Christ Jesus tarried for the Holy Ghost was before the original outpouring on the day of Pentecost. Thereafter, the only way anyone received was with laying on of hands. However, although all in the movement accepted the laying on of hands, many maintained the practice of tarrying in prayer with individuals to receive the baptism of the Holy Ghost if they did not speak in tongues immediately when hands were laid upon them. People began to receive the Holy Ghost by the hundreds with laying on of hands by anointed ministers and saints.

Laying on of Hands
for Healing and Deliverance

The experiential truth of "divine healing" was restored during the Holiness Movement. The main method of receiving healing was through the prayer of faith by elders. The Pentecostals continued the same practice and added the power gifts of the Holy Spirit for healing and deliverance. The "Deliverance Evangelism" ministers believed what the former healing ministers had taught but gave greater emphasis to the practice of "laying on of hands." Hundreds of deliverance ministers arose between 1947 and 1957, conducting healing campaigns around the world. A few of these ministers are mentioned below to show the different aspects of this restorational movement.

William Branham. A Baptist minister who had an angelic visitation that launched him into the ministry of a prophet, Branham ministered in the supernatural gifts of the Holy Spirit. His was the catalyst ministry that inspired and activated most of the other Deliverance Evangelists. His ministry also inspired the small group in Saskatchewan, Ontario, Canada to seek God for a fresh visitation. William Branham was unique in that he not only laid hands on the sick, but also operated in a word of knowledge and a word of wisdom, and sometimes in the discerning of spirits. His ministry as described in the book *A Man Sent From God* reads like the Book of Acts. He was not the typical Deliverance tent-evangelist of the 1950s. He was a forerunner with the "Elijah-type" anointing which shall be upon the Bride of Christ before Jesus returns. Though he started teaching some questionable doctrines before his death, Branham's ministry and gifts were fully accepted by the majority of Pentecostal and Latter Rain believers.

Gordon Lindsay. To become campaign manager for William Branham, Gordon Lindsay left his traveling ministry. He started the *Voice of Healing,* a magazine that was the voice proclaiming the news of what God was doing in the Church around the world. The magazine, headquartered in Dallas, Texas, became the instrument making known the many genuine Deliverance ministries functioning throughout the land. The *Voice of Healing* was phased out with the tent-evangelism ministries, but Gordon Lindsay established the *Christ for the Nations Institute* in the 1970s. It has become a teaching center exposing students to ministries and to teachings representing every segment of truth which has been restored since the beginning of the 20th Century.

T. L. Osborne. This man was used by God to bring mass evangelism to foreign countries. He challenged the people of every religion to believe that Jesus Christ is the Son of God based on the fact that His resurrection could be proven by the healing of the sick and deliverance to the deaf and demonic. Tens of thousands would accept Jesus as Saviour when Christ's resurrection power was demonstrated in miraculous healings and deliverances. He also spread the concept of native evangelism through the T. L. Osborne Evangelistic Association in Tulsa, Oklahoma, which has sponsored thousands of native evangelists around the world.

Oral Roberts. One of the best-known American healing campaign ministers, he traveled around the world for years conducting salvation-healing campaigns in his large tent which seated as many as 18,000 people. Long lines would form all around his tent as people waited patiently for hours in order to pass by Oral Roberts and receive the laying on of hands for the healing of their bodies. Thousands of documented testimonies were given of miraculous healings. His *Abundant Life* periodical (formerly *Healing Waters* magazine) kept his ministry before the church world. In 1955, he launched his first television films, and has continued into the 1980s. He envisioned and built the Oral Roberts University and the great medical complex called the *City of Faith*. Many of the "anti-doctors" and "anti-medicine" Pentecostal and faith-healing brethren have criticized him for building a medical center and for training doctors and nurses in his university. Nevertheless, it is generally conceded that more people have heard about and have seen demonstrated *divine faith healing* with *laying on of hands* from Oral Roberts than from any other Pentecostal, Latter Rain, or Charismatic minister. His main emphasis was the outstretched hand for healing and deliverance.

Many More Could be Mentioned. Typical of the many other deliverance evangelists was **Tommy Hicks** who went to Argentina and preached the gospel with supernatural gifts of the Holy Spirit. "During one night service on May 24, 1954, over 200,000 were in attendance." (John Thomas Nichol, *The Pentecostals,* Plainfield, New Jersey, Logos, 1966. p.224.) Untold thousands were saved and hundreds testified of their miraculous healing or deliverance. Thousands of such reports could be told of great exploits done by scores of "Deliverance Evangelists," such as Jack Coe, William Freeman, Harold Herman, "Little David" Walker, Kathryn Kuhlman, and Kenneth Hagin (Nichol, p. 222). In fact, the "Deliverance Evangelists" that ministered during the 1950s are too numerous to mention.

True Ministries, Questionable Methods. Within 20 years most of the big tent *Deliverance Evangelists* had passed from the scene. Some, such as Jack Coe, were called home to Heaven at the peak of their ministries; some converted from tents to auditoriums, and then to television. Unfortunately, as it has happened in every restorational movement, some went off into false doctrine, some into immorality, some started their own ministerial fellowships, and others built a great following around their ministry. Several "Deliverance Evangelists" used questionable methods of raising offerings in their campaigns which hindered some observers from accepting the truth. As yet there has not emerged a national Christian denomination from the ministries. Nevertheless, the Holy Spirit accomplished His purpose of restoring the doctrine of laying on of hands for *healing* and *deliverance* within the Eternal Church.

10

The Latter Rain Movement

**Restoration of
Laying on of Hands for:**

- *Revealing one's place of ministry in the Body of Christ with laying on of hands and prophecy by presbytery.*
- *Impartation and activation of gifts of Holy Spirit.*

The restoration of this ministry of laying on of hands was the revolutionary teaching and practice which caused the greatest controversy among Pentecostal churches. The Pentecostals were not greatly disturbed doctrinally by the *Deliverance Evangelists* since all Pentecostals believed in divine healing. Divine healing was a part of their "tenets of faith." However, most of these evangelists left their Pentecostal organization and incorporated their own evangelistic association. However, the Latter Rain Movement, with its doctrine of laying on of hands for *other* than deliverance and healing brought about a revolution within Pentecostal circles. It affected the Pentecostal organizations in the same way that the

Pentecostal Movement affected the Holiness Churches, the Holiness Movement affected the Protestant Churches, and the Protestant Movement affected the Catholic Church. In the 1950s there was as much difference between a Latter Rain Christian and a Pentecostal Christian as there was between a Pentecostal Christian and a Holiness Christian.

The new spiritual experiences and teachings incorporated into the Church are listed on the *chart* and will be discussed briefly as has been done with the three previous restorational movements.

The Beginnings of the Latter Rain Movement. The following account is taken from the book *The Feast of Tabernacles the Hope of the Church,* by George H. Warnock:

"In the beginning God . . . So it was that in the spring of 1948, God came forth in answer to the prayer and fasting of His children, poured out the gifts of the Holy Spirit, and revealed the fact that now at this time He would bring His Body together, and make of His Church one glorious Church without spot or wrinkle. It was a day long treasured up in the counsels of God. On February 12 and 13, 1948, the Revival started and on the 14th, the breakthrough came. An eyewitness testifies as follows:

"Three buildings on the Airport at North Battleford, Saskatchewan, composed Sharon Orphanage and schools at its beginning in the fall of 1947. About 70 students gathered to study the Word of God, and fast and pray. After about three months, the Revival suddenly began in our largest classroom where the entire student body was gathered for devotional exercises. One young man told me that when he was five years old, God gave him a vision of that classroom. Everything in it was identical. He saw God moving in a way he could not understand.

"I shall never forget the morning that God moved into our midst in this strange new manner. Some students were under the power of God on the floor, others were kneeling in adoration and worship before the Lord. The anointing deepened until the awe of God was upon everyone. The Lord spoke to one of the brethren, 'Go and lay hands upon a certain student and pray for him.' While he was in doubt and contemplation one of the sisters who had been under the power of God went to the brother saying the same words, and naming the identical student he was to pray for. He went in obedience, and a revelation was given concerning the student's life and future ministry. After this a long prophecy was given with minute details concerning the great thing God was about to do. The pattern for the Revival and many details concerning it were given. To this day, I can remember the gist of the prophecy, and will try to repeat some things here as they were spoken — 'These are the last days, my people. The coming of the Lord draweth nigh, and I shall move in the midst of mine own. The gifts of the Spirit will be restored to my Church. If thou obey me, I shall immediately restore them . . . But oh, my people, I would have you to be reverent before me as never before. Take the shoes from off thy feet for the ground on which thou standest is holy. If thou does not reverence the Lord in His House, The Lord will require it at thy hands . . . Do not speak lightly of the things I am about to do, for the Lord shall not hold thee guiltless. Do not gossip about these things. Do not write letters to thy nearest friends, of the new way in which the Lord moveth, for they will not understand . . . If thou dost disobey the Lord in these things, take heed lest thy days be numbered in sorrow and thou goest early to the grave . . . Thou hast obeyed Me, and *I shall restore my gifts to you.* I shall indicate from time to time those who are ready to receive the gifts of My Spirit. *They shall be received by prophecy and the laying on of the hands of the presbytery.'*

"Immediately following this prophecy a sister who was under the power of God gave by revelation the names of five students who were ready to receive. Hands were laid upon them by the presbytery. This procedure was very faltering and imperfect that first morning, but after two days of searching the Word of God to see if we were on scriptural grounds, great unity prevailed and the Lord came forth in greater power and glory day by day. Soon a visible manifestation of gifts was received when candidates were prayed over, and many as a result began to be healed, as gifts of healing were received.

"Day after day the glory and power of God came among us. Great repentance, humbling, fasting, and prayer prevailed.

"In the beginning God . . . Thank God for the beginning, and also for the continuation of the great work which He started a few years ago. And though men are prone to look for the spectacular, God continues to move silently and below all the noise in the hearts of His people, perfecting that good work which He has begun in them. The place that God chose in which to start the Restoration of this truth is only significant inasmuch as it is the most unlikely of places. No man would have chosen either the town, or the school, or the students, or the ministers, through whom God bestowed His blessing. But that is all most consistent with God's ways; for He chooses what man rejects. Bethlehem was the least esteemed village of the tribes of Judah — but the Son of God was born there. Nazareth was most contemptible in the eyes of the people, but the Great Prophet arose from thence. The Roman cross was an instrument of torture so despicable and so vile, that a great Roman politican once declared it ought never be mentioned in decent conversation; and yet there it was, on a Roman Cross, that God displayed His infinite Wisdom and Power through Jesus Christ.

"Let the saints rejoice, therefore, for the mercy-drops of blessing which He has given — but most of all for the *sound of abundance of rain.* A cloud appears on the horizon! It will not be long ere it covers the earth, and the glory of God shall be displayed throughout all nations, as the waters cover the sea." (George H. Warnock, *The Feast of Tabernacles The Hope of The Church,* North Battleford, Saskatchewan, Canada, Sharon Publishers, 1951, pp. 3,4.)

The following quotations were taken from the book *The 1948 Revival and Now,* by M.E. Kirkpatrick.

"First of all, I should lay down the setting and how all this came about and what the conditions were. At this particular time in Saskatchewan, Canada, a number of we [sic] pastors, evangelists, and workers longed to see a move of God in our churches and meetings. We became alarmed at the spiritual decline and coldness and the lack of spiritual hunger among the people. We were anxious to do something about it, but things seemed to have grown steadily worse. No one seemed to have the answer. The general consensus of opinion [sic] from those who were over us in the Lord was that we were not to expect revival because we were living in the closing days of time and things were going to grow worse, and we were to hold on to the bitter end. We often heard quoted, 'Except those days should be shortened there should no flesh be saved' *(Mt. 24:22).* This only brought more depression in [into] our spirits so we were at the point of despair.

So many of us in this large Pentecostal group, because of our desperation and hunger for God, began to fast and pray. Some fasted three weeks and one brother fasted 42 days. This was even new to us. Many of us gathered in this one place, through a chain of circumstances that is not necessary for us to tell here. God brought us together through a sovereign act at this particular time.

"1948 was the year when many things we could mention began. It was the year the Jews became a nation, the year when unions made themselves known. There seemed to be a general quickening in every department and in every country around the world.

"One particular day a brother stood to his feet and began to prophesy. Until that time we had not heard much prophecy nor very little about the ministry of a prophet. For over one-half hour God spoke through him about visitation. Because of the heavy anointing we knew God had spoken to us through the honest brother. God spoke to us about restoration days and that He would pour out His Spirit upon all flesh. This thrilled our hearts, having lived in an atmosphere of defeatism. It was refreshing, for now we were assured of visitation from God. What joy swept through the camp; what faith and hope were planted in our hearts. *God said He would restore all that the Church had lost.*"

Restoration of the Doctrine of Laying on of Hands With Prophecy for the Revealing of God's Will, Ministry, Calling, and Placement of Members of the Corporate Body of Christ.

"This was new to us in many respects. We had laid hands on the sick, but when the prophet spoke of laying on of hands and prophecy, this sent every one to their knees, faculty and students alike. In those days we sought the Lord to see if those things were scriptural. We took time off for three whole days. All went to their rooms to pray and search the scriptures. On the fourth day all came out with their findings, and everyone without exception said, 'It is absolutely Biblical and scriptural.' They quoted Hebrews 6:2. This speaks of it as a doctrine. Acts 13:1-4 shows that the early church practiced it. I Timothy 1:18, 4:14, and II Timothy 1:6 shows that Paul believed in the laying on of hands and prophecy. Mark 16:18 says, 'They shall lay hands on the sick.' So as far as we were concerned, the doctrine of laying on of hands and prophecy was accepted and we believed the Biblical record.

"It was rather amusing how in the beginning the laying on of hands got started. The question was — who would have the faith to start doing it? Like anything new in the Spirit, it takes faith to begin. God spoke to the brother that gave the first prophecy. He was a bit afraid to lay hands on anyone. At that moment someone in the back of the congregation said, 'My servant — what the Lord has told you to do, do it, don't be afraid.' So who do you think he chose? I was sitting in the middle of the front seat and we were only halfway through the service when he walked over to me and took me by the hand. I thought this was a peculiar time to shake hands, but when he took me by the hand, I felt the glorious anointing. I might say God had prepared my heart. I had been in prayer the night before and for the first time in years was slain by the power of God, and when the brother took me by the hand I felt the same anointing. Then he began to prophesy and mentioned the ministry of the apostle, which of course means a missionary, or a sent one. Then he said, the gifts of the Spirit would come into operation when needed.

This was of course, a confirmation as we had already been doing some of this type of work.

"I must testify and say that the ministry of laying on of hands has given me a greater incentive. Hence, we have traveled to many countries and have seen outstanding results. The gifts of the Spirit have been in operation and brought much blessing. We ascribe all the glory to God the giver of every perfect gift.

"God is raising up the Body of Christ, the Church, from all nations, with power and authority to have an impact upon world governments and leaders in this hour. [*Some fulfillment during Charismatic Movement, more yet to come.*]

"I believe that all past heaven sent revivals and restorational truths that have been established, along with what God is doing today, *will consummate in the mightiest revival and victory against evil that the world has ever known. Do not think for one moment that the church will go down into oblivion.* Not so, the rock mentioned by Daniel, that was cut out without hands will smash the great image.

"When I speak of the 1948 Restorational Movement, I do not discredit or exclude other movements, but rather include them. God has been restoring since Luther's time, line upon line, precept upon precept, that the Church as a unified body will be a power to reckon with before Christ's coming. I have written about the 1948 revival to clear up some misunderstandings and to show that the 1948 movement was God adding to the structure of the Church.

"We were there when the revival came and observed the seven principles that were to guide us. I do not believe any one can Biblically discredit these principles" (Milford E. Kirkpatrick, *The 1948 Revival,* Dallas, Texas, A1 Printing Co., 1954, pp. 2-4).

Latter Rain Doctrine and Practice

Thus was the birth of the Latter Rain restorational Movement. The following material reveals the new spiritual experiences added to the Church and an explanation of the Fourth Doctrine of Christ restored at this time.

Spiritual Experiences (from chart).

Ministration. *Ministration* best describes the spiritual experiences that accompanied this restorational movement. *Ministry* was the main theme: *ministry* of the congregation in praise and worship of God; *ministry* of saints to one another in Body ministry; *ministry of prophecy to the Church for edification, comfort, and* exhortation; *ministry* of the presbytery to the saints with laying on of hands and prophecy; *ministration* of the ascension five-fold ministries of the apostle, prophet, evangelist, pastor, and teacher for the perfecting of the saints: *ministration* of the gifts of the Spirit in evangelism and the upbuilding of the **Church.**

Singing Praises. There was birthed within the Church during this movement a new expression of worship and praise to God. It came as a melodious praise flowing up and down like rhythmic waves of gentle ocean breezes and then rising to a crescendo of melodious praises that is best described by the book of Revelation as the "sound of many waters" *(Rev. 19:6).* As the lifting of hands and shouting praises was the most distinctive characteristic of Pentecostal worship and praise, so the lifting of hands and voices in melodious singing-praise was the most distinctive feature of Latter Rain worship and praise. Old-time Pentecostals shout their praises for two or three minutes in response to a blessing, or in response to an exhortation to praise God. Whereas, the Latter Rain people received a revelation that "God inhabits the praises of His people" *(Ps. 22:3).* They would unanimously begin to lift hands and voices to God in singing praises without a preliminary spiritual "warm-up" from singing hymns and choruses or an exhortation to worship God. In the 1950s, the praise service would flow continuously from 30 minutes to three hours. Most Charismatics of the 1960s and 1970s came into the Latter Rain type of worship more than the Pentecostal ways of worship. Both, however, are scriptural and acceptable before God, especially when the action is motivated by a heart of love and performed as an act of appreciation to God (Col. 3:23; Ps. *68:4, 81:1, 95:1; Acts 10:35).*

Psalms, Spiritual Songs, Worship. Ephesians 5:18 tells Christians to stay filled with the Spirit by speaking to themselves in *psalms, hymns,* and *spiritual songs. Hymns* are normally classified as songs of past movements which have been written in a bound volume called a "Hymnal" or "songbook." A *spiritual song* as manifested in this movement was a song sung extemporaneously from the spirit expressing a prayer or praise to God, or a prophetic utterance in song. It was a song of the spirit, not of the memory or from the hymnal. Some of these were recorded and printed into music sheets and they are now sung by present-day Christians as choruses or hymns. *Psalms:* during this movement hundreds received melodies to Scriptures recorded in the Book of Psalms. Psalm 100 and 150 were two of the most popular Psalms sung during the Latter Rain Movement. Melodious worship was more prominent than jubilant praise in the early days of the movement. In fact, in the early 1950s, most Latter Rain churches removed all song books from their churches, disbanded the choir, and removed most of the musical instruments other than piano and organ, calling all those things "old order." To be "in the move," one had to worship slowly in melodious praise with no clapping, stomping, or extra loudness; *singing praise* in worship and prophecy was the **"move of God"** and being **"in the revival."** However, within ten years the robed choir, all musical instruments, and jubilant praise with dancing and rejoicing were reinstated. A few churches even brought back the hymnals, but most printed all the new choruses and Psalms into chorus books and used these in their singing. Others incorporated the *overhead projector* method of projecting the choruses upon a large screen in front of the audience.

Praise in the Dance. Some independent churches were a mixture of Pentecostal and Latter Rain ways of worship. The all-out Latter Rain Churches mainly worshipped with very little or no jubilant praise, shouting or dancing in the spirit. However, in 1954 during a Latter Rain yearly conference at Crescent Beach in British Columbia, Canada, a sovereign move of the Holy Spirit restored the praise in the dance. A minister, (the writer) who was present at this meeting, tells what happened.

> The congregation of about 800 people had been worshipping God for quite some time. As the worship lowered to a melodious murmur, suddenly a sister began to prophesy, "The King is coming, the King is coming — go ye out to meet Him with dances and rejoicing." She started taking ferns out of the flower basket and waving them in the air and laying some of them as if before the Lord as she praised the Lord in the dance

across the auditorium in front of the platform. The Head of the conference started to stop her but the Holy Spirit spoke to him not to, for it was of God. Within a few moments most of the audience was praising God with legs swinging and bodies moving in rhythmic praise to God.

Latter Rain Praise Dance. Within a short time, most of the Latter Rain churches on the West Coast were praising God in the dance for from five to 25 minutes during every service. This was completely different from the Pentecostal "dancing in the spirit," an uncontrolled, eyes shut, emotional-frenzied dance. These people would begin singing a fast chorus, deliberately leave their pews, walk into the aisle and down to the front, and then begin praising the Lord in the dance. Many of the ladies would remove their high heel shoes so that they would have more freedom. The Charismatics moved into "praise in the dance" rather than the Pentecostal "dancing in the spirit." In fact, the Jesus people and Charismatics added the praise in Jewish-type folk dance (i.e., Christians joining hands in a circle, taking a fellow Christian's hand, and dancing around as in the old western square dance).

There are more biblical examples and Scriptures on praising the Lord in the dance than there are on lifting or clapping the hands, shouting, singing from hymnals, or many other ways in which God is worshipped within Christendom. King David, the man after God's own heart, praised the Lord in the dance (Acts 13:22, II Sam. 6:14-16; Ps. 149:3, 150:4; Jer. 31:4,13; Ps. 30:11; Eccl. 3:14; Mt. 11:17; Lk. 15:25).

Sacrifice of Praise. Dr. Reginald Layzell is recognized among most of those in the movement as the apostle of praise and missions. He preached Psalms 22:3 and Hebrews 13:15 at the yearly Crescent Beach conferences during the 1950s until the message of those Scriptures was birthed within many a minister and congregation. Most of those who came into this movement were Pentecostals. They were accustomed to praising God from their feelings. Pastor Layzell taught that the sacrifice of praise was the "fruit of your lips" giving thanks to Jesus. Feeling had nothing to do with it. One praises God because "God inhabits the praises of His people." It is one of the "spiritual sacrifices" that the *priesthood believer* has the privilege of offering to the Lord. It is not just an emotional response but one of the greatest forces of protection and instruments of warfare ever given to the Church.

There was also much teaching on "sacrifices of joy" and the joy of the Lord. A number of the Scriptures are used for joy and singing praises *(Jer. 31:12,13; 33:10,11; Neh. 8:10; Is. 12:3; Ps. 27:6; 89:1,15; 147:1; II Chron. 5:11-14; 20:18-28; Zeph. 3:17).*

Singing praises was a sovereign move of the Holy Spirit that accompanied the laying on of hands with prophecy doctrine wherever it was manifested. But it was the solid, consistent teaching of Pastor Layzell that enabled churches on the West Coast and in Western Canada to maintain that joyful sound of voluminous melodious praise to the Lord. Those churches never called themselves Latter Rain, but identify themselves as "Revival" churches and their annual conference as "Revival Fellowship." One can attend their conference and hear the same "singing praise" that was the distinctive spiritual manifestation of the Latter Rain Movement.

Body of Christ and Body Ministry

The truths restored in the former restorational movements dealt chiefly with the relation of the believer to God as an individual. They included his personal salvation, individual baptism, holiness before the Lord, personal healing, and baptism of Holy Spirit. The truths restored in this movement were those which affected the Church as a body of believers.

Restoration of Revelation on Body of Christ. Prior to this time when reference was made to the "Church," people thought of the Baptist, Methodist, Catholic, or Pentecostal denominations or some local church building. In this move there came illumination and teaching on the Church as the many-membered corporate Body of Christ. Jesus was exalted as the only head and headquarters of the Church (not the Pope, some bishop, general superintendent, or denominational headquarters). Pentecostals who came into the move were challenged to come out of their doctrinal ditches of "Godhead" concepts, water baptismal formulas, sanctification dogmas, and all other divisive doctrines that had separated the Church (only walls-salvation, gates-praise) *(Is. 60:18)*. Individuals could keep their own personal conviction as long as they based their fellowship around loving and praising Jesus Christ *(I Jn. 1:3)*. Christians from every Pentecostal denomination flowed out of the old-wineskins and into the river of God. They gathered together in love and harmony because they recognized they were all members of the same Body of Christ with the same Headship, Jesus Christ. Many prophecies and teachings came forth on the desire and determination of Jesus for His Church to be one. Fellowship was based on a personal relationship with Jesus Christ, not doctrine.

No Denominations Formed. To this present time, the 1980s, there has been no denomination formed out of the Latter Rain Movement. There are "fellowships," "ministerial associations," and "evangelistic associations." Because of their strong teachings regarding local churches, each congregation is autonomous and self-incorporated with no legal or doctrinal ties with other local churches.

Body ministry was taught and practiced by Latter Rain Christians. They taught that every born-again, spirit-filled member in the Body of Christ has a ministry (though not a minister); that the church service was not just for pulpit and platform ministry, but that the Holy Spirit could use saints in the congregation to bless each other with gifts of the Holy Spirit. The saints as well as the preachers were given the opportunity to minister.

The Ascension Gift Ministries. Much teaching was given on Ephesians 4:8-15. The five-fold administrative offices of the **apostle, prophet, evangelist, pastor,** and **teacher** were emphasized. The Church had for years acknowledged the ministry of the teacher, pastor, and evangelist. These ministers were addressed as "Pastor Jones" or "Evangelist Smith." However, those who had the ministry of the apostle or prophet were not addressed as "Apostle Jones" or "Prophet Smith." The same theologians who taught that the days of miracles and talking in tongues ceased with the Early Church also taught that the office-ministries of the apostle and prophet ceased with the founding of the Church.

Ministry of Ministers. This movement taught strongly Ephesians 4:11-13, emphasizing that all five ministries must continue to function in their ministry of perfecting the saints *until* the Church reaches the "unity of the faith, knowledge of the son of God, [know as we are known], unto a perfect man [mature, fully restored Church] unto the measure of the stature of the fulness of Christ" [each member conformed to the image of Christ]. In other words, Jesus will not return physically until the Church reaches spiritual maturity. The Bride must be matured for marriage to Her heavenly Bridegroom and the Army of the Lord must be equipped and trained in their weapons of warfare which will be needed to fulfill God's plan for the last generation of the mortal Church.

The Gift and Ministry of Prophesying. The gift of prophecy and ministry of prophesying was restored to the Church during the 1948 movement. A portion of the Body ministry was performed by different members in the congregation lifting their voices and allowing the prophetic utterances to come forth to the local church. Pentecostals had maintained the manifestation of the gift of tongues and interpretation of tongues during their worship service, but rarely were there prophecies. The Latter Rain worship service would have numerous prophecies come forth. Pentecostals taught that there could be only two or three tongues and interpretations during one local church service *(I Cor. 14:27)*. Latter Rain ministers taught that "ye may all prophesy one by one, that all may learn, and all may be comforted" *(I Cor. 14:31)*.

The Latter Rain teachers emphasized the difference between prophecy as *forth*telling and prophecy as *fore*telling. New Testament congregational prophesying is not for predicting future events, but simply for "edification, exhortation, and comfort" *(I Cor. 14:3)*. Pentecostals had "testimony time" during their services when different saints would stand in the congregation and testify about their experiences. Latter Rain congregations would stand in worship and allow the Lord to testify in their midst by the spirit and ministry of prophesying. "The testimony of Jesus is the spirit of prophecy" *(Rev. 19:10).*

Present-Truth Charismatics. In the 1950s there was as much difference between a Pentecostal and a Latter Rain church service as there was between a Pentecostal and a Holiness worship service. Most Present-truth Charismatic congregations moved right into the latest restored ways of worship, praise, singing praises, and praising God in the dance, with the music, as a deliberate act of worship before the Lord. Most Charismatics moved into congregational prophesying and laying on of hands in personal prophecy for impartation and activation of the gifts and callings of God.

Laying on of Hands and Prophecy. It has always been a practice of the Church throughout its history to lay hands upon the head of the person being ordained or set apart for a special work, but the doctrine had been reduced to an empty ritual during the Dark Ages. Most of the time it was empty hands laid upon empty heads in a lifeless ceremony. In the 1948 restoration of the laying on of hands doctrine, many of the Scriptures in the Old and New Testaments were illuminated to the ministers. The Holy Spirit revealed the reality and power invested in this doctrine. Every restorational movement takes a truth out of the theoretical, philosophical, doctrinal realm and brings it into experiential actuality and practicable reality. The soverign work of the Holy Spirit demonstrated that as anointed ministers laid hands upon other ministers and saints, there could be a divine impartation and activation of the gifts of the Holy Spirit and ministries of Christ. Not only could healing, deliverance, and the Holy Ghost be imparted, but, by prophecy with laying on of hands, gifts of the Holy Spirit could be given and a person's calling and ministry could be revealed. I Timothy 4:14 was taken to "mean what it says and to say what it means." Paul told Timothy to "neglect not the **gift** that is in thee, which was **given thee by prophecy**, with the **laying on of the hands** of the presbytery."

Same Old Restorational Routine. The majority of Pentecostal denominations rejected this teaching and new type of singing-praise **Latter Rain** worship. Therefore, those who received this revelation and practiced this doctrine had to "go outside the camp bearing the reproach" *(Heb. 13:13)*. The Pentecostal ministers who accepted this movement had to leave their denomination in order to participate, just as the Baptist and Methodist ministers who accepted the Pentecostal movement had to leave their denominations when they received and started preaching the baptism of the Holy Ghost with speaking in other tongues. The same was true when historic Protestants accepted Holiness truth and when Catholics accepted Protestant Movement restorational truth.

The Church Journeys On

The restorational movements of the seven Doctrines of Christ are typified in the experiences the children of Israel had in their journey from Egypt to their Canaan Land. The children of Israel in Egypt, bound in the works of man, are typical of the Church during its Dark Ages under the domain of the Roman Catholic Church. Their coming out of Egypt by the blood of the Lamb is typical of the Protestant Movement. However, unlike the children of Israel, many in the Church built denominations around the truth of "repentance from dead works" and never journeyed on toward Canaan. Some built denominations after they crossed the Red Sea of "believer's baptism by immersion," settling there and journeying no further. Others journeyed on to complete separation through "sanctification" and built their denominations there. Still more journeyed on to the waters of Marah where they entered God's covenant of "divine healing" and then built denominations around that truth, but journeyed no further. There were those who journeyed on to the water from the rock which is typical of the baptism of the Holy Ghost with speaking in tongues, but they built denominations around that water and settled there. Finally, a few journeyed on to Mt. Sinai where they came to know their place in the Body of Christ and their functional position as typified by the arrangement of the 12 tribes and appointments in the service of the Tabernacle. Divine order was established but they were not in Canaan yet.

Trumpet Sounding "Catch-up" Call. The Church has not yet entered its promised Canaan Land. Only four of the seven Doctrines of Christ have been restored in experiential reality to the Church. The restorational trumpet of the Holy Spirit has been sounding forth in a new way for the last 15 years; not only to those camped at Mt. Sinai, but also to all of those dwelling in all their denominational camps, even those still in Egypt. The Holy Spirit is giving the invitation to every person throughout Chrtistendom to march on up to the front line of restored truth, thereby becoming established in all truth that has been restored since the beginning of the reformation up to and including the present truth. This *"catch-up* call" and move of the Holy Spirit has been called the "Charismatic Movement." The last stragglers are coming into present truth.

Trumpet Soon to Sound for Advancement. All things are about ready for advancement. The trumpet is about to sound and marching orders are about to be given for the Church to cross over its River Jordan (Doctrine of Christ #5), possess its promised Canaan Land (Doctrine of Christ #6) and then settle down to reign over its designated domain (Doctrine of Christ #7).

11

The Charismatic Movement

Early Rain, Latter Rain — Both Together. As previously mentioned, the Charismatic Movement was an extension and an expansion of the Latter Rain Movement. The Pentecostal Movement was the "Early Rain" of the 20th Century Church (which many believe to be the last century of the mortal Church). The "Laying on of Hands" Movement was the "Latter Rain" of the last century Church. The Charismatic Movement was symbolic of the outpouring of the "former rain and the latter rain in the first month" *(Joel 2:23).* All of the truths which have been restored since the beginning of the "period of the great restoration" have been propagated throughout Christendom by the Charismatic Movement.

Five-Hundred Years. Generally speaking, the Church had been in progressive restoration for approximately 500 years in preparation for the great Charismatic Renewal. Every Restorational movement since the Reformation had always affected only certain groups of people and countries, but the Charismatic Movement was truly a fulfillment of the prophecy, "I will pour out my Spirit upon **all** *flesh*"

(Acts 2:17). The Latter Rain Movement was primarily among Pentecostals; the Pentecostal Movement mainly affected Holiness churches; the Holiness Movement affected the historic Protestants; and the Protestant Movement mainly affected the Catholics. God did a new thing with the Charismatic Movement as manifested by its effect on every group: all Christendom from Pentecostals to Catholics and Eastern Orthodox; the rich and poor, professionals and laborers, government houses and jail cells, old and young, from national celebrities to the average man in the street. In fact, no segment of human existence was passed over by the Holy Spirit. **All flesh** was given an opportunity to be "established in the present truth" *(II Pet. 1:12)*.

Preparation for the Charismatic Movement

While the **Healing Evangelist** and **Latter Rain** ministers were orbiting the globe with the truth of "laying on of hands," God was building the launching pad for the next thrust of the Holy Spirit. That launching pad was the establishment of the Full Gospel Business Men's Fellowship International (FGBMFI). The ministry of FGBMFI was envisioned by Demos Shakarian, a successful California dairyman. From the 21-member organization that was launched in Clinton's Cafeteria in Los Angeles, in 1951, FGBMFI has expanded to every continent of the world and has chapters in virtually every major city.

New Image Given Tongues-Talkers. These chapters conduct their meetings and banquets in hotel ballrooms. These meetings provided a neutral place for Christian laymen and ministers from all areas of

Christendom to come and be exposed to the Baptism of the Holy Ghost with speaking in tongues. Historic Protestants and fundamentalist Christians had associated "Pentecostals" and "tongues speaking" with the *poor, uneducated* and *lower class* of society. They attributed these ways of worship to ignorance, simplicity, emotional instability and a substitute for a lack of the "better things of life." The wealthy and prestigious Full Gospel Business Men who conducted their chapter meetings in the best hotels available changed this impression. They freely and joyfully testified about their experience of "speaking in tongues" and unashamedly raised their hands and worshipped their heavenly Father. The FGBMFI ministry was used to reach the "up-and-outers" of religion and society as the **Teen Challenge** ministry was used to reach the "down-and-outers" of the ghettos and teenage gangs.

Nationwide Full Gospel television ministries such as **Oral Roberts'** ministry, and outstanding Pentecostal personalities such as **David J. du Plessis** (Mr. Pentecost), were instrumental in impressing the non-Pentecostals in favorable ways. There were many people and ministries that prepared the way for the Charismatic Movement. However, one particular incident is recognized as the time when the Charismatic Movement was launched.

Beginnings Of The Movement: 1960

The Charismatic Movement did not effectively penetrate non-Pentecostal churches on any mass scale until the national publication of Episcopalian Father Dennis Bennett's personal testimony of the baptism of the Holy Spirit with speaking in tongues. Bennett was forced to resign as pastor of the fashionable St. Mark's Episcopal Church in Van Nuys, California, in April, 1960. Leaders in historic denominations became interested in Father Bennett's testimony. These included Larry Christenson of the American Lutheran Church, Harald Bredesen of the Reformed Church of America, John L. Peters of the United Methodist Church, and many others.

The "Blessed Trinity Society", and their publication *Trinity Magazine* was uniquely instrumental in promoting the Charismatic Movement in the historic churches in the early 1960s. Several books and periodicals have been published which present the participants and promoters of the Charismatic Movement. It would require hundreds of pages to give proper recognition and due credit to all who contributed to the Charismatic cause.

The Word —
"Charismatic"

Prior to the mid-1960s very few people had heard the word **Charismatic.** Many had heard the word *"charisma"* used to describe an individual's charming personality and persuasive leadership ability, but had not heard the word used to identify a certain type of Christian or religious movement. The word **Charismatic** became the term used to identify those ministers and individual Christians in the historic and evangelical denominational churches who had received the *gift* of the *Holy Ghost* with *speaking in other tongues.* Those denominational Christians who received this **gift** preferred not to be identified as Pentecostals. Therefore the Greek word for gift *charismata* was used to identify what they had received. The Greek word *glossolalia* was chosen to describe what they did when they received the *charismata*. *Glossolalia* is a combination of two Greek words meaning "tongue-speaking." Those Charismatics did not describe themselves as "Pentecostals" who were *"baptized with the Holy Ghost and spoke in other tongues,"* but rather as those who had *received the "charismata" of the Holy Spirit accompanied with "glossolalia."*

The Pentecostals referred to their Holy Ghost praying as "talking in tongues," "other tongues," and, "praying in the Holy Ghost." The Charismatics described that same manifestation of the Holy Spirit as their "prayer and praise language," "language of the Spirit," and "praying with the Spirit." It was the same experiential truth received and manifested, but different terminology was used to explain the gift of the Holy Spirit.

Two Types of Charismatics

The author feels that *Charismatics can be classified into two main categories:*

1. Denominational Basic-Charismatics.
2. Non-denominational Present-truth Charismatics.

The **Basic-Charismatics** are the Christians who have received the *glossolalia* of the Holy Spirit into their lives but have never progressed into all the blessings of that dimension. To both the Catholic and Protestant Basic-Charismatic, remaining a member of his particular denomination is as important to him as his *glossolalia* experience. He is a secret disciple of the Holy Ghost who justifies his quietness by believing it is a private experience, not for public knowledge. He maintains his spiritual life by occasionally attending Present-truth Holy Ghost meetings, usually outside his denomination. Catholic Charismatics have been allowed to function as a Charismatic community within the structure of their Church.

The Basic-Charismatics will eventually become full fledged fruitful Present-truth Charismatics or they will wither on the vine. They will eventually have to make a decision between staying with their denomination, which may join the antichrist world church system, or going all the way with the anointed Body of Christ. Before Jesus returns, every Christian will have to make a decision between being identified with the humanistic denominational structured church system or the spiritual Present-truth restored Church. Basically, these individuals are called "Charismatic," but they are not the ones who made the Charismatic truths known around the world.

The **Present-truth Charismatics** of the 1960s, 1970s, and 1980s are Christians who have not only received the Holy Ghost with *glossolalia,* but have walked in all the truth which the Holy Spirit has restored to the Church up to the present time. They are the Christians from every segment of Christendom who "went outside the camp bearing the reproach" in order to walk in the fulness of restored truth. They are the ministers who established congregations which manifested all the "spiritual experiences" that have been restored to the Church. These are the ministers who practiced the four doctrines of Christ which have been restored to the Church during the last 450 years.

Catholic Charismatics

Surprised. The Latter Rain and Pentecostal Christians were taken by surprise when historic Protestant ministers began to receive the Holy Ghost. These

Protestants not only began speaking in tongues, but began to move into all restored truth and spiritual experiences. Many of these ministers started teaching and practicing Present-truth without being taught these things by man. It was a sovereign work of the Holy Spirit throughout the church world.

Shocked. However, it was completely shocking and challenging to Protestant Present-truth Christians when the Holy Spirit started filling Catholics with the same Holy Spirit experience and Present-truth knowledge. Many Protestants for over 400 years had identified the Roman Catholic Church as the "Harlot" church, forsaken and forgotten of God; a heathen religion clothed with Christian concepts and terminology. The average Protestant could not visualize Jesus or the Holy Spirit working with a person within the Catholic Church. The only way most Protestants could conceive of a Catholic receiving true salvation, or receiving the baptism of the Holy Spirit, was for him to come out of the Babylonish church system and renounce all ties with Catholicism. But the Holy Spirit refused to be limited and restricted by Catholic and Protestant attitudes toward each other.

Holy Spirit Moving Upon All Flesh. Jesus has decreed that the Holy Spirit shall be poured out upon all flesh. That includes all humanity regardless of whether they are Jew or Gentile; black, yellow, brown or white race; or where they may be found, in heathenism, Catholicism, Protestantism, in every continent on Earth. God is no respector of persons. He is standing at the "door" of every church. He is "knocking" on every heart saying, "If any person hear My voice and open the door, I will come into him and sup with him and he with Me" *(Rev. 3:20)*. "And the Spirit and the Bride are saying, Come. And those that are hearing His voice are saying, Come. And those that are thirsty are coming. And whosoever will, let him come and take of the water of life freely" *(Rev. 22:17)*. All those elected to be true sheep are hearing their heavenly Shepherd's voice and are following Him into all presently restored truth. This includes those within Catholicism.

Development of the Catholic Charismatic Community

"The Charismatic Movement has become a significant feature of a larger religious awakening in the Roman Catholic Church, of which Vatican Council II (1962-5) was the first widely publicized expression. The purpose of calling the council, according to then Pope John XXIII, was to revive and reform the Roman Catholic Church, so that historic divisions of Christendom might be reconciled and reunited in one visible church *(John 17:22-23)*. At the opening of Vatican Council II, Pope John had prayed, 'O Holy Spirit . . . Renew Thy wonders in this our day, as by a *new Pentecost . . .*' (Abbott, *Documents of Vatican II*, 1965.)

"Pope John died in June 1963, and Pope Paul VI directed completion of the work of the council. Church liturgy and government were reformed to remove historic Protestant objections to reunion with Catholics. The liturgy was rewritten in national languages of the people and was revised to permit greater congregational participation. An international, elected Synod of Bishops was organized to provide more representative government, and to inform and advise the pope on the proper application of Scripture to Christian belief and practice. The council's *Decree on Ecu-*

menism (November 21, 1964) was not formally imple-
mented by the Synod of Bishops until 1967, when
Episcopal Commissions on Ecumenical Affairs were
appointed in each National Conference of Catholic
Bishops, including the United States.

"The Vatican Council II *Decree of Ecumenism* provided for three kinds of ecumenical activity with other
Christian denominations, including: (1) home meetings
for prayer and Bible study among laymen on a devotional, but not too intellectual level, under episcopal
supervision; (2) cooperation between Roman Catholics
and Protestants in activities of common concern, such
as public education and morality, or social and cultural events; and (3) theological dialogue between
bishops and official denominational representatives
as a basis for reunion.

"By 1974 such theological dialogue had been established between Roman Catholic bishops and Southern
Baptists, American Baptists, Lutherans, Methodists,
Episcopalians, Presbyterians and Reformed, Disciples
of Christ, and Eastern Orthodox. As a result, 20 consensus statements had been approved for publication
and reaction in each communion. Pope Paul interpreted the council's *Decree on Ecumenism* to mean
that 'the reconciliation of Christians . . . must necessarily start from an inner conversion of heart . . . from
spiritual renewal.' American Catholic bishops urged
'each Christian Church and Community to examine
its own fidelity to the Gospel to eliminate from its
own tradition whatever dims the image of Christ.
Thus renewal becomes a vital part of reunion' (Wessel,
*Celebration of the Tenth Anniversary of the Second
Vatican Council's Decree on Ecumenism,* November
21, 1974).

"Amid such interdenominational revival, fellowship, and dialogue, the Catholic Charismatic Movement came into being. In February 1967 four faculty members of Duquesne University of Pittsburgh received a Pentecostal experience in a Protestant Charismatic prayer group, as a result of reading David Wilkerson's *Cross and the Switchblade* and John Sherrill's *They Speak With Other Tongues.* The home of an Assemblies of God deacon was the place that nine Catholics of Notre Dame received 'the baptism in the Holy Spirit' the following month. They then held a weekend retreat on the campus, attended by 80 faculty and students from Notre Dame, St. Mary's and Michigan State University.

"By November 1969 the Charismatic Movement in Roman Catholic Churches had received the attention of Catholic bishops meeting in Washington, D.C. Under their direction, Roman Catholic Charismatic prayer groups emphasized varied leadership, group edification, private use of tongues, and obedience to the bishops. *Christianity Today* has reported that Roman Catholic pastors are using spiritual gifts in their administration of the sacraments.

"In 1970 Roman Catholics in the United States began holding Annual National Conferences on Charismatic Revewal. In 1973 the first International Conference on Charismatic Renewal was held. The third such conference in 1975 was held in Rome and received the greetings of Pope Paul VI. That pope encouraged delegates to demonstrate their Christian love and joy by gratefully sharing their spiritual gifts with the world.

"The Charismatic and Pentecostal Movements have made rapid advances in South America. Typical is the account of the beginnings of Charismatic Renewal in Buenos Aires, Argentina, in a prayer group of 15 pastors and missionaries of Anglican, Mennonite, and Roman Catholic faiths. In 1972 a Roman Catholic, Pedro Rodriguez, age 19, began preaching in a shopping center in one of the cities of Colombia. Within two years he had organized a church of 600 members, who became active in street preaching, sick visitation, and food distribution to the poor.

"In Brazil, Manoel de Mello in 1974 erected 'the largest Pentecostal temple in the world' seating 25,000. In December 1974 the Jotabeche Pentecostal Methodist Church of Santiago, Chile, dedicated a new temple-cathedral for 15,000. A congregation of 80,000 is now four times the size it was 10 years earlier in 1964. Members attend one service a month on a rotating basis, and on other Sundays attend one of 100 classes in the city, shepherded by assistant pastors. These churches have continued to grow tremendously. The Central Full Gospel Church in Korea is a living example. It has now become one of the largest churches in the world with a congregation of over 100,000.

"Penetration of established denominations by Pentecostal and Latter Rain practices may be expected to have a two-fold effect. Charismatic Renewal will split some churches, as have all historic revivals of the past.

"In the 1970s Charismatic churches were among the fastest growing Christian communities in the world. Because of their phenomenal growth, attitudes began to change from toleration to active interest.

Moves Toward Unity

"The 1977 Kansas City Conference on Charismatic Renewal in the Churches attracted about 45,000 dele-

gates to Arrowhead Stadium for four evenings. *Roman Catholic Charismatic Renewal Services* coordinated the entire conference program planned by a 14-man interdenominational committee. After Catholics, the next largest groups in attendance were the Independents, Lutherans, and Methodists. Other conference sponsoring groups included Baptists, Mennonites, Pentecostals, Episcopalians, Presbyterians, and Messianic Jews.

"A significant achievement of the conference was the establishment of vital spiritual fellowship on a national level between Charismatic Catholics and Protestants — an unusual experience without precedent in the history of the church since the breach of the Reformation Era. Fellowship between Catholics and Protestants at the conference was realized at both devotional and theological levels. Protestant Charismatics probably wish the Roman Church would modify its historic attitude toward veneration of Mary and the saints. As such theological differences continue, Catholics and Protestants, Charismatic among them, will hopefully continue to co-operate in common public interests in a spirit of devotion to Christ" (Christian International College, *Church History Undergraduate Course No. HT-10,* Phoenix, Arizona Christian University, 1978, pp. 69-72).

Holy Spirit Invasion. Recent statistics indicate that millions of Catholics testify to being born-again and baptized in the Holy Spirit. Multi-millions are participants of the Charismatic renewal within the Catholic Church. Every Protestant denomination has been invaded by the Holy Spirit and hundreds of thousands have become participants in the Charismatic renewal. A good number of the Southern Baptist ministers have become Charismatics. The same is true with varying percentages of every Protestant denomination. Some of the ministers and Christian laymen in these various denominations have remained in their denomination as Basic-Charismatics. Others voluntarily and some involuntarily left their denomination and became Present-truth Charismatics.

Development of Charismatic Doctrine

Present-truth Charismatics base their doctrine upon the infallible Scriptures. Their creed is Christ. Their tenets of faith, the whole Word of God. Their unity is based on the love of God and fellowship in the Holy Spirit. More specifically, they accept the Apostles' Creed and practice the *four major doctrines* which have been restored to the Church in *experiential reality*. Their ways of worship include all the *manifestations* and *spiritual experiences* restored to the Church during the last 500 years.

The Extreme Swingers And The Middle Hangers. The Charismatic Movement was not initially instrumental in restoring one of the seven doctrines of Christ, but was mightily used of God. It made known to all Christendom every truth and spiritual experience which the Holy Ghost had restored to the Church. Every truth restored within the last 500 years has produced three classes of participants. Truth is restored like the pendulum of a clock. It swings extremely to the right, and then to the left, and finally hangs in a straight line with a balanced message hanging in the middle of the two extremes.

The Swing
of the Pendulum
# of Restoration-Truth

A brief resume of the major truths restored over the last five centuries will reveal these three groups.

1500s — Justification By Faith

This pendulum of truth swung from one extreme of Salvation by works with no faith, to the other extreme of all faith and no Salvation by works. Those who walked on in the truth came to a balance in the middle. They were justified by faith, demonstrating their faith by works of obedience to righteous living. There were the theological extremes of Calvinism and Arminianism with those who took the balance between the two extremes.

1600s — Water Baptism

There were the extremes of those who preached that a person was not saved until he was water-baptized by immersion versus those who put little value on water baptism. There were those who taught that a baby could receive all the blessings of Christianity through water baptism and there were those who taught a child could receive nothing from the Lord until the age of 12. Those who walked on in truth developed a balance between these extremes.

1700s — Holiness,
Sanctification, and Perfectionism

There were the extremes between legalism and liberty. The legalist believed all sports, amusements, and current fashions were sinful for Christians. The liberty group declared grace gave license for all things proclaiming that "to the pure all things are pure." Sanctification had extremes from *one eternal sanctifying experience* to the need of being *sanctified daily*. Perfectionism had its extremes between those who made no allowance for a Christian ever sinning, and those who believed a Christian must sin a little every day. Thank God there is a balance between these extremes of a divine truth.

1800s — Second Coming of Jesus

There were the extremes between those who proclaimed His imminent return and set dates for His coming, using every world event and calamity as proof, and those who did not believe in a literal return of Jesus Christ. The great theological controversies were over their eschatological viewpoints concerning Pre-millennialism, Post-millennialism, and A-millennialism. Those who were pre-millennialist argued over the time of the rapture, whether pre-tribulation, mid-tribulation, or post-tribulation.

1880s — Divine Faith Healing

The theological controversy was whether the stripes Jesus received provided healing for the physical body as His death on the cross provided forgiveness of sins. In other words, was there physical healing in the atonement of Christ Jesus? Those who did accept the teaching of healing in the atonement developed different beliefs: those who believed that divine faith was the only acceptable remedy for the physical healing of Christians, and on the opposite side, those who exhausted all natural means before turning to Christ Jesus for supernatural divine healing.

1900s — Holy Ghost
Baptism and Other Tongues

The theological problem was whether the "unknown tongues" are the only valid scriptural evidence of one having received the gift of the Holy Ghost. Among the Pentecostals who accepted tongues-talking there were the two groups: those who believed a person was not saved until he spoke in tongues, and then those who believed there were several different divine proofs (such as the Holiness Movement proclaimed) of the Holy Ghost baptism other than tongues. The Pentecostals also went to extremes in Godhead concepts of Jesus Only and tritheism. They also developed hard religious attitudes concerning water baptism formulas.

There were differences of opinion concerning the proper terminology for describing this "other tongues" experience; whether *baptized* or *Spirit-filled;* whether *gift of* or Baptism *with, in, into, by* or *of* the Holy Ghost. The terminology used did not hinder the Holy Spirit from baptizing the believers.

1940s — Laying on
of Hands and Prophecy

The issue was whether Holy Ghost-filled ministers had the right and power to impart and activate spiritual gifts within the believer; whether personal prophecy by prophets and other ministers could be used to reveal the calling and ministries of members in the Body of Christ. This pendulum of truth had its far swings to the right and left before becoming balanced in the middle. Some Latter Rain Ministers relegated prophecy to certain appointed apostles and prophets, while others allowed anyone, at any time, without proper supervision, to prophesy to anyone else.

1950s — Worship and Praise

The difference in scriptural emphasis was whether saints should shout or sing praises in worship; whether praise and body ministry should play a major or minor role in the church service. Again, there were the extremes — those who believed the gathering together of the saints was only for worshipping God and perfecting each other in Christ and those who believed the whole role of the Church was to evangelize the world with very little time being given to long church services of praise and prophecy.

1960s — Demonology

One of the first controversies to develop within the Charismatic Movement was that of the relationship of demons to Christians. The issue was whether a born-again, Holy Ghost-baptized Christian could have demon activity within his or her life to the extent that the demons needed to be cast out. The controversy developed between those who taught that every negative thought, action, and physical affliction was a demon which had to be exorcized before the Christian could change or be healed; and those who maintained that, because a person had at one time had all his past sins covered by the blood of Jesus, a devil could not cross the blood line. In the second case, the Christian would be immune from any demonic activity within his or her life or body. By the mid-1970s most Charismatics had developed a balanced doctrine and practice concerning demonology.

1970s — Discipleship and Church Structure

The Holy Spirit was preparing the Church for great numerical growth. Many churches in South America and Korea developed the concept of one large church congregation with numerous cell groups meeting in homes of the Church members. The Holy Spirit was seeking to bring mutual respect among the ministers and a willing recognition and submission to each other. The Holy Spirit was restoring theocratic government to the Church and restoring the proper chain of command. There was a restoration of family life. Ministers developed proper priorities: God first, wife and family second, and then ministry.

However, when the pendulum of truth swings, some are pushed into extremes. Some taught and developed a Christian leadership pyramid, chain-of-command. The Pastor became almost a papal leader to those under him. All single Christian women had to have a male headship covering to be in divine order. All decisions had to be made by leadership, even daily and personal activities of members. Some groups went to other extremes of doing away with church structure by changing from pastorship to co-eldership. Some disbanded the weekly united meeting of a large congregation, breaking it up into small house meeting cell groups only.

There was a "Jesus Movement" that came out of the worldly young peoples' rebellion against society (the hippie movement). They were more inclined to anti-church structure. Nevertheless, they helped deliver the Church from some of its ritualistic traditions.

Before the end of the decade most non-denominational Present-truth Charismatic churches had developed a balance in doctrine and practice concerning *discipleship, shepherding, family life,* and *Church struc-ture.* The Eternal Church moves to the Middle of the Stream of restored truth and flows toward God's sea of fulness of truth.

1970s — Prosperity, Faith Message, Word People

For years God had been trying to deliver the Church from its teaching that spirituality and poverty were synonymous. The practice of monasticism and asceticism that developed during the Dark Ages were still influencing the Church. Those from the Holiness, Pentecostal, and Latter Rain movements were still under the impression that it was worldly and carnal to have wealth, modern conveniences, and wear and drive the latest and best.

Oral Roberts was one of the first to propagate the idea that God is a good God and desires Christians to be in health and prosper even as their soul prospers. But it was not until the 1970s that the truth started being practiced enough to become a world wide controversy in the Church. The teaching of victorious, prosperous, healthy living in the natural and spiritual came from three different camps: (1) Oral Roberts' ministry of teaching the seed faith principle of sowing and reaping, of sowing finances to reap finances; (2) Robert Schueller's ministry of positive living and success principles; and (3) the group of ministers who became known as "prosperity preachers," "the Faith Message," "Word people." A few of the well known leaders were Kenneth Hagin, Kenneth Copeland, Hobart Freeman, and many more. The Holy Spirit was striving to bring the Body of Christ to a new faith level and a greater revelation of truth found in the Holy Scriptures. Nevertheless, as in the activation and restoration of every truth, different groups became "stuck" on the extremes of the swing of the pendulum of truth.

Some groups taught and developed the attitude that any Christian who was not wealthy and healthy was either an unbeliever or out of fellowship with God. They taught that all trials and tests were of the devil, that God does not try the righteous. If you did not have a miracle every day and prosperity all the way, you were not a faith person. Others went to extremes on confession and positive declarations until it approximated the doctrine of Christian Science. Still others swung to the opposite side, declaring that believers have no control over their lives. They must accept whatever comes their way as the will of God; that poverty and sickness are used of God to perfect the saints. Therefore, sickness and poverty must be suffered gracefully and thankfully.

Also, the old controversy that arose during the divine healing movement of the 1800s arose among the faith people. Anyone who used medicine, consulted a physician, or had surgery was looked down upon by the "Faith people." Regardless of the differences in the various camps, these ministers were instrumental in establishing the Church on the biblical principles of overcoming faith, prosperity, faith healing, power of the Word, and the necessity of a continual positive confession. They wrote hundreds of books and made thousands of cassette tapes giving scriptural principles for prosperity, health, and happiness.

1980s — Unity of Church, Gifts of Spirit, Resurrection Life

There will be many issues that will come to the forefront among the Present-truth and Charismatic Christians. There will be major issues and minor issues. Some of the minor issues will be as follows:

1. Controversies over the "Electronic Church" i.e., what part Christian television plays in church structure. Regardless of the opposition from some organizations and ministers, Christian television networks will play a major role in God's eternal plan for the last generation Church.

2. God's preparation and perfecting of the Body of Christ will be intensified during the 1980s. Some of the greatest supernatural performances ever recorded by the Church will occur. At the same time the Church will enter into its *baptism of fire,* thus purging the Church and burning up all the *chaff* and *dross,* leaving the *wheat* and *pure gold.*

3. There will be great discussions among the Charismatics concerning the relationship of Natural Israel (Jews) and the Church; whether there will be a Jewish group of believers to carry on the work of the Lord, or whether there will be one great Body and Army of the Lord. Before the 1980s are finished there will come a true insight from the Lord which will enable the true believers to come to unity of the faith. Of course, many of the old issues will remain among some, concerning the time of the rapture and how the end time will be climaxed.

The Unity of the Church. There will also be some major issues which will cause great excitement in the Church. The number one issue that will arise among those who are believing for the full restoration of the Church, and among Charismatic and Evangelical Christendom, will be the fulfillment of the prayer of Jesus in John 17 for the unity of the Church. Some will zealously push unity to the extent of deleting important restorational truth for the sake of unity among Charismatics, Pentecostals, and Evangelicals. Others will be so afraid of compromise that they will stay in their own little corner of the kingdom of God and refuse to flow together with the whole Body of Christ. There will be two drives during this time, one a true move by the Holy Spirit, and the other a counterfeit by the spirit of deception.

Part Played by World Council. The World Council of Churches will be spearheading a move for all religions of the world to come together under one head as a great world church for the purpose of unity and the preservation of peace. Satan's goal is to set up a millennium of peace without the Prince of Peace. The Holy Spirit is working night and day around the world throughout the Body of Christ motivating anointed ministers to speak of unity and the fulfilling of Jesus' prayers for the oneness of the Body of Christ. His prayer will be fulfilled, but the Holy Spirit will have to give the revelation and application for its fulfillment.

The second major issue will arise within the Charismatic-Present-truth churches. There will come great discussions concerning the operation of all the gifts of the Spirit. Should every saint function in one or more of the gifts of the Spirit, or should just a few proven ministries participate? Should the operation of these gifts be controlled and delivered only from the pulpit or should they be opened up to the whole body of believers? It will be a time similar to the days of Martin Luther. The pope said it would be dangerous to put a Bible in every believer's hands. But Luther said he would make every believer a priest unto God and as knowledgeable of the Scripture as the pope himself. There will be modern day Luthers with the same attitude concerning the saints and the gifts of the Spirit.

A third issue to come forth in the late 1980s and possibly into the early 1990s will result from the greatest restorational revelation ever to come to the Church since the beginning of the Reformation. The Holy Spirit illumination of the Scriptures on the last day truth will bring the Church to the experiential fulfillment of Doctrine No. 5 of Hebrews 6:1,2. It will be as revolutionary and world shaking to the 20th Century Charismatic Christian world as Paul's teaching on "salvation without the law and circumcision" was to the Jews of his day, and as Martin Luther's teaching on "justification by faith without pope, priest, or doing penance" was to the Catholic Church of his day.

Latter Rain
Charismatic Movement Churches

Three Restorational Divisions. No denomination has been formed from any of the *three divisions* of this movement; not from the Deliverance Evangelism, Latter-Rain or Charismatic divisions. Although no denomination has been formed, numerous evangelistic centers, ministerial fellowships, and thousands of independent, nondenominational churches have been established.

Deliverance Evangelism Division

Hundreds of evangelistic centers were established throughout the world. Four, among many, are mentioned.

1. **Oral Roberts' Evangelistic Association.** Oral Roberts' ministry evolved from that of pastor in the 1940s to tent-evangelist, to radio and television minister, to establishing Oral Roberts University and now the City of Faith Hospital and Health Center in the 1980s. His membership (mailing list) numbers into the millions.

2. **T. L. Osborne Evangelistic Association.** He is not as well known today as other television ministers, such as Oral Roberts and Rex Humbard, but he played a vital role in this movement. Most of his ministry of healing and miracles was conducted in overseas missions.

3. **Voice of Healing and Christ For the Nations Institute (CFNI).** Gordon Lindsay established *The Voice of Healing* magazine and headquarters in Dallas, Texas, in the early 1950s to promote the hundreds of Deliverance Evangelists. He wrote hundreds of books dealing with different aspects of the movement. In the early 1970s, he established the Christ For the Nations Institute. CFNI trains hundreds of students each year in the present truths of this movement.

4. **Kenneth Hagin and Rhema Bible Institute.** Kenneth Hagin was one of the early deliverance ministers. He faithfully ministered the Pentecostal truths and faith principles of which E. W. Kenyon wrote. He started teaching the pro-

sperity faith message and produced some strong ministers in this area such as Kenneth Copeland. He established the Rhema Bible College which is training hundreds in the message of faith healing, deliverance, and financial prosperity.

Latter Rain Movement Division

The Latter Rain Movement never developed a national headquarters, but each section of North America developed a strong church which became a rallying point and example for the others. Five of these will be discussed.

1. **Western United States and Canada.** Crescent Beach Bible Conference. This conference was directed by the Rev. Reginald Layzell, pastor of Glad Tidings Temple, Vancouver, British Columbia, Canada. It was the yearly meeting place for the Latter Rain (Revival Fellowship) churches on the West Coast. This yearly conference was started in the early 1950s and continued until the mid-1960s. It evolved into the present day Revival Fellowship convention which meets annually during the last week in January in Southern California. There were other Latter Rain churches on the West Coast such as Wings of Healing in Portland, Oregon, and the Rev. Earl Lee's Church in Los Angeles.

2. **Midwest United States (Bethesda Missionary Temple, Detroit, Michigan).** This church was co-pastored by M. D. Beall and her son James Beall. Bethesda Temple was instrumental in exposing hundreds of ministers to the Latter Rain Movement and thousands of Chris-

tians were brought into the movement through the church. Bethesda Temple is one of the few churches in the midwestern United States which has maintained a balance in Latter Rain doctrine and practice. Dr. James Beall has continued into the 1980s as pastor of the church, which presently has a weekly attendance of approximately 4,000. Pastor James Beall and his sister, Patricia Beall Gruits, have published several books which are used among Latter Rain and Charismatic churches.

3. **East Coast United States (Elim Bible Institute, Lima, New York).** Elim Bible Institute was founded by Ivan Q. Spencer in 1924 as a Pentecostal Bible college. However, when the Latter Rain Movement came, they accepted its scriptural practices and teachings. The founder and his son, Carlton, who was made president of EBI in 1951, became influential ministers in the movement. EBI remains an active college training its students in the Word of God, including Latter Rain doctrine.

4. **Australia and New Zealand. Ray Jackson,** after returning to America from missionary work in Japan and Indonesia, attended the meetings in Saskatchewan, Canada. Hands were laid upon him by the presbytery and prophecy came forth that God wanted him to go to Australia. He became an apostle of this movement in Australia and New Zealand. Jackson is presently pastoring a large Present-truth church in Melbourne, Australia. **Rob Wheeler,** a New Zealander, was a co-laborer with Ray Jackson. He is pastoring a large congregation in Auckland, North Island, New

Zealand. **Peter Morrow** and **Kevin Conner** were outstanding ministers of this movement in these countries. *Peter Morrow* is presently pastoring Christ's Church New Life Center in South Island, New Zealand. *Kevin Conner,* an Australian, has travelled around the world as a conference speaker, authored several books and is presently in the United States serving as dean and teacher at Portland Bible College.

5. **Missionary Outreach: World M.A.P.** Ralph Mahoney envisioned the World MAP (Missionary Assistance Plan) in the late 1950s. It has grown into a worldwide ministry reaching into over half the nations of the World. Ralph Mahoney is in fellowship with all of the aforementioned Latter Rain restorational church groups. The World MAP vision and ministry is to inspire and establish Missionaries and National Church leaders in Present-truth Charismatic realities. This is accomplished by "Spiritual Renewal Seminars for Church Leaders," Tape-a-month, *Acts* Magazine, *World Map Digest,* and many other means.

Ralph's heartbeat is a strong, united Church in the Third World. He devotes all of his time and resource to see Church leaders in Asia, Africa, and Latin America come into the dynamic of the Spirit-filled life. *(World MAP Digest,* 900 Glenoaks, Burbank, California 91502, March, 1981 issue, p. 5.)

Most Latter Rain churches during the 1960s established their own local church-oriented Bible colleges.

Charismatic Division

It is difficult to specify any particular rallying point for Charismatics. It depends on their denominational origin more than geographical location. The Catholic Charismatics have their meeting places and yearly conventions. There are historic church Charismatics such as Episcopalian, Lutheran, and Presbyterian which have their own annual meetings. Many of the Evangelical-Fundamentalist churches such as the Southern Baptist Charismatics have their annual conventions besides their regular Southern Baptist Convention. There are Pentecostal and Latter Rain Charismatics who have their own separate yearly and regional conventions. Almost every major city in the United States and Canada now has an outstanding Charismatic church with a thousand or more members. In the writer's home city of Phoenix, Arizona, there are scores of Charismatic churches, three of which have a weekly attendance of 1,200 to 3,500. To designate one as more influential than the others would create more division and strife than unity. Most Charismatic churches in a local area do not have fellowship meetings. In some areas the Charismatic ministers will have an occasional ministers' breakfast.

Charismatic magazines and Christian television stations have become more of a rallying point for the worldwide Charismatic Movement than certain churches or cities. A few of the prominent Charismatic magazines and Christian television networks are listed.

Charismatic Magazines

1. **The Voice.** This magazine was envisioned by Demos Shakarian, president of the Full Gospel

Business Men's Fellowship International (FGBMFI). It was developed to be the voice of the FGBMFI chapter meetings, regional, and national conventions. It also gave notice of Charismatic conventions and testimonies of thousands of people from all walks of life who had received the baptism of the Holy Ghost. Ministers from every Christian denomination gave their testimonies of receiving the *charismata* of the Holy Ghost with *glossolalia*. This magazine has probably influenced people toward the Charismatic Movement more than all others.

2. **Logos Journal.** Dan Malachuk envisioned and produced this magazine and a book publishing house called *Logos International. Logos Journal* has made the Christian populace knowledgeable about the Charismatic Movement with its announcements, articles, and numerous book reviews. Logos International has become the largest and most widely known publisher of books by Charismatic authors.

3. **New Wine.** Originated to give emphasis to the discipleship teaching of the Charismatic Movement, its main contributors of articles being Don Basham, Bob Mumford, Derek Prince, Ern Baxter, and Charles Simpson.

4. **Charisma.** The *Charisma* magazine was a latecomer to the Charismatic Movement but has become an outstanding magazine in quality and content. The Rev. Roy Harthern, pastor of Calvary Temple in Orlando, Florida, inspired and supported its publication.

5. **Christian Life.** This magazine for years functioned as a voice for fundamental-evangelical-

ism. However, in the 1970s, it began to favor and cover more of the activities of the Charismatic Movement.

Christian Television Networks

1. **Christian Broadcasting Network** (Virginia Beach, Virginia). CBN was the first Charismatic television station to reach national prominence. It was envisioned by Pat Robertson, a Charismatic Baptist minister and the son of a United States Senator. In its early days of broadcasting, it had a tremendous number of Charismatic manifestations of praise with uplifted hands, joyful weeping and rejoicing, gifts of the Holy Spirit, miracles of healings and answered prayers for all kinds of human needs. The people knelt and prayed, clapped their hands, and rejoiced. Thousands of testimonies were received over and over again describing outstanding healings and miracles of answered prayer. The network did not come into existence as a profit-making business. CBN was built and supported by supernatural supply through the donations and free will offerings of the Body of Christ members. (A few sinners gave some too.) Charismatic Christian television was taking the full Gospel into homes of those who would never have knowingly darkened the door of a Charismatic church. The 700 Club became the doorway for hundreds of Charismatic ministries to be exposed to a greater segment of the Body of Christ.

2. **Trinity Broadcasting Network** (Santa Ana, California). Paul and Jan Crouch pioneered the TBN Christian television network into its

present worldwide ministry. They, likewise, came into prominence through determination, prayer, tears, and the supernatural enablement of the Holy Spirit. They are seeking to bring outstanding conventions and meetings to the Christian world via the television medium. More than anything else, television has been used as a rallying point for all Charismatics.

3. **Praise The Lord Television Network** (Charlotte, North Carolina). The PTL Christian television network was the result of the vision and ministry of its president, the Rev. Jim Bakker. It was produced, as was CBN, by supernatural directions and financial donations of the Body of Christ. Jim Bakker had the original idea for a Christian talk show on Christian television. It was only natural, therefore, for him to develop the PTL Club which functioned similarly to the 700 Club. Jim and his wife, Tammy, have sought to keep the program's ministry in the original vision and to allow Pentecostal-Charismatic manifestations in the power of the Holy Spirit on the PTL Club and other programming.

Future for Christian Television

What part will television play in this last generation of the mortal Church? *Television* has done and will continue to do for the Charismatic Movement and the next restorational movement what the *printing press* did for the Reformation. Every movement has had new inventions in communications and travel come into existence to carry that truth to the ends of the Earth. The **Protestant Movement** had the *print-*

ing press. The **Holiness Movement** had its truths spread around the world faster by the invention of *steamships, trains, telegraph, telephone,* and *newspapers.* The **Pentecostal Movement** was given the *automobile, radio,* and *propeller airplanes.* The **Charismatic Movement** was equipped with the *jet airplane, television,* and *electronic recording equipment.*

Greater Works. A minister today can preach in the major cities of the world faster than John Wesley in his day could preach in the major cities of one state. Television ministers can reach more people with one television broadcast than past movement preachers reached in a lifetime. However, the Church has barely scratched the surface concerning the way God has planned to use *television* in fulfilling His eternal will in this world.

Related Events During the Charismatic Movement

Most of the "isms" and "schisms" of past movements were still plaguing Christendom. Most of the Latter Rain participants came out of Pentecostal organizations. They were far removed from many of the battles that the Evangelicals and historic Protestants were waging. Nevertheless, many things were happening which affected this movement.

The World Council of Churches was birthed in 1948. It promoted religious modernism, liberal theology, and even agnosticism in some of the seminaries under its influence. A spirit of lethargy and competition between Jewish, Catholic, and Protestant religions enabled Madalyn O'Hara, an athiest, to entice Congress to remove prayer from the public schools. With God taken out of public schools, and the teaching of

Freudian psychology and "Spockism" to our young people, a willful and rebellious generation of young people was produced.

At the same time, America was facing a cultural revolution. The assassinations of President Kennedy and Robert Kennedy, the shooting of the champion of integration — Martin Luther King, the Watergate episode and the resignation of President Nixon, race riots, the hippie movement, college campus sit-ins, union strikes, America's involvement in "no-win" wars in Korea and Vietnam, caused many Americans to become disillusioned with their government and its society. The "God is dead" doctrine, prayer taken out of public schools, the rise of homosexuality and sexual permissiveness, motivated by rock and roll music and gyrating singers and rock bands, along with the invasion of drugs producing dope addicts, acid heads, and street gangs, developed a godless and immoral generation of Americans.

The devilish spirit of Communism was spreading like a cancer throughout the world. All of China fell to Communism in the late 1940s. The Iron Curtain was drawn across Northern Europe enslaving most of the Slavic nations under its godless and cruel control. Germany was split in two by its Berlin Wall. The whole continent of Africa went through revolutions, inner strife and war as colonies and states sought their independence and self-government. The Far East was having its historic wars. The Korean conflict and Vietnam conflicts were catastrophic and debasing to American prestige.

A Year of Important Happenings, 1948. The most significant prophetic occurrence in the world situation was the establishment of Israel as a self-governing state, a nation unto itself. The Jews were in their own country again for the first time in more than two millennia. May 14, 1948 was a memorable day in the annals of history. Israel became a time-clock of the prophetic times to the dispensationalist theologians. The Six-Day War in 1967 was further proof of God having a hand in their return and preservation as a nation.

From Atomic to Space Age. The world had come into the atomic age and was moving into the space age. Russia and America were sending space capsules into space. Men went around the world in space and landed on the moon. New inventions of war arsenals became so vast and mighty, staggering the imaginations. Russia and America alone have enough destructive power stockpiled to annihilate every living creature on planet Earth.

Bible Translations. Positive things were happening too. The 20th Century Church was experiencing what the 16th Century Church experienced in the translation of Bibles. More translations were produced during the period of this movement than had ever been produced before.

God's Counterattack. The *Jesus Movement* and *Teen Challenge* became God's answer to the hippies and teenage gangs. The *Charismatic Movement* was the answer to the drug culture and to an immoral and godless society. The supernatural reality and joy of the Holy Ghost presented a Christianity which offered substance and reality to the disillusioned generation.

Billy Graham. The Holy Spirit raised up a 20th Century "John the Baptist" in the person of **Billy Graham.** He became a national evangelical figure in

1948 and has continued as a prominent minister during the full time of this movement. Graham never did publicly accept or reject the Charismatic Movement. He was the one great figure in Christendom who held the respect of both Evangelicals and Charismatics. He filled some of the largest stadiums in America and around the world. Thousands were saved in almost every meeting. He shook lukewarm Protestant Christianity with his message of repentance and the necessity of being born again. Graham was instrumental in making the church world conscious of its need for a personal relationship with Jesus Christ. He will go down in church history as one of the greatest evangelists of the 20th Century.

More recently, the church world has had its Carl McIntires, who warned of the evils of Communism and the World Council of Churches; its present-day James Robinsons and Jerry Falwells, who preached against corruption, immorality and promoted the Moral Majority.

Dr. Don Howard with the ministry of the Accelerated Christian Education schools and others such as Omega and Beca gave the Christian an alternative to godless, immoral public schools. Almost every large Evangelical and Charismatic Church now has an ACE school, grades Kindergarten through 12, or one similar to it. Christian International and other similar extension colleges are producing self-teaching Bible college courses and helping churches throughout the country to start their own Bible college program within the local church.

The Church has been a *sleeping giant,* but it is now *awake* and *on the move.* It is now being prepared to begin its conquering march as the Army of the Lord.

The **inventions** that affected communications and travel are the jet airplane with its capacity for commercial travel; the multiplicity of automobiles with faster speeds and greater efficiency; television, video tapes, eight-track and cassette tapes; and satellite broadcasting by radio and television.

The Latter Rain-Charismatic Movement Summarized

Its **purpose** was to restore the experiential reality of the biblical practice of "laying on of hands," thereby restoring to the Church the Fourth Doctrine of Christ. The **place** of its birth (Latter Rain emphasis) was Canada. It then spread throughout the United States and the world. The Latter Rain-Charismatic Movement has never recognized any man or group as head of the Movement, but certain men were notable in making known and maintaining certain truths: laying on of hands for healing, Oral Roberts; laying on of hands with prophecy by the presbytery for revealing one's place in the Body of Christ, Reginald Layzell. Originally making known Charismatic truths to the rest of the church world were Demos Shakarian, David du Plessis, and Dennis Bennet. Making historic Charismatics conscious of the reality of demon activity was Derek Prince. Kenneth Hagin proclaimed the faith message for prosperity and health.

The majority of the **people** who participated and the **ministers** who propagated "Deliverance Evangelism" and "Latter Rain" truths came from the Pentecostal Movement churches. Those who originally were called Charismatics were ministers and members of historic Protestant churches, then Catholics, Holiness/Evangelical/Fundamentalist. Finally many Pentecostals and Latter Rain brethren reluctantly accepted the word "Charismatic" to identify those who were Holy Ghost-filled, tongues-talking, praising God, Present-truth Christians.

The **message** was three-fold:

1. Laying on of Hands for *healing, Holy Ghost baptism, deliverance, Body of Christ member-ship ministry,* and *activation of gifts of Spirit.*
2. Proclaiming all the Pentecostal and Latter Rain Movement truths to denominational Christians and members. (This was mainly done by newly Holy Ghost-baptized denominational ministers.)
3. Preaching the maturity of the Body of Christ and victorious Christian living spiritually, physically and financially.

The **ministry** was preaching of the Word accompanied by healings, prophecy, and revelation gifts. This caused many souls to be saved, spiritual growth of Christians, numerical growth of churches, and the prosperity of the saints.

The **result** was that the Eternal Church reached its Mt. Sinai experience and remained there until divine order was established, until all Christendom had an opportunity to move to the front line of present truth. The Church has now been encamped at this mountain of Truth for over 30 years. The angel of the Church is about to sound the trumpet declaring, "**You have been here long enough.** Start moving toward the Jordan River. Prepare to possess the promised possessions that God has preordained for the per-fected Church to possess."

The

Destination

Of The

Church

RESTORATION AND DESTINATION OF THE CHURCH

(Restoration Movements and N.T. Restorational Truths
Correlated with O.T. Historical Happenings and Types)

Restoration Movements	Spiritual Experiences	Doctrines Of Christ (Heb. 6:1,2)	Journeys Of The Children Of Israel	Ezekiel's Bone Yard (Ezek. 37)	Water From Temple (Ezek. 47)	Tabernacle of Moses (Ex. 25-40)
1. Protestant	1. Justification	1. Repentance from Dead Works	1. Passover	1. *Breath* Enter	1. To Ankles	1. Brazen Altar
2. Holiness	2. Sanctification	2. Faith toward God	2. Red Sea, Banks; Marah-Water	2. Lay *Sinew* upon you	2. To Knees	2. Laver, Table of Shewbread
3. Pentecostal	3. Manifestation	3. Doctrine of Baptisms	3. Water from Rock	3. Bring up *Flesh* upon you	3. To Loins	3. Candlestick
4. Charismatic	4. Ministration	4. Laying on of Hands	4. Mt. Sinai	4. Cover you with *Skin*	4. To Swim in	4. Boards, Altar of Incense
5. Body of Christ	5. Glorification	5. Resurrection of Dead	5. Crossing Jordan	5. Ye shall *Live*	5. Life	5. Vail and Coverings
6. Army of Lord	6. Adjudication	6. Eternal Judgment	6. Conquering Canaan	6. Exceeding Great *Army*	6. Miry Place Judged	6. Ark and Contents
7. Queen Church	7. Administration	7. Ultimate Perfection	7. Canaan Conquered	7. Davidic King one Shepherd	7. Rest and Life	7. Mercy Seat
8. Eternal Church	8. Continuation	8. New Earth and New Heavens	8. Ruling and Oc-cupying Canaan	8. Tabernacle of God With Man	8. Temple of God With Man	8. New Temple

Dr. W. S. "Bill" Hamon, P. O. Box 27398, Phoenix, Arizona 85061 ©Christian International Publishers

REITERATION OF RESTORATION OF THE CHURCH

1500	Justification	1	Repentance From Dead Works	Baptism of Repentance . . . Blood	Protestant
1800	Sanctification	2	Faith Toward God	Baptism of . . . . Water	Holiness
1900	Manifestation	3	Doctrine of Baptisms	Baptism of Holy . . . . . . Spirit	Pentecostal
1950	Ministration	4	Laying on of Hands	Christ's Corporate . . . . . Body	Charismatic

DESTINATION OF THE CHURCH

Approx. Date	Spiritual Experiences		Doctrines of Christ Hebrews 6:1,2 Acts 3:21	Three Baptisms	Three Witnesses	Restoration Movements
19??	Glorification — High Praises, Righteousness, Agape Love, Divine Unity	5+	**Resurrection of the Dead.** Gifts: Working of Miracles, Discerning of Spirits. Prelude: Purified, Spotless, Full Maturity in Christ Jesus. Result: Redemption of the Body. Mortality ended in Life. Victory over the Last Enemy	Purified by . . .	Fire	**Body of Christ** — One United and Perfected Church
19??	Adjudication — 7-Fold Spirit	6+	**Eternal Judgment.** Gifts: All Gifts and Fruits. Joel's Army of the Lord. Manifestation of Sons of God. Saints Execute Judgment Written	Fulness of . . .	Love	**Army of Lord** — Overcomers, Bride of Christ
????	Administration	7+	**Ultimate Perfection.** God's Seventh Day of Rest. 1000-Year Reign of Peace on Earth. Overcomers Rule and Reign with Christ	Perfected . . .	Wisdom	**Queen Church** — Kingdom on Earth
Endless Ages	Continuation	8+	**New Heavens and New Earth.** Redemption of Creation. Restoration of the Earth. Church begins Eternal Ministry	Performance in . . .	Fulness	**Eternal Church** — Universal Reign

Dr. W. S. "Bill" Hamon, P. O. Box 27398, Phoenix, Arizona, 85061 © Christian International Publishers

1

Reiteration And Review Of Church Restoration

We have now studied the **Church** from every aspect except from the aspect of its *eternal destination*. A review is in order before discussing the future of the Church.

Conceived in Eternity, Birthed in Time. This writing has emphasized the fact that the Church was eternally conceived in the mind of God before the foundation of the world. The purchase price of its redemption was the sacrifice of the life of Jesus on the Cross of Calvary. The resurrection of Jesus confirmed and authorized the coming forth of the Church. The Holy Spirit caused the Church to be birthed on the day of Pentecost. Through this process the Church had its **origination.**

One Church in Heaven and on Earth. This book has studied the Church scripturally to determine what it is and what it takes to be a functioning member of the Eternal Church. We found the Church to be one body of believers made up of saints who have lived and died during the whole Church Age. Some are in Heaven and some are still on Earth, but the Church members are not spiritually separated by time or distance, life or death. Their universal and endless union is based on their relationship with the eternal Head of the Church, Jesus Christ. Though part of the Church is made up of mortal humans here on Earth, they are not earth-bound. These redeemed mortal members have been lifted up in their spirit and made to sit in heavenly places with Christ Jesus.

One Continuous Church. Christ has only **one** Church. The First Century Church and the 20th Century Church are not separate entities. The Church that was birthed on the day of Pentecost and portrayed in the Book of Acts is the same Church of today. It is operating under the same Headship, governed by the same principles and endowed with the same power and privileges. There is neither a Jewish Church nor a Gentile Church. There is One Church consisting of both Jew and Gentile. All race distinctions are dissolved when people become members of the Body of Christ. They become citizens of a new race, the *Church race.* In the Church, people are no longer black or white, Oriental or European, male or female, slave or master. They are neither superior nor inferior to one another, but fellow citizens of the Church-nation. Citizens of the nation of America are called Americans, those from Africa are called Africans, but those who belong to the nation of the Church have the universal identity of "Christians."

Definition. Based on the scriptural study given in an earlier chapter, the following definition of the Church was found to be the most complete and accurate: **the one universal many membered corporate Body of Christ.**

Deterioration. The Church was examined as to its early performances. It was seen that the Church reached its apex of power and performance in its First Century. Then it began to decline. The **deterioration** of the Church was revealed through our study of the Dark Ages. The reasons why the Church deteriorated and what eternal purpose could have possibly been accomplished by over 1,000 years of barreness and bondage were discussed.

Restoration. God then made the necessary preparation for the beginning of *"The Period of the Great Restoration."* The **restoration** of the Church has been followed step by step through each supernatural restorational movement. If careful reading, meditation, and study was given, the reader should have a clearer understanding of the Body of Christ and of Christendom in general. One should have a better understanding of why there are many different Christian denominations within Christendom; why there are different theological beliefs; why mainline Christendom is broken up into five major groups:

1. Catholic
2. Protestant
3. Holiness/Evangelical/Fundamental
4. Pentecostal
5. Charismatic

The reader should have a better understanding and appreciation for each group.

Christian heritage to be Understood and Appreciated. If one finds his or her identity within the five major groups, then one should have a greater insight concerning what one believes and why. Christians in the last restoration group should have a greater appreciation and understanding of their Charismatic Christian heritage.

The Purpose of This Book. The whole purpose of this book is not to give a sense of spiritual superiority or inferiority to other Christian groups. Rather, it has been designed to help people understand that Jesus wanted a Church, and He wants individuals to be a part of that Church. Christ Jesus died and rose again to make it possible for mankind to be members of His Eternal Corporate Body. One is not alone as a member, but integrally united with all other mortal members of the Body of Christ around the world, and the departed members who are now in Heaven. As a Christian, one becomes a member of a universal family; Jesus is the head of the family and all true believers in Him are brothers and sisters. We are family, we are one.

Not Known by Earthly Titles. There is no competition in the Body of Christ. No two members have the same ministry. God has a unique function for each of the tens of millions of members to personally perform. People should not allow man-made distinctions to separate them from any of the members of the Body of Christ. Jesus does not know any of His children by their earthly titles of Catholic, Baptist, Assembly of God, or Charismatic. If their sins have been washed away by His precious blood and His Spirit is dwelling within, and the love and Word of God is the motivating force of their life, then they are truly His children.

Be One for Jesus' Sake. All of God's children may not be perfect yet in doctrine, holy living, and powerful performances, but if they are truly "blood-washed" members of the Body of Christ, they are blood brothers and sisters and must treat each other as such. There is no place for jealousy, resentment, condemnation, judgement, strife, bigotry, religious conceit, or any other impure motive or action among the members of the Body of Christ. Jesus paid a tremendous price to have His Church with Him and unified. If we really love and appreciate what He has done, then for His sake, let us love one another and be one great united family of God.

The Future Destiny of the Church

The Origination, Deterioration and Restoration of the Church has been covered in detail. This should have given a foundational understanding and knowledge of the evolvement of the Present-truth Church. There will not be time or space to give a detailed study of the next four phases of the Eternal Church. It will require another book to do justice to this area of the Church. Sufficient information will be given for a general outline of what may happen in, with, and through the Church.

Exciting and Tantalizing. It is exciting and tantalizing to study the future ministry of the Church. It is interesting to speculate about the chronological order of events to take place in these last days and the consummation of the ages. However, it is much more important to know what it takes to be a part of that ministry. Jesus only shows us the future and what it holds in order for us to make proper preparation. Jesus, *"for the joy that was set before Him, endured the cross despising the shame" (Heb. 12:2).* Jesus does not give us glimpses into the eternal ministry of the Church to satisfy our curiosity, but to excite and encourage us to "press toward that mark for the prize of the high calling of God in Christ Jesus *(Phil. 3:14).* It will be worth all our suffering of

the flesh, self denial, separation from the world, death to self and conformity to Christ when we receive our "overcomer's reward." "If we suffer with Him we shall also reign with Him" *(II Tim. 2:12; Rom. 8:17).*
He lets us know we shall have an eternal reign with Him so that we will be willing and able to suffer with Him while in our mortality.

Preparing to Progress to Perfection. Glimpses into the future of the Church are given in order to encourage the reader to incorporate into his or her life all present truth which has been restored to the Church. One should make sure he or she has experientially received all of the **"Spiritual Experiences"** of *justification, sanctification, manifestation,* and *ministration.* Then the reader will be more properly prepared to enter into the next four Spiritual Experiences of *Glorification, Adjudication, Administration,* and *Continuation.* It is important to make sure one has more than an intellectual knowledge of the four doctrines of Christ which have already been restored to the Church.

A doctrine of Christ is not just a creed one agrees with, but a living reality one experiences and practices. If a person has experienced the Doctrines of *Repentance from Dead Works, Faith toward God, Doctrine of Baptisms,* and *Laying on of Hands,* he or she is in a better position to participate in the living realities of the next *three* Doctrines of Christ: *Resurrection of the Dead, Eternal Judgement,* and *Ultimate Perfection.* These will activate the participants into an everlasting ministry in the *Eternal Church.*

2

Introduction
To Fifth
Doctrine
Of Christ

Questions to be Answered. Did God know that the mortal Church would still be alive and active in the 1980s? Did God make plans and provisions for this generation of the Church? Is the Church drifting or being divinely directed? Is this the day that the Lord hath made? Is this generation destined to experientially restore the last truth and thereby bring about the close of the **"Period of the Great Restoration?"** Will the next two decades of the Church see the *"restoration of all things?"* Will the generation of the Church alive today be responsible for fulfilling the last Scriptures ordained to be fulfilled, thereby releasing Jesus from the Heavens to return for His Church-Bride? Is this the generation upon whom the consummation of the ages has come? Is the Church still here by accident or by divine purpose?

Progression According to Plan. God had in mind an ultimate purpose for the Church to fulfill when He birthed it into this world. Everything He has done and is doing in the Church is by divine design. Truth is being restored in the chronological order that Jesus preordained. Each step of restoration brings the Church closer to its last-day ministry.

Restoration Before Rapture. If the only thing Jesus has left for the Church was a sovereign rapture with no preparation and participation by the saints, then He could have raptured *(immortalized)* the Church anytime during the last 1,950 years. The fact is that He did not. He has not translated the Church because there is a special work that He wants to accomplish in and through the last generation Church.

Church not in Suspended Animation. The Church is not in suspended animation awaiting the restoration of Israel or the fulness of wickedness in the world. The Jews will undoubtedly be restored and the world's cup of iniquity will become full. But that is not what has prolonged the duration of the Church Age. There is a work of preparation and restoration that must be accomplished **in** the Church before Christ Jesus can fulfill His ultimate purpose **for** and **through** the Church. He must come **to** His Church in full restoration before He comes **for** His church in translation. All restorational work of the Holy Spirit has been progressively preparing the Church for this day and hour. The Fifth Doctrine of Christ can only be fulfilled by the last generation of the mortal Church.

Four to Three Odds. The first *four* of the *seven* doctrines of Christ have come to pass in the chronological order in which they are listed in Hebrews 6:1,2. If restorational fulfillment continues in the same order, then the next doctrine of Christ to be fulfilled in demonstrable reality is "Resurrection of the Dead."

Redemption to Whole Man. Every restorational truth of the Holy Spirit brings more redemption to the whole man. Each additional truth has enabled the Church to appropriate more of the full redemptive work of Christ. The Holy Spirit has been commissioned by Jesus Christ to lead the Church into **all truth.** Fulness of truth will bring fulness of life. When the Church reaches the full maturity in the life of Christ, it will come into all that Christ presently is "as He is so are we in this world" *(I Jn. 4:17).*

The Purchased Possession. Truth is parallel and progressive with an ultimate objective, that is, the redemption of the whole man: spirit, soul and body. " . . . ye were sealed with the Holy Spirit of promise, which is the earnest of our inheritance *until the redemption of the purchased possession" (Eph. 1:13,14).* What is the "purchased possession" waiting to be redeemed of which the Holy Spirit is the "earnest" or guarantee that it will be redeemed? The *physical body* of the saints is the *"purchased possession"* which is still awaiting redemption. The Church has yet to receive its full inheritance. Our spiritual birth and baptism of the Holy Spirit is only the "earnest" of our inheritance.

From Religious Platitudes to Living Principles. Every restorational truth has brought the scriptural meaning back to its original application as intended by the Holy Spirit when He inspired its writing. Each period of restoration has taken a group of Scriptures that religious men have placed in the mythical, allegorical, spiritual and futuristic realm and made them a workable reality in the life of man. Jesus inspired the writing of the Scriptures, not to give man a set of idealistic philosophies and platitudes to be eulogized by great religious leaders, but to give mankind truths: living principles and promises which will work in meeting every need of humanity. Every Scripture which has been spiritualized in the ethereal will be fulfilled in the literal. As has been revealed, each movement did that for the four doctrines of

Christ and the spiritual experiences that accompanied their fulfillment. During the Dark Ages most of the scriptural blessings we now enjoy were kept from the Christians by religious leaders who spiritualized them into some ethereal realm or off into some future age.

All of the seven Doctrines of Christ relate to the Church. They will be fulfilled **in, by,** and **through** the Church. The four which have been restored required an act of faith and obedience to receive the benefits of that truth. For instance, Jesus died on the cross to provide salvation for all humanity, but a person does not receive that salvation simply because he or she is a member of the human race. Eternal life is the sovereign gift of God. It is given by the unmerited favor of God. An individual cannot give oneself eternal life and neither can God give it, unless that person believes on Jesus Christ and receives Christ into his or her heart. There are strong scriptural indications that the Church will be brought to translating faith in preparation for the immortalization and glorification of the Church.

> "This means that all hindrance to the believer's deliverance clear up to total glorification is on the human side. One man, Enoch, proved, verified, and confirmed this principle by appropriating faith for glorification *(Gen. 5:24; Heb. 11:5)*. Enoch's experience proves that there is a legal basis for full deliverance in this life from every result of the Fall for every child of God." (Paul E. Billheimer, *Don't Waste Your Sorrows,* Fort Washington, Pennsylvania, Christian Literature Crusade, 1977. p. 103.)

Translation in the Old Testament. There are two types of the translation of the Church in the Old

Testament, *Enoch* and *Elijah*. Elijah had a revelation and witness that he was going to be translated. He even knew the general time in which he was going. Enoch had the testimony that he pleased God and walked with God. The New Testament reveals that Enoch had a revelation of Christ coming with His saints *(Jude 14,15)*. He evidently understood that the saints would be translated. He received a word from the Lord. Enoch laid hold of that Word and applied it to himself. Hebrews 11:5 states that "By **faith** Enoch was **translated** that he should not see **death.**" Enoch is a type of the last generation of the corporate Body of Christ who shall be translated and not see death.

No Private Translations. The author can see no scriptural basis to believe there will be any "by faith private translations" prior to the worldwide, instantaneous, momentous translation of the corporate Body of Christ. The writer does not claim to have a complete revelation or detailed understanding of how all this shall transpire. He only knows that all of the Scriptures on death and immortality that the Church has up to this time applied only to the spirit and soul will at that time be applied and fulfilled in the physical body of the saints. When the time arrives for the restoration of this truth, the Holy Spirit will bring the revelation and faith for its fulfillment.

Fifth Doctrine
of Christ Scriptures

No doubt, a new understanding will come to the Church on such Scriptures as:

> "Jesus Christ, who *hath abolished death,* and hath brought *life* and *immortality* to light *through the gospel*" *(II Tim. 1:10).*

"The law of the spirit of life in Christ Jesus *hath made me free* from the law of sin and **death"** *(Rom. 8:2).*

"If the Spirit of Him who raised Jesus from the dead is living in you, He who raised Christ from the dead will also give *life to your mortal bodies* through His Spirit who lives in you" *(Rom. 8:11 NIV).*

"Christ in you the hope of glory" *(Col. 1:27).*

"Jesus said unto her, *I am the resurrection and the life;* he that believeth in Me though he were dead, yet shall he live: And whosoever *liveth and believeth* in Me shall **never die. Believest thou this?"** *(Jn. 11:25,26).*

"Verily, verily, I say unto you, if a man keep my saying, he shall **never see death"** *(Jn. 8:51).*

"I am the living bread which came down from heaven, if any man eat of this bread he shall live forever. This is that bread which came down from heaven: not as your *fathers did eat manna, and are dead:* he that eateth of this bread *shall live forever"* *(Jn. 6:51,58).*

"Mortality is swallowed up of life" *(II Cor. 5:4).*

"Death is swallowed up in victory. The sting of death is sin; and the strength of sin is the law. But thanks be to God who giveth us the victory through our Lord Jesus Christ" *(I Cor. 15:54-57).*

"The last enemy to be destroyed is death. Christ must reign till He hath put all enemies under His feet" *(I Cor. 15:26,27).*

> "And hath put all things under His feet
> [Jesus is the Head, Church is the Body, feet
> are in the body] and gave Him to be head
> over all things to the Church which is His
> body" *(Eph. 1:22).*

> "Just as man is destined to die once, and
> after that to face judgement, so Christ was
> sacrificed once to take away the sins of many
> people; and He will appear a second time,
> not to bear sin, but to *bring salvation to
> those who are waiting for Him" (Heb. 9:27,28
> NIV).*

It is appointed unto man once to die, but the prophetic Word declares that there will be a generation
that praises the Lord who are in Mt. Zion that shall
break the appointment with death, *"to loose those
that are appointed to death" (Ps. 102:16-21).*

Scriptures Fulfilled Literally. Theologians and
preachers know the spiritual application of these Scriptures to mankind's spirit and soul and have rightly
used them so for years. But just as being born again,
healing for the body, speaking in other tongues
and many other truths have been brought out of the
ethereal realm and made living realities within the
lives of the saints, so shall these Scriptures on *life,
death* and *immortality* be applied to the whole man,
including his *body.* The hour is coming closer. The
Holy Spirit is causing a cry to arise within the hearts
of the saints for their full sonship, full rights, full redemption and all of their inheritance.

> "We ourselves, who have the firstfruits of the
> spirit groan inwardly as we wait eagerly for

our adoption as sons, the redemption of our bodies" *(Rom. 8:23 NIV)*.

"We wait for that *redemption of our bodies* which will mean that at last we have realized our *full sonship in Him" (Rom. 8:23 Phillips)*.

"We, too, wait anxiously for that day when God will give us *our full rights as His children,* including the new *bodies He has promised us — bodies that will never be sick again and will never die" (Rom. 8:23 LB)*.

"When Jesus comes back He will take these dying bodies of ours and change them into **glorious bodies** like His own, using the same mighty power that He will use to conquer all else everywhere" *(Phil. 3:21)*.

Same Experience but Different Terms and Approaches

All Bible-believing Christians acknowledge this truth, but approach it from different directions and use different terms to describe its fulfillment, such as *rapture, translation, immortalization, the change, first resurrection, manifestation of the sons of God, manchild company, restoration of last truth to the mortal Church, Christ coming to be glorified in His saints, overcomer's exaltation, second coming of Christ, Omega generation, beginning of the millennium,* and various other terms. Regardless of the eschatological approach or theological terms used, the end result is the same: immortalization and escalation of the Church with Christ into an indestructible and invincible Army of the Lord. It will definitely result in the literal fulfillment of the Fifth Doctrine of Christ, **Resurrection of the Dead.**

Get Ready for New Restorational Movement

Oh, present generation of the Church, you that are young in heart "and your eye has caught the vision and your heart has felt the thrill, to the call of the Master, and your heart has said, I will. Ready for the conflict of the ages, oh his fury is upon us, is upon us today." Those are more than words to a chorus, they are the cry of the Holy Spirit to this generation. You that have never been a part of a restorational truth move of the Holy Spirit, get ready! And get excited! There is another restoration truth coming to the Church that will bring us into full reality. But be assured it will be the same among Christendom during this time as it was when Israel was challenged to go in and possess their promised possessions. Twelve Israeli spies went into the land of Canaan. They all saw the same bountifulness and truthfulness of which God had told them about the land. But 10 of them were overwhelmed with the giants and walled cities and fortified areas. Joshua and Caleb saw the impossibilities in the natural, but they believed God's promise and said, "We are well able to overcome and possess." The 10 unbelieving spies said, "We be not able" *(Num. 13:30,31).*

Two Family Camps — The "Ables" and "Not-Ables". This next challenge of the Holy Spirit to the Church will sound just as unreasonable, irrational, impossible, and ridiculous to the majority of present-day ministers as it did to the 10 natural, humanistic minded Israelis. If this Old Testament type holds true in the percentages, it means that for every two ministers who are preaching this truth there will be 10 against it. Every minister in Christendom, and even those among the Charismatics, will be faced with a decision. The Church will be separated into two camps; the "we are able" group and the "we are not able" group. The majority has never been right. God is not looking for a multitude but for a few people who are willing to cross their "Jordan of death to self," arise in *resurrection life* and be united with the believers into a mighty army that shall go in and possess their promised possessions.

Old Truth Revived — New Truth Restored. New truth is about to be restored. With the restoration of every new truth greater enlightenment and reality is brought concerning the old truths. Nothing is lost but everything is enhanced. Any supposedly new truth that deletes, belittles, or does away with an old truth is not a truth at all, but a lying deception and a counterfeit from Satan. New truth may delete the traditions of men that were tacked on to a restored truth, but it will not change the basic truth.

I feel like Martin Luther did when he was presenting the revolutionary truth of justification by faith and anti-papalism, relics, images and church paraphernalia. There were the scripturally uneducated and spiritually unstable who went to extremism and fanaticism. But every restorational move has had its extremes when the pendulum of new truth began to swing and mark a new time of advancement for the Church. If I am privileged of the Holy Spirit to be a Joshua or a Caleb to this new generation, then I shall do all in my power to maintain a balance by the grace, wisdom, and maturity of the Head of the Church, Himself, Jesus Christ our Lord.

3

Explanation of Chart Subjects

Approximate Date: 19??

Knowledge of this doctrine is made known from the Holy Scriptures, although it has not been fulfilled in its experiential reality. The only Man in Heaven or Earth who knows the year, day and hour of its fulfillment is the Man, Christ Jesus. Evidently, Jesus did not know the chronology of the end time while in His mortal humanity *(Mk. 13:22)*. "But when He ascended back to the Father all things were given unto Him and He shewed them unto John," *(Rev. 1:1)*. Any attempt to put an exact date to it would be foolish, speculative, immature and presumptuous. Nevertheless, the author's expectation and conviction is that it will take place before the year 2000. For that reason the date is placed on the chart as 19??.

Spiritual Experiences

Spiritual Experiences
Glorification
High Praises
Righteousness
Agape Love
Divine Unity

There will be new spiritual experiences added to the Church just prior to and immediately after this next restorational move. This book will only deal with those which it is believed will be added while the Church is still in its mortal state.

Glorification

Other synonymous words could have been used such as "translation" or "immortalization" to be the heading for these spiritual experiences. Glorification was chosen because of its broader meaning. It has application both to the mortal and the immortal Church. Romans 8:17 and II Thessalonians 1:10 will have a three-phase fulfillment, just before, during, and afterwards. Christ will come and be "glorified" in His mortal saints in one of the greatest world-shaking revivals ever to be experienced on Earth. The Church will demonstrate all the attributes of the Kingdom of God to all the world before the translation and establishment of the literal Kingdom of God on Earth. Many of the Scriptures which the extreme futurists have put off to the millennium will have a fulfillment in the last generation Church. Christ will be glorified in His mortal saints in the full splendor of His power. His "glory" will cover the Earth as the waters cover the sea *(Is. 11:9; Num. 14:21; Hab. 2:14)*. Glory may be described as the expression, manifestation, demonstration, and personification of the invisible God. Jesus was the personification of Jehovah. The Church is the extension and personification of Christ Jesus. The Church is His *"glory"* that He shall cause to cover the Earth as the waters cover the Sea. The "Last Truth Church" will be a personification of His person, demonstration of His *dunamis,* performance of His principles, portrayal of His presence, manifestation of His ministry, and glorification of His grace, goodness and glory.

High Praises

Based on Psalms 102:16-21; 149:6-9; and scores of other Scriptures, those who break the appointment with death and are used to execute God's judgments on the world will have the "high praises" of God in their mouths and a two-edged sword in their hands. That generation that shall be created shall "praise the Lord." The Altar of Incense (praise) was the last performance of the priest before going through the veil and entering into the Holy of Holies. The Pentecostals praised the Lord in response to God's presence, the Latter Rain brethren praised the Lord to produce the presence of God, the Charismatics praised the Lord as a positive force to answered prayer. The next movement will bring an even greater revelation and application of praise. It will give that generation of the Church an invincibility and powerful force beyond the wildest imagination and present understanding of the Church.

Righteousness

The Holiness Movement taught inner sanctification of the soul for holy living, but ended up being preoccupied with pruning the saints of worldliness. "And now the axe is laid unto the root of the trees" *(Mt. 3:10)*. This righteousness will be nothing short of conformity to the image of Jesus Christ. The Church will be taken beyond imputed righteousness for justification to Holy Spirit-accumulated righteousness for transformation into the very nature and character of Christ Jesus. We must have His "right-in-us": right attitude, right thinking, right principles, right doctrine, right actions, right relationship with God and all fellow members in the Body of Christ. "Sow to yourselves in *righteousness,* reap in mercy; break up your fallow ground: for *it is time* to seek the Lord, till He come and *rain righteousness upon you*" *(Hos. 10:12).* "For I tell you that unless your righteousness surpasses that of the Pharisees and the teachers of the law, you will certainly not enter the kingdom of Heaven" *(Mt. 5:20 NIV).*

Love

The King James Version uses the word "charity" to denote this *agape* love which is the very essence of the nature and character of Christ *(I Cor. 13:4-8).* Paul knew by revelation that the Church would never reach full maturity until fulness of love was obtained. Therefore, he tells the Church, "I pray that you, being rooted and established in love, may have power, together with all the saints, to grasp how wide and long and high and deep is the **love** of Christ, and to **know this love** that surpasses knowledge — that you may be filled to the measure of **all** the **fulness of God**" *(Eph. 3:17-19 NIV).*

The Determining Factor for Participation. The ultimate criterion and determining factor for those who will be participants in the next restorational move is whether the **love character** of Christ has become the inner motivating force of their lives. Fellow Present-truth Charismatics should not base future participation on present-day manifestations. The Early Church Charismatic apostle, Dr. Paul, wrote the following words under the inspiration of the Holy Spirit:

"If I speak in the tongues of men and of angels . . . If I have the gift of prophecy and can fathom all mysteries and all knowledge . . . but have not **love,** I am only a resounding gong or a clanging cymbal . . . I gain nothing." [Prosperity preachers and faith people must also listen to what the Holy Spirit has to say.] "If I have a faith that can move mountains . . . If I give all I possess . . . but I have not love, I am nothing . . . I gain nothing." [To the historical and evangelical Christian who rests his confidence in being conservative, caring for the poor and meeting the practical needs and a life of self-sacrifice, hear what the Spirit saith . . .] "If I give all I possess to the poor . . . and surrender my body to the flames . . . it profiteth me nothing and I am nothing" *(I Cor. 13:1-3 NIV).*

Spiritual manifestations or good works will not open the door, but those who have the love character of Christ will have an open door set before them which no man can shut.

Unity of the Church: Prayer of Jesus, St. John 17

The prayer of Jesus concerning the oneness and unity of the Church will be fulfilled prior to the immortalization of the Eternal Church. The Holy Spirit will bring a new revelation and activation of divine grace which will enable the Body of Christ to become one. The Church will be made **one,** one way or the other, through willful obedience of its members or through great persecution from outside sources. Jesus intensely desires the **unity** of the Church more than its worldly comforts. If it becomes necessary He will strip the Church of all its buildings and everything that separates Christians until all that is left is each other. However, the author does not believe this is His first choice.

Divine Unity is Not Uniformity. The Church, right now, has the wherewithal to be one. Jesus said in John 17:22, "And the glory which thou gavest me **I have given them: that they may be one even as we are one.**" It is not a lack of available grace, it is a lack of desire and determination to be one.

Divine **unity** is not outward uniformity. It cannot be accomplished by man-made methods, ecumenical councils or denominational conglomerates. It must start in the spirit and work out into relationships. **Unity** is a spirit and divine grace, not a program or gathering together in one geographical location. One can tie the tails of two cats together and hang them over a clothesline and have togetherness, but not unity.

Preachers Are the Key to Unity. The saints cannot produce unity. It can only be done by ministers; the leadership, the shepherds leading the sheep, willingly submitting themselves to one another in the fear of God and love of the Lord Jesus. The saints are not against mixing and mingling in unity and fellowship. It is the fearful, proud, personal-kingdom building, insecure and possessive preachers who are the number one problem. Fellow ministers of the Church, Almighty God will hold us responsible for the part we play in helping or hindering the fulfillment of Jesus' prayer for the **unity** of His Church.

Unity will take place. The Church, the true Body of Christ, will be **one** before Jesus returns. It can happen. It will take place. Jesus prayed it. God decreed it. Nothing or no one can stop it. The Holy Spirit has started things in motion that will clear the way for it to take place. Judgment is beginning at the house of God. Jesus has begun the purging of all things from His Kingdom that offend and hinder the fulfillment of His will. Fellow ministers and fellow members of the Body of Christ, if we cannot be motivated by love, then let us be motivated by the fear of God. For Christians will either submit to His purging through the baptism of fire or baptism of love, or become outcasts. The Holy Spirit must be allowed to deliver us from self-righteous, narrow-minded, argumentative attitudes. We must allow Him to deliver us from the theological and philosophical reasons which we have used with pet Scriptures to justify our divisive, exclusive, and separatist actions and attitudes. We have slipped by in times past and God has winked at our ignorance and immaturity, but not any more. God is demanding manhood of his ministers. Many will become sickly and die an early death because they will not rightly discern the Body of Christ, nor work for its unity.

Ministers separated from Bride. Denominational pride or an independent self-willed and proud spirit will separate a Christian minister from the Bride of Christ just as it separated Lucifer from being a minister of God in His heavenly domain. God sacrificed Jesus for the formation of the Church and its perfection in unity. How much more will God sacrifice any minister who is hindering the perfection and unification of His Church? No individual is indispensable.

Jesus died for every individual and longingly desires with unfathomable love that every person become a member in His great Corporate Body, the Church. However, the ministers who manifest the spirit of the 10 unbelieving Israeli spies, who hindered the children of Israel from entering into God's promised land, will be left behind to wander in the wilderness while the Joshua and Caleb ministers lead Christ's Church into the Promised Land. The choice is ours to submit, believe, and become one with the whole Body of Christ or rebel, refuse, stiffen our necks and be devoured.

Not God's Will. It is not God's will or holy desire for sinners to die and go to Satan's Hell, but millions do every year. It is not His will that Christians fall away from the faith, but many do. It is not His will that any minister or Christian walk short of present truth, but thousands do so daily. True unified fellowship is based on our fellowship with the Father and His Son, and walking in the light as He is in the light. We must be established in all presently restored truth and actively promote the **unity** of the Body of Christ.

Thy Will By Done. "Lord Jesus, cause our will to be in unity and intensified with your will, and then let us work together for your will to be done, for it is your will that the **Church** be **One**."

4

Ministry
Of The Last
Generation Church

Fifth Doctrine of Christ: Resurrection of the Dead. It would require scores of pages to cover in detail all the subjects presented with this doctrine. There are over 100 Scriptures alone dealing with the three phases of this fifth restorational Doctrine of Christ. It would require numerous pages to hermeneutically and expositorily deal with each. The Lord willing, this will be done in a detailed manner in a future writing. The book could be called *The Future Ministry of the Church,* or the *Destiny of the Church.* It would cover in detail Doctrines of Christ numbers 5, 6, 7 plus 8 (the number of the new beginning) which deals with the Eternal Church and Her ministry with Christ throughout the endless ages to come.

Three Phases of Resurrection of the Dead

First Phase — Resurrection Life

A supernatural flow of divine life will come into the progressive Present-truth Church a few years prior to the time of the translation. This will not initially be for the bodily immortalization of the saints. It will enable the Church to demonstrate Jesus Christ, not only as Savior of man, but as Lord of all, including His Lordship over all nations of the world. All of the works that Jesus and the First Century Church did, the latter-day Church shall do also, and to an even greater extent. "The glory of this latter house shall be greater than of the former, saith the Lord of Hosts" *(Hag. 2:9; Jn. 14:12).*

Ephesians 3:10 reveals that the Church is destined and designed to demonstrate the manifold wisdom of God to all eternal creatures, according to the eternal purpose which He purposed in Christ Jesus our Lord. There are still parts of that eternal plan which the Church has not understood nor demonstrated to all creation. The mortal Church still has a part to portray.

Gospel of Kingdom in Resurrection Life. The Gospel of the Kingdom (not just salvation, but a full demonstration of God's power, splendor, and sovereign majesty) shall be preached in all nations for a witness (that He is Lord of all), then shall the end come. Super-abundant *resurrection life* shall be divinely imparted in order to demonstrate that the Head of the Church is living in His Corporate Body as a supernatural resurrected Christ. Illustrations of what will happen during this time are given under "Gifts" "Prelude" and "Results."

Counterfeits Reveal There is the Real. Oh, Body of Christ, do not be swept into a substitute or counterfeit of this Resurrection Life, but press on to perfection until the Holy Spirit brings forth this new restorational movement. God is going to do a "new thing." It will not be a reviving of the old erroneous "longevity" or "never die" doctrine. It will not come as a confirmation to this book nor to some small group who are waiting for God to vindicate them to the rest of Christendom. This restorational move of the Holy Spirit will not be done in a corner, nor just with some small exclusive group hidden away. When it comes, it will have to be birthed somewhere, but it will immediately and simultaneously spread to the whole Body of Christ around the world. It may start as a small flame in some obscure and insignificant place as all movements have. But it will quickly spread into a roaring flame which shall sweep around the world. It will be shouted from the housetops and carried to the ends of the Earth. It will become the most controversial and revolutionary issue ever to arise in Christendom or the world. It shall cause the rise and fall of many nations and peoples.

Phase Two — First Resurrection and Translation

The **First Resurrection** is the bodily resurrection of the saints who have physically died; that is, their spirit body departed to be with the Lord in Paradise while their physical human body was left here on Earth to decompose *(Eccl. 12:7; Lk. 16:22-31; Phil. 1:20-23; II Cor. 5:4; Rev. 6:9-11).* Jesus will bring these departed saints with Him at His coming at the end of this age. Jesus will come back in His resurrected human body, but they will return in their spirit bodies. As they descend to Earth Jesus will give a shout, the trumpet shall sound, and their decomposed human bodies will be immediately reformulated and resurrected simultaneously. Their resurrected human bodies will be joined with their spirits, thus making them physically redeemed and restored to a total human entity according to the original pattern of spirit, soul, and **body.** They will then be totally restored human beings with bodies like unto the glorious resurrected human body of their Lord and Savior Jesus Christ *(Phil. 3:21; I Thess. 4:14-17).*

The **translation** does the same thing for the living saints who are still functioning in their mortal bodies, as the First Resurrection does for the saints who lost their mortal physical bodies through death. Those saints who are alive and remain unto the time of the translation will have their mortal, physical human bodies changed "in a moment, in the twinkling of an eye" into immortal, physical human bodies. Also during that "moment" every physical imperfection and abnormality caused by the curse will be eradicated, youth will be renewed, and their bodies will be purified, perfected, and changed into immortal, indestructible, eternal human bodies *(I Cor. 15:51-54).* As Paul stated, this is a great mystery; only God knows how all of this can and will be accomplished. He who originally made man's body from the dust of the Earth has the wisdom and power to resurrect and translate.

Justification-Salvation . . . gives eternal life to man's *spirit.*

Sanctification-Transformation . . . transforms man's *soul* (mind, emotions, will) into the thinking attitude and temperament needed for His eternal function.

Glorification-Translation . . . gives immortality and eternal life to the physical *body.*

Phase Three —
General Resurrection of
the Rest of Humanity

The resurrection of the dead unto the White Throne Judgment is expressed in the Apostles' Creed. It is taught by every mainline church group within Christendom. Most Christians accept it but many do not understand the purpose and significance of the bodily resurrection of the unrighteous. Chapter 20 of the book of Revelation states the First Resurrection is for the righteous dead in Christ only and that this resurrection occurs at the beginning of the 1,000-year period. The resurrection of all the rest of humanity takes place at the end of the 1,000 years.

All Resurrected. The Bible teaches that all humans who have breathed the breath of life in a mortal body will be resurrected with immortal indestructible bodies. The righteous will be resurrected to blissful life with Christ Jesus in His new Heaven and new Earth. The wicked will be resurrected to suffer in torment with the devil in that hellish eternal state of existence called the Lake of Fire.

The eternal heavenly world of the righteous will be an everlasting memorial unto all eternal creatures of God's love, merciful forgiveness and righteous goodness *(Eph. 2:7)*. The forever existing world of the unrighteous will be an everlasting memorial and reminder to all eternal creatures of God's righteous judgments against all rebels, who would not live according to godly principles which are for the preservation and perpetuation of God's universal eternal creation *(Dan. 12:2; Jn. 5:28,29; Acts 24:15; I Cor. 15:12-22)*.

Prelude to the Church's Resurrection and Translation

For over two centuries Church leaders have been saying, "The next important event on God's calendar is the second coming of Christ." They would use world events, signs in the Heavens and Earth, and their interpretation of certain Scriptures to verify their predictions. They sensed in their spirit that something was about to happen and God was planning a new event for the Church. What they interpreted to be the literal coming of the Lord turned out to be a restorational movement of the Holy Spirit to restore another truth to the Church. Most men of God who become involved in predicting the time of the coming of the Lord become guilty of this misinterpretation.

This writer is no exception: from the year 1954 until the end of 1962, I preached with great inner conviction and persuasion that the rapture of the Church would take place sometime in 1963. This conviction was based on several things, but mainly on the decreased time periods between each restorational movement: 1,000 years of Dark Ages; then 300 years between the restoration of the First and Second Doctrine of Christ; then 100 years between restoration of the Second and Third Doctrine, then approximately 50 years between restoration of the Third and Fourth Doctrine of Christ. Evidence was that God was shortening the periods between the major restorational movements. Matthew 24:22 says that God is going to do a quick work and cut it short. The time periods were being shortened and cut to one-third of the previous one: 1,000, 300, 100 and then 50. The Laying on of Hands doctrine was restored in 1948, approximately 45 years after the doctrine of Baptisms. I used the figure of one-third of 45 (15) and added that to 1948 to come up with 1963. I also used Scriptures concerning Israel, world conditions, and many other means in making this prediction. Several other influential ministers had made predictions concerning 1963. I became convinced that 1963 was the year.

During those years my first son, Tim, was born in 1956, Tom in 1959 and Sherilyn in 1961. Hundreds of times I made statements that "my son will never start to school, for Jesus will come before that time." Well, Tim has graduated from college with an engineering degree, is married and has a family; Tom has graduated from Bible college and is now in the ministry and married. My daughter is married and in the ministry. It is still hard for me to grasp that this is the 1980s, the world is still going around, and Jesus has not come. Nevertheless, I still believe He is coming soon!

Prediction Wrong Because of Perception. We were wrong to predict that the coming of Jesus would take place at that time, but were correct in feeling and believing that something worldwide was going to happen to the Church. It did happen. Not the literal personal coming of Jesus, but another spiritual coming of a global move of the Holy Spirit. The great Charismatic Renewal swept throughout Christendom during the mid-1960s. Because we saw no more truth to be restored or Scriptures to be fulfilled concerning the Church, we assumed that the only thing left for the Holy Spirit to accomplish was the translation of the saints. We made the same mistake that virtually every preacher of prophecy has made for the last few centuries of the Church; that the next thing on God's agenda is the "Second Coming of Christ."

Another Restoration Before Rapture. Many Evangelical and Charismatic ministers of the late 1970s, and now those of the 1980s, are predicting that the second coming of Christ is the next thing on God's schedule of events. However, I believe they are misinterpreting that stirring of the Holy Spirit within them. The Spirit is saying "He is coming soon!" But before His literal coming takes place, there is first coming another worldwide truth-restoring mighty move of the Holy Spirit. This will be a **prelude** to the literal coming of Christ. It will include one of the mightiest manifestations of God's power ever to take place in the Church. It will enable the Church to take its final step of restoration bringing about purification, perfection, unity, and maturity of the Church. The last member will be brought into the Body of Christ fulfilling the *quantity* needed. Those members will be brought to the *quality* needed to meet God's standard for the last generation of the mortal Church.

No Going Up Until Grown Up. This is not the time for the Church just to sing and daydream about "going up" but it is the time to become involved in "growing up." The Church will not "go up" until it is "grown up." If evangelical and Charismatic Christians would get as excited about *growing up* as they do about *going up,* the Body of Christ would reach its maturity much sooner, fulfill all Scriptures, restore all things, and thereby "bring back King Jesus."

Gifts of the Holy Spirit: Working of Miracles

I Cor. 12:10; Mt. 10:7,8; Acts 10:38 cf. Jn. 14:12; Dan. 11:32; see earlier chapter dealing with the supernatural and the miraculous in the Book of Acts. What was in the beginning will be

doubled at the end of the Church Age — double manna on the
sixth day in preparation for Sabbath. Performance of the Last
Century Church will be greater and more glorious than the
First Century Church Hag. 2:9; Mal. 4:5 cf. Mt. 17:11; Rev.
11:3-15.

The gift of miracles will be restored to its full
function during this next restorational movement. All
other gifts which have already been restored and are
active in the Church will be brought to a higher level
of performance.

Creative Miracles. The working of miracles will
cause creative miracles among the maimed and de-
formed. New limbs will grow back where they had
been removed or never developed. Not only will there
be creative miracles in the human body, there will
also be creative miracles performed in nature. There
will be undeniable miracles taking place of such pro-
portions that it will affect whole nations. The Church
was given a short example in Indonesia of what the
Holy Spirit could do with the working of miracles.
Such things as Mel Tari describes in his book, *Like a*
Mighty Wind will be regular and worldwide occur-
rences.

Book of Acts Re-enacted. God will not do these
things just to confirm someone's revelation or spirituality; to satisfy curiosity, or just a desire to see the
miraculous. As needs arise, the working of miracles
will enable the Church to "walk on water," be transported by the Spirit from one geographical location to
another as Phillip the Evangelist; multiply the loaves
and fishes to feed the multitudes when there are no
other resources; supernaturally, preach to a nation in
its own language; have supernatural preservation during calamities; be miraculously directed, and involve

a greater number of incidents of people being raised from the dead.

Spirit World Activity Increased. Satan's demonic activity will be accelerated. As we enter the final years of this age, every person will become either more evil spirit-possessed or more Holy Spirit-possessed. The ministry of "casting out devils" will be accelerated. The veil between the natural world and spirit world will be opened wider. This will allow the saints to have more angelic visitations and communication.

The spirit beings from the underworld of Satan's domain will be cast out of their self-appointed realms and forced into greater activity among humanity *(Rev. 12:9).* The ministering spirits of God's angelic host shall descend to work more intimately with the Church. **Heaven and Hell will meet face to face within the human race.**

Kingdom Message with Supernatural Signs. The Gospel of the Kingdom will be preached to all nations accompanied with the gifts of the Spirit and especially the *working of miracles.* Anointed ministers as led by the Holy Spirit will pronounce judgments upon opponents of the Gospel, as Apostle Paul did by proclaiming blindness upon Elymas, the sorcerer. Prophets will prophesy great changes in nature and nations. They will accurately predict earthquakes, tidal waves, and other catastrophes of nature. These prophecies given in the name of Jesus Christ will come to pass exactly as predicted. This will cause the fear of Jehovah God to come upon the people. Whole nations are going to turn to God. Others will resent

Christ and rebel against His power. It will be like the days when Moses demonstrated God's power to Pharoah. The two witnesses of revelation are symbolic of the power and authority that will be demonstrated in this "Elijah company" that will be raised up for this special day of God's visitation to the Earth and final restoration of all things.

Eternal Church Greater Than Samson. Just as Samson, after his hair was fully restored, killed more of the enemy than he did in all of his previous years and exploits, in like manner the fully restored Church will affect more people for Jesus Christ and do greater exploits during this Last Century of the Church than all the preceding 1,900 centuries.

Imagination Insufficient. The statements given here are but a minute insight into the activity of the last generation Church. Eye has not seen nor ear heard all that God has prepared for them that love Him, but His Spirit has revealed a few of these things to us, enough to get us excited about pressing on with dedicated determination to make sure we are one of the participants in this next restorational movement.

Discerning of Spirits

(I Cor. 12:10; Is. 11:2-4; Mt. 24:4,5,11,24; 25:1-13; II Tim. 3:13; I Pet. 5:8; Rev. 16:13,14) Those Christian groups who do not have a mature proven ministry in their midst with the gift of discerning of spirits are going to be placed in precarious situations. During the days of this next restorational move of the Holy Spirit, Satan will arise and use every cunning and deceitful power available to deceive and destroy the true Church. False christs will arise with supernatural demonstrations so close to the genuine that it will

require the discerning of spirits to determine the difference. Those groups who do not have mature ministry with the wisdom of God directing them will be drawn after these counterfeits and ensnared. There will be troublesome times for the scripturally uneducated, spiritually immature, and for those whose oil is about run out and whose wicks are not trimmed. Woe to the foolish virgin saints of that day and hour *(Mt. 25:1-13)*.

Jesus said, "The very elect would be deceived if possible." False apostles and prophets will arise. They will sound very Evangelical and Charismatic in their words and actions. On the surface everything will look and sound right. But they will be wolves in sheep's clothing.

The true Church will not judge after the seeing of the eye, or hearing of the ear, but will judge in the righteousness of God by the spirit of discernment. Those who are saturated with the whole Word of God, who have the love of God in their hearts, who are filled with the Holy Spirit, and know the eternal purpose of God for His Church will not be led astray.

Purified, Spotless, Glorious Church *(Eph. 5:27)*

Full Maturity in Christ, Perfected *(Eph. 4:11-15)*

This truth has been emphasized over and over again throughout this book. Scores of Scriptures have been given to prove that the Church is going through a process of "going on" and "growing up" until it reaches the *perfection* of *purity* and *performance* and *manhood* of *maturity* and *ministry*.

Peak of Performance. Jesus will continue to arise within His true apostles, prophets, evangelists, pastors and teachers, until the saints are perfected and moving in their ministry; until the whole Body of Christ is fully built up and comes unto the "unity of the faith, knowledge that God's Son has, unto a perfect man, even the measure of the stature of the fulness of Christ." Some are destined to "grow up unto Him in all things, which is the Head, even Christ." The Church-Bride will not be a little girl (immature) or an old woman (fallen away, deteriorated) but a fully developed and grown young woman in Her prime and at the peak of Her performance.

Prerequisites for Participation. Those who shall be participants in the resurrection life ministry will not be there simply because of their revelation, faith, or preaching. Participants and leaders of past restorational movements were mightily used even though they were immature and carnal in areas of their lives. But those days have come to a close for the last generation Church. The only Christians who will participate fully in this resurrection life ministry will be those who have died the death to sin and self. Galations 2:20 will have become a life-style reality to them. Every attitude and action contrary to divine principle will have to be purged. Nothing short of conformity to the image of Jesus Christ will suffice.

Last Day Ministry of Prophets and Apostles. As the ministry of the apostle and prophet founded the Church, so shall the ministry of the apostle and prophet put the finishing touches on the Church. Prophets will be raised up in the Church to purge the ministry and the believers. There is a great lack of the reverential fear of God within Christendom. Christians, even Charismatic Christians come to church services with all types of sin in their lives, ranging from sexual immorality to gossip, jealousy, and party spirits. They sing, praise, rejoice, prophesy, and testify as though there were nothing out of order in their lives. Anointed ministers and especially prophets will move into a new realm of prophecy, word of knowledge, and discerning of spirits. They will expose this hypocrisy and cause the reverential fear of God to fall upon the congregations. Christians will come to the place where they examine their lives in prayer and with the Word of God before entering the church building to make sure every sin and selfish act is under the blood of Jesus. The religiously proud who try to justify themselves by lying to the Holy Ghost who is speaking through these ministers will receive the same judgment of God as Ananias and Sapphira did when they lied to the Holy Ghost speaking through the Apostle Peter.

Soldiers in the Making. The final days of the Church's "boot camp" training are here. Blanks have been taken out of the guns and real bullets put in. The ministry will not be just a noise anymore, but it will be in the power and demonstration of the Holy Ghost. Keep your head down in humbleness and follow Holy Ghost orders. For if you rise up now in self-will and rebellion, you will become a casualty. You may be killed by the bullet or wounded so badly that you will not recover sufficiently to be a qualified soldier in the coming Army of the Lord.

Results

Redemption of the Body .... Romans 8:23
Mortality swallowed up of life ... II Corinthians 5:4
Victory over the last enemy .... I Corinthians 15:26
Translation of the saints ..... I Thessalonians 4:17

We have already discussed the fact that the Holy Spirit, grace, and power that redeems the spirit and soul of man is the same Spirit, grace and power that redeems the body of the saints. If that Spirit, grace, and power is not already working in a person, there will be no redemption of his or her body. Jesus is the way, the truth and the **life.** He is the resurrection and the (resurrection) **life.** If Christ is our **life** then shall we appear with Him in glorified bodies. Jesus, through death, destroyed the devil who controlled death. When He arose from the grave, He gained the victory for His Church. Christians have eternal life in their spirit body now. They have everlasting life. They will never die spiritually. Jesus said the time is coming when those who are alive physicially and are believers will never see physical death. They will not go the way of the grave. Jesus died that they might live physically, as well as spiritually. The Early Church saints were sown throughout the Earth in Martyrdom that the last generation Church may be reaped throughout the Earth in immortalization of their bodies without death. The Church will gain victory over the last enemy, death. Victory speaks of a battle being fought. The last day saints will wage and win a warfare against death. The last generation saints will come to translating faith in preparation for participation in the translation.

Sovereignty or Faith-Maturity. Most Evangelical and Charismatic churches teach the translation of the Church, but each approaches this truth from one of two directions.

1. The total sovereign act of God with no preparation or participation by the Church required, except believing that Jesus is the Son of God and that He arose from the grave.

2. A sovereign act of God, but precipitated by the Church reaching maturity, fulfilling all Scripture and restoring all things, thereby releasing Jesus from Heaven to come back and translate His Church-Bride.

Regardless of which direction a person approaches the translation from, the end result is the same: the instanteneous, world-wide immortalization of the Church.

Purpose of Rapture — Translation. A Christian's concept concerning the *time* and *purpose* of the rapture-translation determines his or her approach. Those who believe the main purpose of the rapture is to remove all Christians from the Earth before the great tribulation and before God pours out His wrath upon the wicked, preach *total sovereignty rapture.* Those who preach the maturity of the Church and restoration of all scriptural truths believe the purpose of the rapture-translation is strictly for the *immortalization of the saints.* The purpose for the immortalization of the physical bodies of the saints is to enable them to participate with Christ in the next phase for the Church. The next phase for the Church is the mobilization of the saints into an invincible Army which shall follow its King of Kings as He goes forth conquering and to conquer. Immortalization of their bodies puts them in that glorified state where they can be with Him and function on His level as co-reigners and executioneers of His will upon planet Earth and throughout the universe.

Preparation and Purification by Fire!

There is a *"baptism of fire"* reserved for the last generation Church. Each restorational movement has had its own "baptism" revelation and experience: Pro-testant-*baptism of Repentance;* Holiness-*water;* Pentecostal-*Holy Ghost;* Charismatic-*Body of Christ;* United and Perfected Church-*Baptism of Fire.*

The Baptism of Fire

These divinely inspired words will especially apply to this generation: "He shall baptize you with the Holy Ghost, and with **fire**: Whose fan is in His hand, and He will thoroughly purge His floor, and gather His wheat into the garner; but He will burn up the chaff with unquenchable **fire**" *(Mt. 3:11,12)*. The Baptism of **Fire** within the saint burns up the chaff in his or her life, leaving nothing but the pure wheat. The Baptism of Fire is more than the burning zeal of the Lord within our soul.

Fire for Pruning, Purifying and Processing. Christ Jesus uses the Baptism of Fire in His Church as the farmer uses pruning shears in his orchard. The Baptism of Fire is God's way of pruning the individ-ual Christian of those things in his or her life which would hinder progressive growth and proper fruit pro-duction. God uses the Baptism of Fire to purify His saints as the goldsmith and silversmith use the fur-nace to purify gold and silver. Gold is not purified by only one process, and neither is the Baptism of Fire a once-in-a-lifetime experience. If we Christians are to be a manifestation of the pure Word of God then we will be immersed again and again, "as silver tried in a furnace of earth, purified seven times" *(Ps. 12:6)*. No overcomers will escape this Baptism of Fire. No amount of faith and positive confession can deliver a person from it, only through it. "The **fire** shall try *every man's work*" *(I Cor. 3:13),* so "think it not strange concerning the **fiery** trial which is to try you" *(I Pet. 4:12)* for "the trial of your faith is more precious to God than gold is to mankind" *(II Pet. 1:7)*. To reject the Baptism of Fire is to reject God, "For our God is a consuming **fire**" *(Heb. 12:29)*.

Some Christians may say "I am the temple of God, I am seeking the Lord and delighting in Him. Therefore, there is no need for me to be *tested, tried,* and *purified."*

> "Behold . . . the **Lord** whom you *seek,* shall suddenly come to His *temple,* even the messenger of truth whom ye *delight* in: Behold, He shall come, saith the **Lord** of hosts. But who may abide the day of His coming? and who shall stand when He appeareth? for He is like a refiner's **fire,** and like fuller's soap: And He shall sit as a refiner and purifier of silver: and He shall purify the sons of Levi, and purge them as gold and silver, that they may offer unto the **Lord** an offering in *righteousness"* *(Mal. 3:1-3).*

Most Christians want to be among Gideon's 300-member elite army that was left after God reduced them down to the *third part.* Jehovah God speaks through the prophet and says "I will bring the *third part* through the **fire,** and refine them as silver is refined and will try them as gold is tried" *(Zach. 13:9; Jud. 7:1-8).*

One should not fear or dread the Baptism of Fire anymore than the three Hebrew young men feared their fiery furnace. It will do for the Bride what it did for them: the **fire** will burn off the bondage put on by man, give a revelation of Jesus and bring the believer into an intimate relationship with the Son of God; and cause a whole nation to recognize that Jesus Christ is the living God *(Dan. 3:1-30).*

God's Firebrands. Those who go through the **fire** will become His firebrands. "He maketh His ministers a flame of **fire**" *(Ps. 104:4)*. "Behold, I will make my Word fire in thy mouth, and these people wood" *(Jer. 5:14)*. These Holy Ghost Church firebrands and flames of fire shall be united with their consuming-fire-God into that great Army of the Lord. They shall be one with Him "when He shall come to be glorified in His saints, . . . in *flaming fire* taking vengeance on them that know not God, and that obey not the gospel of our Lord Jesus Christ" *(II Thess. 1:8-10)*. Will it be worth it all? Jesus says to the Church, "I counsel thee to buy of me gold, tried in the **fire**" *(Rev. 3:18)*. If so, you will gain the overcomer's reward. And besides that, He promises "when *thou* walkest through the **fire,** *thou* shalt not be burned; neither shall the flame kindle upon *thee.* For I am the Lord *thy* God" *(Is. 43:2,3)*.

One Unified and Perfected Church

"Behold how good and how pleasant it is for brethren to dwell together in **unity.** For there [in the unity of the Church] the **Lord** commanded the blessing even **life** for evermore" *(Ps. 133)*. Unity will bring about the *resurrection life* and result in the immortalization of the Church.

The Church Cost the Most. To Jesus, bringing about the One United and Perfect Church is what it is all about. "Jesus *loved* the **Church** and gave Himself *for the* **Church**" *(Eph. 5:25)*. He wanted the Church more than He wanted life itself. The Church means more to Christ Jesus than all the wealth of the universe and all creation in Heaven and all nations of humanity on Earth. For all that it cost Him to produce all other earthly and heavenly things was the energizing of His creative power and the speaking forth of His creative Word. In extreme contrast what did it cost Him to produce the Church? It cost Him humiliation, suffering, death on a cruel cross, and His own life's blood. He purchased the Church with His precious blood and then sent His own Holy Spirit to birth His Church into existence. He has worked patiently for nearly two millennia to bring Her to the position of a fully matured, united, and perfected Church.

The Greatest Joy of Jesus. He did not return immediately for the Early Church because it was still in its infancy and without a sufficient number of members to satisfy Him. Jesus could not be satisfied with a one-person bride as the first Adam was, because He is so full of love that it will take a Bride consisting of many millions of saints to satisfy the heart of Jesus. No one individual is capable of absorbing His love, no more than a sponge could soak up all the water in the ocean. Not even a body of billions could exhaust the love He has for His own. Unlimited indescribable love beyond compare is flowing from the heart of Jesus to His Bride. He has been longing for the day when She will be wholly and eternally joined unto Himself. Just as a man's greatest joy is when he becomes physically one with his long-awaited bride, so the greatest joy of Jesus will be when His Bride is physically resurrected and translated bodily to meet Him in the air.

Seeing and Sensing the Heart of Jesus. The Holy Spirit directed the author to write this book for Jesus, about His Church and to His Church. The writer believes he was given a divinely inspired insight into what is taking place in the heart of Jesus as He sees this long-awaited moment approaching, and what He will do when it arrives.

Jesus is Getting Very Excited. At this very moment, Jesus is filled with an incomprehensible amount of heart-throbbing love and longing excitement. His anticipation has been progressively building for the last 2,000 years. It has become intensified during the last few centuries of the Church as He has beheld His Bride becoming more mature and prepared for marriage. He knows it won't be long now. The heartbeat of His love is increasing; every molecule of His resurrected human body is vibrating with divine desire; His emotions are spiritually inflamed with the passionate fire of holy love, reaching a sublime magnitude beyond human description.

Behold Now His Performance as All Things Are Accomplished for His Return. When the actual *moment* arrives for the consumation of the ages and the marriage to His Bride, He leaps from the throne and triumphantly sweeps down toward planet Earth. When He reaches Earth's atmosphere, He releases His pent-up love by jubilantly bursting forth with a victorious shout. When He releases that shout, it reverberates from the corridors of Heaven to the ends of the Earth. The spirits of the departed saints are gathered around Him with tingling excitement. As the archangel announces the momentous news and the trumpet of God is sounded, the bodies of the departed saints are immediately joined with their spirits as the first resurrection takes place. The living saints are instantaneously changed from mortals to immortals. This has happened so quickly that before one twinkle of His eye flashes by, the Bride is in His presence, fully united and clothed with their eternal bodies, joined together with their eternal Bridegroom in an endless union of living, loving, and reigning together forever and ever. Hallelujah! Amen.

5

Introduction To Sixth Doctrine Of Christ

The study of the Church will now venture into an area that is very sensitive to most theologians and preachers as well as to some lay-Christians. However, please keep in mind the author's major goals for each reader of this writing: first, to bring the individual reader into a personal relationship with Jesus Christ, the Head of the Church; second, to help that person become a knowledgeable and faithful member in the Universal Body of Christ; third, to help each person know his or her membership ministry in that Body; fourth, to encourage each person to be a faithful member within a local congregation of believers.

Respect for All Members of The Eternal Church. May the truths presented within this book lift the reader above the earthly things that divide the Body of Christ. May they lift the Christian into the higher realm of love and respect for all members of the Universal Body of Christ regardless of his or her earthly, independent, or denominational tag of Catholic, Protestant, Holiness, Pentecostal, or Charismatic.

The overall objective of the book is to present a panoramic view of the Church without becoming bogged down in the doctrinal differences within Christendom. The last four "Spiritual Experiences" of glorification, adjudication, administration, and continuation are mentioned for the sole purpose of giving the Church members inspirational insight into the possibilities of their future ministry with Christ Jesus our Lord.

A New Look at the Old Book. The challenge is given to fellow ministers and theologians to take a **new** look at the **Old** Book. Let us allow the Holy Spirit to lift our vision above man's perspective and into the very heart of Christ and seek to see the Church through the eyes of Jesus. This can only be done as we lay aside our eschatological categorizing, doctrinal dogmatisms, hermeneutical hang-ups, denominationalism, preconceived concepts, personal prophetic persuasions, and the habit of pigeon-holing every point presented under some theological terminology.

Only Jesus Sees the Whole Picture. There is not a mortal man on Earth who has a complete, clear, accurate, and detailed understanding of the end times. Jesus will never reveal the whole plan to any one man regardless of how prestigious he is within the Church. However, He is revealing by His Spirit all things to the Corporate Body of Christ. It is the revelation, teaching, ministry, and books written by all God-ordained ministers and anointed saints that make the whole Church picture clear. As individial ministers, we *know in part and perceive prophecy in part* but when the Church is united as one perfected Body, then the whole jigsaw picture puzzle of God's eternal plan for man will be revealed and fulfilled. This new wine will come from the cluster not from just one grape. The newness and fulness of truth is in the whole Body of Christ; it is not in just one denomination, fellowship, congregation, or individual Christian. Comprehensive as this book is, it does not give all the pieces to the puzzle. There are other good books which present pieces of the puzzle from the perspective of God's dealings with the wicked nations of the world, with Israel, and with the Jews. But this writing looks at all of God's works from the perspectives of the Church and God's eternal plan for Jesus and His Bride.

Our Relationship. It is not that I have no concern for the wicked world and the natural Jew, but I am convinced that my relationship *with* and ministry *to* them will be as a member of the Church. My eternal citizenship is in the Church. I am a native of the Church-nation, a member of the new race of humanity called the Church-race. My revelation and anointing is as a prophet *in* the Church and *to* the Church. My eternal function will be as a member of this Church. The destiny of the Church is my destiny. If you are a member of this One Universal, Many-Membered, Corporate Body of Christ, then your destiny is in the Church, and our destiny is together in Christ. There is no higher calling, created race, nation on Earth, or world in the universe that equals the Church-Bride of Christ. The highest privilege ever offered to any of God's created beings is that of being a member of the Body of Christ. Let us now look at some of the things that may be in our future as members of His Eternal Church.

Concerning the Chart. Since sections 6, 7 and 8 on the chart are all futuristic, the former pattern of explaining, under separate headings, each point presented will not be followed in the same detailed manner. A minimal general explanation will be given, and then a summarized conclusion of *"My Present Personal Perception"* concerning the future performance of the Church.

Time in the Hands of the Eternal

No **approximate date** is given for "Adjudication" for the same reason one was not given for "glorification." Deuteronomy 29:29 states, "The secret things belong unto the Lord our God: but the things which are revealed belong unto us and to our children for ever, that we may **do** all the words of this law." Jesus said, "It is not for you to know the times or the season, which the Father hath put in His own power. But ye shall receive power, after that the Holy Ghost is come upon you" *(Acts 1:7,8)*.

"Time" is one of God's secrets which is rarely shared with the Church or individuals. More important to Him is the *preparation* and *power* required to be a part of His *plan*. The Scriptures definitely speak of all the ideas presented on the chart. They shall come to pass. My dispensational theology background and understanding of the restoration of the Church causes me to believe these things will happen within the next 50 years, possibly before the year 2,000; they could be fulfilled almost anytime, for final preparation is in progress now.

Which "Mill" is Right? The chart is not offered to promote any particular eschatological viewpoint (doctrines concerning end time events). No attempt is made to prove pre-millennialism, post-millennialism, or a-millennialism. It is doubtful that any one of the views is 100 percent right. There is some truth in each viewpoint. This book presents a post-millennial view of a restored victorious Church at the end of the Church Age as well as the "pre-mill" view that the translation of the Church will be followed by a 1,000-year reign of the saints with Christ; and agrees with the a-millennialists that "Believers are already in heavenly places in Christ Jesus and reign in life by Him; Satan is a defeated foe, and believers triumph over him in Christ." (Baker's *Dictionary of Theology,* p. 354.) The **"pan-mill"** view is presented more than anything else; that is, everything is going to **pan-out** according to God's eternal purpose. Thank God that man's various eschatological viewpoints will not change the way He has predestined for it to happen.

Preparation Not Time-Period. To those with the view of the Eternal Church, the post-tribulation, mid-tribulation, or pre-tribulation rapture viewpoint is not the issue. The issue is preparation, purification, and perfection of each person for proper performance. Those who receive all that the Holy Spirit requires for the last generation Church will be a part of that Church. They will remain with the Church whether it stays and the wicked go or the wicked stay and the Church goes; whether its translation takes place in the beginning, middle, or end of that controversial seven-year period.

Is It Possible?

The Church is now moving toward the unity of the Spirit, but will it ever reach the unity of the faith? The Scriptures emphatically declare that the five-fold ministry of the apostle, prophet, evangelist, pastor and teacher must function until the Church reaches the "unity of the faith" *(Eph. 4:11-13)*. "For they [the Church] shall see eye to eye when the Lord shall bring again Zion" *(Is. 52:8)*. How can this ever become a reality with all the various viewpoints within Christendom? Most Catholic and historic Protestants are *a-millennialists,* and interpret the book of Revelation from the *historicist* view. The majority of Holiness Movement churches are *post-mill* and *pre-mill* with a few being *a-mill.* Nearly all Pentecostal Movement churches are *pre-mill* and *pre-trib* rapture and are *futurist* in their interpretation of the book of Revelation. However, because Present-truth Charismatics come from all of these major denominational backgrounds, one can find all of these various beliefs concerning end time events among their preachers.

The Greatest Challenge. The Holy Spirit has before Him the greatest challenge of all, to bring the Church not only to the unity of Spirit but also to the unity of the faith. The Holy Spirit is already at work. When I travel among the various Charismatic churches I find they are beginning to believe and practice the same things. Preachers and priests with such extreme backgrounds as Catholic and Pentecostal, and ministers with such different approaches as Southern Baptist and Church of Christ, are no longer promoting their old denominational eschatological doctrines but have come to a new unified position concerning God's plan for the Church. Most Charismatic ministers are preaching the same things throughout the world even though they have had no personal communication or doctrinal discussions. The Holy Spirit does not hold "forty-eleven" different views concerning the Church. The Holy Spirit will fully fill, enlighten, and control the last day Church and will bring it to the fulness of truth. Those who are filled with the Holy Spirit and are the Mt. Zion of God will come to see eye to eye. The Holy Spirit will not give up on or fail in His task of bringing the Church to maturity in the unity of Spirit and faith.

Washington for Jesus, 1980

Rev. John Gimenez inspired and launched the incredible vision of "Washington for Jesus." The result was "More than 500,000 gathered at Capitol Mall during the WFJ Rally held April 29, 1980." *(AFJ Publication,* Vol. 1, No. 1, p. 9.) It was the largest non-denominational Christian gathering ever recorded in history. Though WFJ was played down by the "secular media", it merited mention in the *1981 Book of the Year,* page 605, of the Encyclopedia Britannica. John Gimenez is now National Chairman of "America for Jesus" (AFJ). The National Executive Committee of AFJ reads like a "Who's Who?" list of Evangelical and Charismatic leaders. Plans are being made for another "Washington for Jesus" in 1982. Those who desire further information may write to "America for Jesus, P.O. Box 62524, Virginia Beach, Virginia 23462.

A Prototype of Universal Potential. A living example and prelude to what could be done in the Universal Body of Christ was demonstrated on April 29, 1980, at the Washington for Jesus rally in front of the capitol. Over one-half million people gathered for a day of repentance. A unified effort was made to present the One Universal Body of Christ to the world. All the presidents of the Christian television networks were represented. Ministers from virtually every Christian denomination were represented and many spoke to that great gathering of the Body of Christ. Even the Eastern Orthodox Church was represented as well as Catholic, historical Protestants, Evangelicals, Fundamentalists, Pentecostals, and prominent Charismatic leaders.

Historical Happening. This assembly was an unprecedented historic occasion beyond anything recorded in church history. There was nothing but love and unity flowing from the platform and throughout that great congregation of saints. My wife and I were greatly moved as we marched with the Arizona delegation. The streets were lined on each side with Christians as we turned back toward the park. As familiar faces were seen, hands would be raised and great shouts of recognition and rejoicing would ring forth.

What a Day That Will Be! It caused us to think of how we will feel when we march through the portals of glory and find the saints of past ages awaiting our arrival. They will smile and wave and rejoice and welcome us into the everlasting unity and brotherhood of the Eternal Church. Oh, what a day that will be. It will take millions of years just to personally greet each of the billions of saints that will be together with Christ. Hallelujah! We will forever have eternal gratitude for the privilege of being a child of the King of Kings and a member of the Eternal Body of Christ.

6

The Eternal Judgement Ministry

The Church is destined to experientially receive and manifest the *Sixth Doctrine of Christ* "Eternal Judgment." The author is not making references to the *"Judgment Seat of Christ"* or the *"White Throne Judgment,"* but rather to *Christ's judgment of the world and angels through the church.* "Do you not know that the saints will judge the world? . . . Do you not know that we the Church, are to judge angels" *(I Cor. 6:2,3 RSV)?*

When Will it Happen? The *Eternal Judgment Doctrine* will be fully manifested when Jesus activates His Church into the Army of the Lord and fulfills Revelation 11:15. "The kingdoms of this world are become the kingdoms of our Lord and of His Christ; and He shall reign forever and ever." This Scripture is applicable to our Lord Jesus and His Church. The Church is Jesus' *"christos,"* anointed one, as Jesus is God's *christos,* anointed one. The church is called the Body of Christ, or it would be the same to say the Body of the Anointed, or Jesus' Anointed Corporate Body. The Church is one body of believers referred to in the singular not the plural. The Church is our Lord's anointed one. Followers of Christ are called Christians, Christ-ones, *"Christianos."*

Pre-Immortalization Ministry

The Church Army of the Lord will enter into a last-day ministry before its immortalization, and into an even greater ministry afterwards. God's ultimate goal for this age is a matured Church with the fulness of Christ's life, an equipped Army ready to arise with Christ Jesus to fight and win the greatest battle of all ages.

Jesus Waiting on the Church. There are many Scriptures relating to the ministry of the Church which have not been fulfilled. As was discussed in a previous chapter, we found that according to Acts 3:21 (LB), **"Jesus must remain in heaven until the final recovery of all things from sin as prophesied from ancient times."** All that the fall of man and sin has taken away from humanity, Jesus, through His Church, shall restore. Jesus Christ, through His death, burial, and resurrection, provided all things necessary for His Church to bring about the "recovery of all things." King David of old provided all things necessary for the building of the temple, but it was turned over to his son, Solomon, for its completion. Jesus provided the plan and provision for the recovery or restoration of all things and the building of His kingdom, but it was turned over to His many-membered corporate Son, the Church, for its fulfillment. David through death had to leave his son to work alone, but Jesus through His death and resurrection came back in the power of His Holy Spirit and is now living and working within His Corporate Son.

It Takes Two to Make One. Jesus has fully identified Himself with the Church. He and His Church
are one: He is the head, Church members are the
body; bone of His bone and flesh of His flesh. It takes
both a head and a body to make a functioning being,
it takes Jesus and His Church to make one functioning ministry. As husband and wife are one flesh in
God's sight *(Eph. 5:31),* so Jesus and His Church are
one in spirit and ministry *(I Cor. 6:17).* The Eternal
designed it that way and it is the greatest delight of
Jesus for it to be so.

Jesus Completed His Personal Part. When Jesus
declared "It is finished," and "Father, *I have finished
the work which thou gavest* **me** *to do,"* it revealed
that Jesus had finished the work which had to be
done by Himself, personally, alone. Jesus is thrilled
that His independent, individual ministry is over forever. Never again will He have to do anything alone.
Whatever else is to be done will be done **with** the
Church. Paul E. Billheimer in his book *Destined for
the Throne,* p. 27, emphasizes this point:

> That this is God's glorious purpose for the
> Church is authenticated and confirmed by
> the apostle Paul in I Corinthians 6:2,3. "Do
> ye not know that the saints shall judge the
> world? . . . Know ye not that we shall judge
> angels?" This is an earnest of what Jesus
> meant when He said, "The glory that thou
> gavest me I have given them" *(Jn. 17:22).*
> This royalty and rulership is no hollow,
> empty, figurative, symbolic, or emblematic
> thing. It is not a figment of the imagination.
> The Church, the Bride, the Eternal Compan-
> ion is to sit **with Him** on His throne. If His
> throne represents reality, then hers is no fan-

tasy. Neither joint heir can do anything **alone** *(Rom. 8:17).* In law a joint heir can do nothing alone, nothing without the other.

Co-Laborers Together Forever. Jesus Christ purchased His Church to be His co-laborer, His united Bride, one with Him in *all that He* **was,** *shall ever* **be** *or shall ever* **do.** *Everything that Jesus shall ever do again from now to eternity will be done* **in, through,** *and* **with** *His Church.* **He will never do anything ever again without His Church-Bride being a part with Him in its fulfillment.**

From Origination to Eternal Destination. Jesus has eternally joined Himself unto His Church. He united Himself with His Church in its origination, and did not forsake His Bride during Her deterioration. He has continued to give Himself to His Church time after time in restoration, and will continue until She reaches Her ultimate destination. He has delegated His power of attorney unto His Church for the performance of His eternal purpose. **All things** yet to be **revealed, restored,** or **fulfilled** will be accomplished **in, by** and **through** His Church. The Church-Bride is now functioning as co-executor of His Word and also will continue this ministry after Her resurrection-translation.

The Church is Eternal. Members of the Body of Christ, let your heart rejoice and be glad for the ministry of the Church is destined never to deactivate or end, but to escalate and begin on a higher realm. The Body of Christ will never be dismembered or disbanded, but will become more fully united and eternally magnified in Her ministry with Christ Jesus. Hallelujah, Amen!

Nothing Can Separate. Be convinced, along with the Apostle Paul, that the Church can never be separated from its love, life, reality, and ministry with Christ Jesus. Paul had the clearest and most complete revelation of the Church of any of the biblical writers. As a member of Christ's great Corporate Body he spoke emphatically with great conviction to the Church at Rome concerning the united ministry and relationship with Jesus. "For I am persuaded that neither death, nor life, nor angels, nor principalities, nor powers, nor things present, nor things to come, nor height, nor depth nor any other creature, shall separate us . . . " *(Rom. 8:38,39)*.

Nothing Can Stop Him. Absolutely nothing can stop Jesus from ultimately fulfilling His purpose in and through His Church. Death can't; nothing in life can; demons in Hell or the devil himself cannot, and not even angels in the Heavens. The Church is so interwoven into every fiber, life, and purpose of Christ's being that all of Heaven would have to be ripped apart and the eternal Godhead destroyed in order to separate the Church from Christ. The Church is in the Father's hand and no man can pluck it out *(Jn. 10:28,29)*.

Four Have Been — Three Shall Be. Since nothing can stop Jesus Christ from fulfilling His purpose in His Church, the last three Doctrines of Christ will be fulfilled just as surely as the first four have already been fulfilled and restored. Just as the Church has experientially entered into Justification, Sanctification, Manifestation, and Ministration, it will now begin to enter into its time of Glorification, Adjudication, and Administration with eternal Continuation into the endless ages to come.

Saints Are Christ's Living Letters *(II Cor. 3:12)*. Since the mortal Church must fulfill all Scriptures pertaining to it before Jesus can return, it is beneficial to look at some Scriptures which should be fulfilled in and through the Church before its translation. The following Scriptures are by no means exhaustive, but hopefully they will motivate Christians to read the Bible with this thought in mind: Is this Scripture an experiential reality within the Church, and if so, is it a living experience in my life? If it is not active in the Church, then begin to pray and believe for it to be activated and fulfilled.

Scriptures to be Fulfilled in Fulness

"Behold, I give unto you power . . . over all the power of the enemy: and **nothing** shall by **any means** hurt you." [To be fulfilled physically as well as spiritually] *(Lk. 10:19).*

"As ye go, preach, saying, The kingdom of heaven is at hand. Heal the sick, cleanse the leper, **raise the dead,** cast out devils: freely ye have received, freely give" *(Mt. 10:7,8).*

"As thou [Father] hast sent me [Jesus] into the world, even so have I also sent them [the Church] into the world" [with the same commission, power and authority] *(Jn. 17:20).*

"Verily, verily, I say unto you, He that **believeth** on me, the works that I do shall he do also; and **greater works** than these shall he do; because I go unto my Father" [to send back the Holy Ghost which will give the power to do these works] *(Jn. 14:12).*

Search For More. There are scores of other Scriptures that reveal the power within the Church. A few individuals have learned how to release this power but the Body of Christ as a whole has not. The Church is operating on candle light power and not using the Holy Spirit dynamo which is capable of generating a million volts of divine-light-power. All of the fruit and gifts of the Holy Spirit and the seven-fold spirit of God will be activated into the Church during the last days of its mortal ministry in the world.

7

The Army Of The Lord

The Church has always been an "Army", but has gone through stages of "active" and "inactive," cold wars and hot wars. The Church was reactivated into a militant army and has been engaged in a hot war since the beginning of the *"Period of the Great Restoration."*

Church Forts Captured. The Kingdom of the Church was overrun by the devil during the deterioration of the Church when it went through its Dark Ages. Satan established his forts of dead religion and false concepts of God throughout the Church.

Church's Counter-Attack. The Reformation was the beginning of the sounding of the trumpet for the Church to begin its conquering march. The Church was destined to recapture every fortified area of which Satan had stolen. Since the Church is more than a conqueror it shall not only reclaim the truths that were lost but also reclaim and restore what Satan stole from Adam. He tore down Adam's fortified area of continuous physical life and broke his intimate fellowship with God. The devil then established his fort of rebellion and physical death in the human race.

Church Truth-Forts Recaptured and Restored. Each restorational movement has destroyed Satan's fort and reestablished the "fort of truth" in all its experiential reality. The Catholic Church held the fort of basic Christian truths found in the Apostles' Creed for over a 1,000 years; then the campaign for the full restoration was activated. The division of the Protestant Movement, commanded by General Luther, destroyed Satan's fort of religious dead works and reclaimed that territory for the Church-Kingdom. It then established the true fort of justification by faith. The Holiness Movement took more territory away from the devil and reestablished the fort of believer's baptism, sanctification and divine healing. The Pentecostal Movement reestablished the powerful fort of the baptism of the Holy Ghost and several gifts of the Holy Spirit. The Latter Rain-Charismatic Movement recaptured more territory and reestablished the "Truth-Forts" of laying on of hands, man's whole being involved in praise and worship, deliverance from demons, disease and sickness.

Formidable Fort Facing Present Generation. At the present, the Church is engaged in a battle to take one of the most fortified strongholds of Satan. Ministerial leaders in this Army of the Lord are challenging Christians to live above the world system; to live in divine health, to get out and stay out of debt, to practice the principles that produce physical and materialistic prosperity for the advancing and establishing of the Church-Kingdom. Satan has held that which belongs to the Church long enough. The Body of Christ is now awakening to the fact that the

"Earth is the Lord's and the fulness thereof" *(Ps. 24:1).* All of its wealth and means of commuting and communicating belong to the Church for the propagation of the gospel and fulfillment of the purpose of God in the Church.

Hold the Fort. The taking of every fort has brought casualties to extremism and waywardness, but a large percentage remain faithful to hold that fort of truth. Each restorational advancement of the Army of the Lord has established denominational forts that are given the responsibility to maintain the purity and power of that truth.

Storm the Fort. New recruits are now being drafted and trained and older soldiers and generals are being put through intensified training for the next advancement of the Church-Army. They are being purified by the Baptism of Fire, and everything that can be shaken within them is being shaken that that which cannot be shaken may remain *(Heb. 12:27).* The Church is being prepared and equipped with the revelation and power to go against the most formidable fortress Satan has ever built. There is no biblical record or church history account of one member of the Body of Christ winning the battle against this fort of death. Not one Christian has gotten out of this world alive in his physical body. Satan is determined that none ever will, but Jesus has other plans.

Let's Go Up to Mt. Zion. The last great stronghold to fall to David when he arose to be king of all Israel was the fortified area that later became known as Mt. Zion. After Mt. Zion was taken, David set up his throne and appointed those who helped him wage successful warfare in positions of ruling and reigning with him. Satan's last stronghold is death. When the Church and Jesus take Mt. Zion (victory over death) then Jesus will set up His kingdom over planet Earth and His saintly warriors will rule and reign with Him. When Christians sing about going up to Mt. Zion, they are singing about taking the last fortified stronghold of Satan and setting up the city of God and the throne of their Eternal King David, Jesus Christ our Lord. The Holy Spirit will soon cause the cry to arise within the Church. "Let's go up to Zion, let's go up to Zion, the city of our God!"

An Invincible Army

No weapon that is formed against thee shall prosper; and every tongue that shall arise against thee in judgment thou shalt condemn. This is the heritage of the servants of the Lord, and their righteousness is of me, saith the Lord *(Is. 54:17)*.

Who is she [Bride of Christ] that looketh forth as the morning, fair as the moon, clear as the sun and terrible as an **Army** with banners? *(Song. 6:10)*. Return, return, O Shullamite [Church]; Return, return, [be restored, be restored], that we may look upon thee. What will ye see in the Shullamite? As it were the **company** of two **armies** *(Song 6:13)*.

Blow ye the trumpet in Zion, sound an alarm in my holy mountain [Church]; let all the inhabitants of the land tremble: for the *day of the Lord* [when He comes to be glorified in his saints] cometh, for it is nigh at hand. [It will be a day of darkness and gloominess for the world but the dawning of a new day for the Church.] . . . as the morning spread upon the mountains: [The Church-

Army becomes His firebrands.] A fire devoureth before them . . . and nothing shall escape them . . . like the noise of a flame of fire that devoureth the stubble, as a strong people **set in battle array** . . . They shall run like mighty men; they shall climb the wall **like men of war;** and they shall march every one on his ways, [know their membership ministry in Body of Christ] and they shall not break their ranks [faithful, submissive and consistent to their calling]; neither shall one thrust another [unity and love]; they shall walk everyone in his path [faithful to his position and performance]: And when they fall upon the sword, they shall not be wounded [death to self, fulness of life and one with the Word-sword]. They shall run to and fro . . . The earth shall quake before them, the heavens shall tremble . . . and the **Lord** shall utter *His voice* before **His Army;** for *His camp* is very great: for He is strong that *executeth* His Word *(Joel 2:1-12).* [This is the prophet Joel's description of the Church-Army of the Lord.]

Christ Says to His Army: "Thou shalt not be afraid for the terror by night; nor for the arrow [rockets and missiles] that flieth by day; nor for the pestilence that walketh in darkess [germ warfare]; nor for the destruction that wasteth at noon day [atomic warfare]; . . . A thousand shall fall at thy side, and ten thousand at thy right hand; but it shall not come nigh thee. Only with thine eyes shalt thou behold and see the reward of the wicked. There shall no evil befall thee, neither shall any plague come nigh thy dwelling. Thou shalt tread upon the lion and adder, the young lion and the dragon shalt thou trample under feet. With long life [resurrection life] will I satisfy him [the Church] and show him my salvation [glorification] *(Ps. 91).*

. . . and behold a white horse: and he that sat on him had a bow: and a crown was given unto him: and he went forth *conquering and to conquer (Rev. 6:2).* We are more than conquerors through Him *(Rom. 8:37).* And behold a white horse; and he that sat upon him was called Faithful and True, and in righteousness He doth *judge* and *make war* . . . on His head were many crowns . . . He was clothed with a vesture dipped in blood: And His name is called the Word of God. And the **armies** which were in heaven followed Him upon white horses, clothed in fine linen [the righteousness of the saints], pure and clean. And out of His mouth goeth a sharp sword, that with it He should *smite the nations* and he shall *rule them with a rod of iron:* And He treadeth the winepress of the fierceness and wrath of Almighty God. And He hath on His vesture and on His thigh a name written, **King of Kings, and Lord of Lords** *(Rev. 19:11-16).*

Adjudication and Administration of the Church

Adjudication is the act or process of hearing and deciding judicially; making a judicial sentence, judgment or decision. *Administration* is the act of administering the affairs of others; directing, managing, and dispensing justice. An *administrator* is the chief agent in managing public affairs. A president administers the law when he executes it, or carries it into effect. A judge administers the law when he applies it to a particular case or person.

King Jesus and Queen Church Rule the Universe

Jesus, as Commander in Chief of His Church, will subdue all things under the feet of His Corporate Body. The Church, which has functioned as the Bride of Christ, will then be fully joined unto Christ Jesus as His Wife. She then becomes a part of the sovereign Lordship which is over all the universal affairs of the Kingdom of God on Earth and throughout the universe. Jesus will be recognized by all creation as King Eternal and His Bride-Church as Queen Eternal. Together They execute God's "Eternal Judgments." They sit in the throne together as co-administrators. They rule and reign together as They adjudicate and administer the affairs of Heaven and Earth.

Malachi Makes Mention of Ministry. Probably Malachi 3:16, 17 and 18 gives the clearest picture of the next three phases of the Church. Verse 16 reveals its present time of preparation, meditation and communication. Verse 17 speaks of glorification and translation. Verse 18 makes known the Church's ministry of adjudication and administration.

8

The Reign
Of The
Queen Church

Ruling and Reigning — Reality or Allegory? Most Evangelicals, Pentecostals and many Charismatic Christians talk about being "raptured" and "ruling and reigning" with Christ. However, the majority leave it in the ethereal, mystical, and abstract realm. They rarely think it through to its literal conclusion. If Christ is speaking about a real ministry and not just figurative and allegorical talk, then it is a reality and not a fantasy. Let us try to project ourselves to that time and "think it through" and visualize how it could be in living reality.

You Have Just Been Raptured!

Jesus has just returned with a shout, the trumpet has sounded and you have been translated into an immortal Church member. You now spend seven years, 3½ years, or five seconds with Christ in the heavenlies as He organizes His Church into the Army of the Lord. Jesus goes forth with His Church to establish His Kingdom upon Earth. You, as a member of the Queen Church are now ready to "rule and reign" with

Christ, not as a robot or preprogrammed computer. But you are to function as a redeemed, creative thinking and knowledgeable human being. Jesus comes to you and says, "Sister Faithful or Brother Goodman, I am appointing you administrator over this part of Earth called Japan. There are still millions of mortals living on those islands. I want you to establish **My** Kingdom there. Do everything according to My ways and principles. Change every law and practice they have which is contrary to My principles. I want peace to reign supreme, therefore, establish divine guidelines which will maintain cooperation and unity among the people and with the rest of the world. Make sure you do everything according to the divine pattern as is revealed in the Book of the Kingdom. The Bible is the constitution and the by-laws of the government of the Church Kingdom. I hope you studied it carefully, understand it thoroughly, and that all of its precepts are the motivating principles of your life and the meditations of your mind. It's in your hands now. You said you were ready to rule and reign with Me. Bye! I will return in about a year to see if you have done all things according to My will and way."

Are You Ready? Where do you start? What will you do? A new government must be established, a new way of life for those millions of people. You are now ready to rule and reign on your overcomer's throne! But are you? Do you really want to rule and reign with Christ? *Rapture is not retirement.* Heaven is not one eternal hallelujah holiday. Glorification is not becoming good-for-nothing. Victory over the last enemy does not mean eternal vacation. There will be joy unspeakable and full of glory, rest, excitement, eating, drinking, and playful activity. But that is not why Jesus died for the Church and then spent 2,000 years preparing and perfecting the Church. He created the human race in order to redeem a people unto Himself to work with Him in fulfilling His eternal purpose. The Church has a great work to do with Christ in Her mortal state and an even greater work to do with Christ after Her immortalization. Let us now see if the Scriptures really speak of the saints working with Christ in the executing of His Word, will, and wrath.

Saints Executing Judgment With Christ

Let the **saints** be joyful in glory. Let the high praises of God be in their mouth and a two-edged sword [Word of God] in their hand: To **execute** vengeance upon the heathen and punishments upon the people; to bind their kings with chains, and their nobles with fetters of iron: **to execute** upon them **the judgment written**: This **honor** have all His **saints** *(Ps. 149:6-9).*

. . . and **judgment** was given *to* the **saints** of the most High; and the time came that the **saints** possessed the kingdom . . . But the **judgment** shall sit . . . and the kingdom and dominion, and the greatness of *the kingdom under the whole heaven shall be given to* the people of the **saints** of the most High, whose kingdom is an everlasting kingdom and all dominions shall serve and obey him *(Dan. 7:22,26,27).*

Behold the Lord cometh **with** ten thousands of His **saints, to execute judgment** upon all . . . the ungodly . . . *(Jude 1:15).*

He that hath an ear let him hear what the Spirit saith unto the Church. He that *overcometh* and keepeth my works unto the end, to him will I give *power over the nations:* And he [the overcomer] shall *rule them with a rod of iron;* as the vessels of a potter shall they be broken to shivers: even as I received of my Father. To him that overcometh will I grant to **sit with Me in My throne** even as I also overcome, and am set down with my Father in His throne *(Rev. 2:26,27; 3:21).*

And I saw thrones, and they [Church overcomers, saints] sat upon them, and judgment was given unto them . . . and they lived and reigned with Christ a thousand years. . . . They shall be priests of God and of Christ and shall **reign with Him** a thousand years *(Rev. 20:4,6).*

If we be dead with him we shall also live with him: If we suffer, we shall also **reign with Him** *(II Tim. 2:11).*

Heirs of God and **joint-heirs with Christ;** if so be that we suffer with Him that we may be also **glorified together** *(Rom. 8:17).*

Church Headquarters — Planet Earth

Thou [Jesus] hast redeemed us to God by thy blood out of every kindred, and tongue, and people, and nation. And hast made us unto our God kings and priests and we [the Church] shall **reign** on the **Earth** *(Rev. 5:9,10).*

For evil doers shall be cut off: but *those that wait upon the Lord,* they shall *inherit* the **Earth;** For such as be blessed of him shall inherit the **Earth;** and they that be cursed of him shall be cut off. The righteous shall inherit the land and dwell therein forever *(Psa. 37:9,22,29).*

Blessed are the meek for they shall inherit the **Earth** *(Mt. 5:5).*

For thus saith the Lord, that created the heavens; God himself that formed the **Earth** not in vain, He formed **Earth** to be inhabited *(Is. 45:18).*

And the **Lord** said . . . But as truly as I live **all** the **Earth** shall be filled with the glory of the **Lord** *(Num. 14:21).*

Come behold the works of the Lord, what desolations He hath made in the **Earth.** He maketh wars to cease unto the end of the **Earth** . . . Be still, and know that I am God; I will be exalted among the heathen, *I will be exalted in the* **Earth** *(Ps. 46:8-10).*

For the **Earth** is the Lord's and the fulness thereof *(I Cor. 10:26; Ps. 24:1; 50:6).*

The Lord is in his holy temple: let all the **Earth** keep silence before Him . . . For the **Earth** *shall be filled* with the knowledge of the glory of the Lord, as the waters cover the sea *(Hab. 2:14,20).*

All the ends of the **Earth** shall see the salvation of our God *(Is. 52:10).*

[Even] . . . the **Earth** which he hath established forever *(Ps. 78:69).*

Thy kingdom come. Thy will be done in **Earth,** as it is in heaven *(Mt. 6:10).*

And the seventh angel sounded; and there were great voices in heaven, saying, The kingdoms of this world are become the *kingdoms of our Lord, and of His Christ;* and He shall reign forever and ever *(Rev. 11:15).*

And they [the Church] sung a new song, Thou art worthy to take the book, and to open the seals thereof: For thou [Jesus] wast slain, and hast redeemed us to God by thy blood out of every kindred, and tongue, and people, and nation; and hast made us unto our God **kings** and **priests** and **we shall reign on the Earth** *(Rev. 1:5,6; 5:9,10).*

Redemption of Creation and Restoration of Earth

All of God's creation that has unwillingly been contaminated by the pride, rebellion, and fall of Lucifer and Adam shall be redeemed, renewed, and restored (not speaking of unsaved dead or of fallen angels). Natural creation fell into the bondage of decay and death along with Adam when he sinned. The realms where Satan has functioned since his fall shall be renovated by God's cleansing fire. The Earth shall be cleansed by fire and all the works of fallen man that are therein shall be burned up. "And He that sat upon the throne said, Behold, I make all things new" *(Rev. 21:5).* He did not say He would make all new things, but that all things which have been in existence since the fall of Lucifer will be made new.

But the day of the Lord shall come as a thief in the night; in the which the heavens shall pass away with a great noise, and the elements shall melt with fervent heat, the earth also and the works that are therein shall be burned up. Seeing then that all these things shall be dissolved, what manner of persons ought ye to be in all holy conversation and godliness, looking for and hasting unto the coming of the day of God, wherein the heavens being on fire shall be dissolved, and the elements shall melt with fervent heat? Nevertheless we, according to his promise, look for new heavens **and a new Earth,** wherein dwelleth righteousness *(II Pet. 3:10-13).*

"And I saw a new heaven and **a new Earth**" *(Rev. 21:1).*

Earth will have its change similar to the bodies of translated saints.

Manifestation of the Sons of God

The Earth and all of creation is waiting for the manifestation of the sons of God, the time when they will come into their maturity and immortalization. "For the earnest expectation of the creature waiteth for the *manifestation of the sons of God*" *(Rom. 8:19).* When the Church receives its full inheritance and redemption then creation will be redeemed from its cursed condition of decay, change and death. The "Phillips" translation says, "The whole of creation is on tiptoe to see the wonderful sight of the sons of

God coming into their own." For an expanded insight read Romans 8:18-23 in various translations.

Creation Awaiting Church's Redemption. The Church has a responsibility and ministry to the rest of creation. Earth and its natural creation is anxiously waiting for the Church to reach full maturity and come to full sonship. When the Church realizes its full sonship, its bodily redemption will cause a redemptive chain reaction throughout all of creation.

Mysterious Scriptures. There are numerous applications and interpretations of Isaiah 65:17-25. The most popular being that it is a description of the state of affairs and activities of the mortal humans on Earth during the millennial age. It is a most interesting set of Scriptures. Without divine enlightenment, it produces more questions than answers.

Isaiah 65:17-26 NIV

"Behold, I will create new heavens and a new earth. The former things will not be remembered, nor will they come to mind.

"But be glad and rejoice forever in what I will create, for I will create Jerusalem to be a delight and its people a joy.

"I will rejoice over Jerusalem and take delight in my people; the sound of weeping and of crying will be heard no more.

"Never again will there be in it an infant that lives but a few days, or an old man who does not live out his years; he who dies at a hundred will be thought a mere youth; he who fails to reach a hundred will be considered accursed.

"They will build houses and dwell in them;

they will plant vineyards and eat their fruit.

"No longer will they build houses and others live   in them, or plant and others eat. For as the days of a tree, so will be the days of my people; my chosen ones will long enjoy the works of their hands.

"They will not toil in vain or bear children doomed to misfortune; for they will be a people blessed by the Lord, they and their descendants with them.

"Before they call I will answer; while they are still speaking I will hear.

"The wolf and the lamb will feed together, and the lion will eat straw like the ox, but dust will be the serpent's food. They will neither harm nor destroy in all my holy mountain," says the **Lord.**

9

Personal Perception Of The Higher And Eternal Realm

My Present Personal Perception. Based on my scriptural understanding, and some Holy Spirit enlightenment, the following is a condensed version of what I foresee for the future of the Church.

Purification, Perfection and Power. During these final years of the mortal Church, there will be great restoration and revival. The Body of Christ will be purified by the Baptism of Fire and by immersion in His love, which will bring about the unity of the Church. The true *ecclesia,* the called out and pressing-on Church, will become perfected in purity and maturity. She will preach the gospel of the Kingdom of God in all nations in full power and demonstration of the Holy Spirit.

Christian Communities. Christian groups will establish Christian communities which will meet the total needs of man — spirit, soul, and body. There will be seminars for ministers establishing them in all presently restored truth, Bible colleges, schools of the Holy Spirit teaching saints how to receive and manifest the gifts of the Holy Spirit. Christian schools with grades Kindergarten through 12, marriage counselling retreats, training in trades, divine healing for the body and inner healing for sanctification of the soul. Most of these centers will be outside the metropolitan city areas. Some of these communities will evolve into small Christian cities which will be a prelude and prototype of the Kingdom to come. Christians will invent many things which will make their cities self-sufficient and independent of government control. Some will even develop factories to manufacture their inventions and products. People will come from all parts of the world to receive instruction and ministry at these total Christian communities.

Whole Nation Converted. There will be greater miracles of quality and quantity performed than have ever been recorded in church history. This will cause hundreds of millions to turn to Christ. In some instances, whole nations will be converted to Christ, forsaking their former Muslim, communist, Buddhist or heathen beliefs. Their leaders will believe on Jesus Christ and declare Him to be the only true God and Christianity the true religion.

One-World Church, One-World Government. While the true Body of Christ is being made one in Christ, the devil will be working on producing the counterfeit church. The anti-Present-truth "Christian" denominations who are pro-humanist, modernistic, and liberal will work with the rest of the religions of the world to form a one-world church and one-world government. These two opposite church groups will come into great conflict before Jesus returns. The antichrist church system will put great pressure and persecution upon the Body of Christ. It will martyr many members of the Body of Christ. This will be done in the name of God and the antichrist system will declare it is doing

God a service by destroying those who are in rebellion against the unity and existence of its world-church system.

Too Hot to Handle or Hinder. The Body of Christ will become too powerful in the supernatural power of God for the ungodly to be able to restrict or to destroy them. Angels of the Lord will deliver the saints out of prison as one did Peter. If the world system refuses to sell tickets for them to travel, then the Holy Spirit will supernaturally transport them where they need to go. If they will not allow members of the Body of Christ to buy or sell, then the gift of miracles will cause the food to be multiplied sufficiently to feed thousands of Christians. The fear of God will come upon the people as the Church prophets proclaim judgment upon nations and individuals.

Quota Met — Quality Acquired. When the true Church has demonstrated the Gospel of the Kingdom in all nations for a witness to the Lordship of Christ, then the end of this age will be brought to a close. At the same time, the Church will have reached the *quota of members needed* to meet God's eternal requirements. Most individuals that become members of the Church during that time will go from infancy to maturity in one generation. "The plowman will overtake the reaper" *(Amos 9:13)*.

Army of Lord Activated Against Antichrist. When all Scriptures pertaining to the mortal Church have been fulfilled, the Period of the Great Restoration completed, and the "recovery of all things from sin" has been accomplished, then Jesus shall be revealed from Heaven to activate the resurrection of the dead saints and translation of the living saints. Jesus will then organize His Church into that immortal, indestructible and invincible Army of the Lord. Jesus as **King of Kings and Lord of Lords** will lead His Church-Army and angelic-army against the antichrist, beast-system and false prophets. While natural Israel and other mortal world nations are engaged in mortal combat on Earth at the Battle of Armageddon, the Church will be warring against Satan and his host in the Heavens. (It is possible that the Church-saints may wage their part of this warfare during their mortality in Christ's supernatural *Resurrection Life and Power.)* The Church-Army and angelic-army will win their war against Satan and his host thereby enabling natural Israel and her allies to win their war. The devil and all his fallen angels and demonic host are then removed from all of their positions in Heaven and Earth. Satan and all of his host will be bound in the bottomless pit for a 1000-year period *(Rev. 20:2,3)*.

Ruling and Reigning a Reality. The resurrected and translated members of the Body of Christ will then fill all those positions vacated by Satan's angelic and demonic host, just as the Children of Israel filled all the places vacated by the overcome and destroyed "ites" of Canaan Land. The *Queen Church* with her *Husband King, Christ Jesus,* will then take over the dominion and directing of all nations and mortals on planet Earth. Every saint will be given the privilege and responsibility of administration according to his or her maturity, overcoming grace, wisdom, biblical knowledge, conformity to the character of Christ and the principles of the Kingdom of God, which were obtained during that person's mortal life on Earth. Some saints will reign over continents as kings, others will have responsibilities according to the individual's ability, such as, being president of a nation, governor of a state, or mayor of a city. Some will only be capable of governing just one family and others capable of governing just one individual. Others will not have stationary areas of administration but will travel around the Earth performing specific ministries for Christ and to mortals on Earth.

Unlimited Ability. The glorified saints will be able to do all in their immortal bodies that Christ presently does in His resurrected human body: travel in space, become visible or remain invisible when working with mortals; be able to influence mortal humanity by becoming visible and engaging in verbal communication or through undetected spirit influence.

Incomprehensible Ability and Activity. All this sounds strange when you try to describe it as experiential reality, but there is another dimension and world in which the immortalized human saints shall function. The Church will always be real people functioning in a real world. Human imaginations are incapable of portraying the fulness of all the activities and joys of the Eternal Church. Eye hath not seen nor ear heard what God has prepared for them that love Him, but His spirit has revealed some things *(I Cor. 2:9,10)*. These few statements are but glimmering glimpses into the activity of the Church during the millennial reign.

Why a Millennial Reign? Certain theologians can see no value or purpose for a literal 1000-year period. What value or purpose could there be for a millennial reign of Christ with His saints? If there is no millennial then when will Scriptures like Isaiah 65:17-25 be fulfilled? If Christ has a millennial planned then He must have many reasons for it. I only know of two at this present time:

1. Ever since mankind has been on planet Earth, he has had the devil to blame for his rebellion, wickedness and failure to do God's will. Man is

going to have his day — "One day is a thousand years with the Lord" *(II Pet. 3:9)* — to prove himself. God is going to demonstrate to all eternal creatures throughout the universe that humanity is still unable to do righteously without their Maker abiding within them. "None righteous, no not one" *(Rom. 3:10)*. Even under the direct influence of the godly, unredeemed mankind can remain selfish and contrary to God in his spirit. The only humans who can do good are those who have the Christ-life integrated into their very being. Goodness and godliness only dwell in Christ Jesus.

2. Jesus wants to rule and reign with His Church while there are still mortal humans and nations on Earth. This will be the Church's advanced "on-the-job-training" for Her permanent eternal ministry in the *"endless ages"* to come. The Church is destined not only to rule over the Earth, but to have a *"universal reign"* over all eternal creatures and galaxies throughout the endless universe.

Eternity Begins

At the end of the 1000-year period, Satan and his hordes shall be loosed again upon mortal humanity. All mortals who have not learned that Jesus is the only way, truth, and life will become followers of Lucifer through his false leaders and prophets. Satan and his host will try one more time to overthrow God's Kingdom. But Jesus Christ with His Church-Army and angelic band shall defeat Satan and all his followers and cast them into the lake of fire, which will then be their eternal abode.

New Earth — Headquarters of All Heavenly and Universal Activity

God shall make all things new by cleansing them by fire. This divine fire will rid Earth of all contamination caused by the rebellion of Lucifer and fall of man. New Earth will be central to all universal activities. Jesus and His Church will set up Her headquarters on planet Earth. The redeemed and restored Earth will be more dazzling and beautiful than the description of the new Jerusalem in Revelation. The throne of Jesus and His Church will be the eternal Mt. Zion of this new Jerusalem. The Queen Church now begins Her eternal ministry which will continue forever into the endless ages of eternity.

What Can Christians Do Now??

We can make sure we have a thorough understanding and experiential reality in all of the Doctrines of Christ which have been restored to the Church. Receive and enter into all of the spiritual experiences available in the restored Church. Make sure we are members of the One Universal Many-Membered Corporate Body of Christ. Read and study the Bible consistently. Be open to new truth but not gullible to deception. Prove all things and hold fast to that which is good. Do not become involved in denominationalism, doctrinal differences, and prophetic predictions which bring disunity to the Body of Christ. Die the death to ourselves, and sacrifice everything necessary to become a matured member of the Body of Christ. Press on toward the mark for the prize of that high calling of God in Christ Jesus. If we are each a member of the Church, the Corporate Body of Christ, then we will want to know as much about this great *body of believers* as possible; especially know our Headship, Jesus Christ, and how we can more perfectly relate and function in Him. That is the purpose of this book.

The Time is Now! If the reader is not a born-again member of Christ, the time has come to become one. For if we are members of this great Universal Body of Christ, then we are part of a divine living organism that has been established, not for time alone, but for eternity. As a member of this One Body we are placed in an eternal position of performance and pleasure forevermore. We are each a fellow member with all true Christians on Earth and the departed members of the Body of Christ in Heaven. We are members of Christ's one and only world-wide Church. This Church is destined never to deactivate or end, but to escalate and begin on a higher realm. This Body of Christ will never be dismembered or disbanded, but it will become more fully united and eternally magnified in its ministry with Christ Jesus. To Christ Jesus, who is the ever living Head of this forever functioning Body, be the everlasting praise; and unto God be glory **in the Church** by Christ Jesus throughout all ages, world without end *(Eph. 3:21)*. Amen and amen!

Appendix

The following research sources are listed for those who want a "key" text that will lead them into an exhaustive study of that area of the Church. They are listed according to book title rather than by the author. The chronological order is according to the flow of this book in relation to the past, present and future of **The Eternal Church.**

Strong's Exhaustive Concordance of the Bible by James Strong. Thomas Nelson Publishers, Nashville, Tennessee.

Baker's Dictionary of Theology, © 1960. Baker Book House, Grand Rapids, Michigan.

An Expository Dictionary of New Testament Words by W. E. Vine. Thomas Nelson Publishers, Nashville, Tennessee.

Christian Theology by Emery H. Bancroft. © 1971, Zondervan Publishing House, Grand Rapids, Michigan.

Lectures in Systematic Theology by Henry C. Thiessen. © 1949, William B. Eerdmans Publishing Company, Grand Rapids, Michigan.

Historical Theology — An Introduction by Geoffrey W. Bromily. © 1978, William B. Eerdmans Publishing Company, Grand Rapids, Michigan.

Halleys Bible Handbook. © 1965, Halleys Bible Handbook Inc., Zondervan Publishing Company, Grand Rapids, Michigan.

The Christological Controversy edited by Richard A. Norris, Jr. © 1980, Fortress Press, Philadelphia, Pennsylvania.

Clarke's Commentary, 5 volumes, by Adam Clarke. Abingdon Press, Nashville, Tennessee

Ellicott's Commentary on the Whole Bible, 8 volumes, by Charles J. Ellicott, Zondervan Publishing House, Grand Rapids, Michigan.

Foxe's Christian Martyrs of the World by John Foxe. Moody Press, Chicago, Illinois.

Interpreting the Scriptures by Kevin Conner and Ken Malmin. The Center Press, Portland, Oregon.

Hermeneutics by Christian International College, Course #PM30. Christian International Publishers, Phoenix, Arizona.

Christianity Through the Centuries by Earle E. Cairns. ©
1954, 1967; Zondervan Publishing Company, Grand Rapids,
Michigan.

The Story of the Christian Church by Jesse L. Hurlbut. ©
1970, Zondervan Publishing House, Grand Rapids, Michigan.

Eerdmans' Handbook to the History of Christianity. ©
1977, William. B. Eerdmans, Grand Rapids Publishing Company,
Grand Rapids, Michigan.

Eusebius' Ecclesiastical History, © 1955, Baker Book House,
Grand Rapids, Michigan.

History of the Christian Church by Philip Schall, 8 volumes
© 1910. Eerdmans Publishing Company, Grand Rapids,
Michigan.

A Manual of Church History, 2 volumes, by Albert Henry
Newman. Judson Press, Valley Forge, Pennsylvania.

Who Was Who in Church History by Elgin S. Moyer. © 1962,
Moody Press, Chicago, Illinois.

The Church: From Pentecost to Present by Carl S. Meyer. ©
1969, Moody Press, Chicago, Illinois.

Church History by Christian International College, Course
#HT10. Christian International Publishers, Phoenix, Arizona.

Church History by Christian International Graduate School,
Course #HT50. Christian International Publishers, Phoenix,
Arizona.

The Light and the Glory by Peter Marshall and David Manuel.
© 1977, Fleming H. Revel Company, Old Tappan, New Jersey.

The Reformation by Hans J. Hillerbrand. © 1978, Baker Book
House, Grand Rapids, Michigan.

The Reformation of the Sixteenth Century by Roland H.
Bainton. © 1952, Beacon Press, Boston Massachusetts.

The Gospel of Healing by A. B. Simpson. © 1915, Christian
Publications Inc., Harrisburg, Pennsylvania.

Handbook of Denominations by Frank S. Mead. © 1975,
Abingdon Press, Nashville, Tennessee.

The Holiness Pentecostal Movement in the United States
by Vinson Synan, © 1971, William B. Eerdmans Publishing
Company, Grand Rapids, Michigan.

The Pentecostals by John T. Nichol. © 1966, Logos International, Plainfield, New Jersey.

A Man Called Mr. Pentecost, David Du Plessis as told to
Bob Slosser. © 1977, Logos International, Plainfield, New
Jersey.

Aspects of Pentecostal — Charismatic Origins by Vinson
Synan. © 1975, Logos International, Plainfield, New Jersey.

Nine O'Clock in the Morning, by Dennis Bennett. Logos International, Plainfield, New Jersey.

The Holy Spirit and You by Dennis and Rita Bennett. © 1971, Logos International, Plainfield, New Jersey.

The Gordon Lindsay Story by Gordon Lindsay. Voice of Healing Publishing Company, Dallas, Texas.

The Catholic Pentecostals by Kevin and Dorothy Ranaghan. © 1969, Paulist Press, Deus Books, New York, New York.

The 1948 Revival and Now by M. E. Kirkpartick. Missionary Outreach, 611 North 5th Street, Temple, Texas 76501.

Present Day Truths by Dick Iverson. Bible Press, 7545 N.E. Glisan Street, Portland, Oregon 97213.

Pastor's Pen by B. M. Gaglardi. New West Press, 3456 Fraser Street, Vancouver, B.C. V5V 4C4, Canada.

Unto Perfection by Dr. Reginald Layzell. The Kings Temple, 21701 Avenue West, Mountlake Terrace, Washington 98043.

The Path of the Just Volume II, by Pastor B. Maureen Gaglardi, New West Press, 3456 Fraser Street, Vancouver, B.C. V5V 4C4, Canada.

The Tabernacle of David by Kevin J. Conner. The Center Press, 7626 N.E. Glisan Street, Portland, Oregon 97214.

Contemporary Options in Eschatology by Millard J. Erickson. © 1977, Baker Book House, Grand Rapids, Michigan.

Dispensationalism and Covenant Theology by Christian International Graduate School, Course #TH64. Christian International Publishers, Phoenix, Arizona.

Destined for the Throne by Paul E. Billheimer. © 1975, Christian Literature Crusade, Fort Washington, Pennsylvania.

Revelation by Christian International Graduate School, Course #NT65. Christian International Publishers, P.O. Box 27398, Phoenix, Arizona 85061.

For additional copies of this book and tapes or to contact the author write or call:

Dr. Bill Hamon
Christian International
P.O. Box 27398
Phoenix, AZ 85061

Trade Discounts to Bookstores, Bible Colleges & Churches.